AN ELEMENTARY ODYSSEY

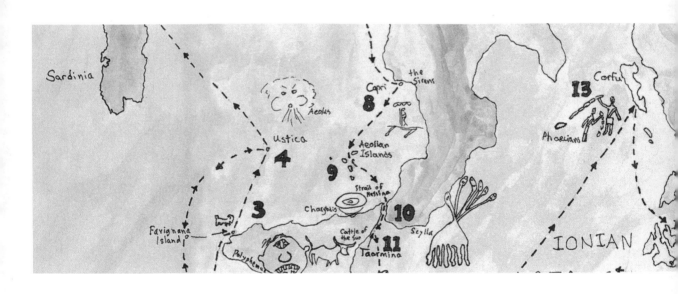

AN ELEMENTARY ODYSSEY
TEACHING ANCIENT CIVILIZATION THROUGH STORY

DAVID H. MILLSTONE

HEINEMANN • PORTSMOUTH, NH

HEINEMANN
A division of Reed Elsevier Inc.
361 Hanover Street
Portsmouth, NH 03801-3912

Offices and agents throughout the world

Every effort has been made to contact the copyright holders for permission to reprint borrowed material where necessary. We regret any oversights that may have occurred and would be happy to rectify them in future printings of this work.

The author and publisher wish to thank those who have generously given permission to reprint borrowed material:

"Ithaca" from *The Complete Poems of Cavafy,* © 1961 and renewed 1989 by Rae Dalven, reprinted by permission of Harcourt Brace & Company.

Acknowledgments for borrowed material continue on page 212.

Library of Congress Cataloging-in-Publication Data

Millstone, David H.
    An elementary odyssey : teaching ancient civilization through story / David H. Millstone.
        p.   cm.
    Includes bibliographical references.
    ISBN 0-435-08841-6 (acid-free paper)
    1. Social sciences—Study and teaching (Elementary)
    2. Civilization, Ancient—Study and teaching (Elementary)   3. Homer.
    Odyssey.   4. Storytelling.   5. Interdisciplinary approach in
    education.   I. Title
    LB1584.M55 1995   94-48431
    372.83—dc20   CIP

Editor: Carolyn Coman
Production: Vicki Kasabian
Text and cover design: Jenny Jensen Greenleaf
Cover illustration: Laura Schned

Printed in the United States of America on acid-free paper
99 98 97 96 95 EB 1 2 3 4 5 6 7 8 9

For my parents,
Mae and Harry Millstone,
who taught me to love words
and to love the world

CONTENTS

ACKNOWLEDGMENTS

My interest in teaching Homer to fifth graders was kindled at a 1984 summer institute at Georgetown University. It was a turning point in my life. Thanks go to Joseph F. O'Connor, who directed the institute, and whose welcoming personality and continuing professional support made my introduction to classics a pleasure.

Closer to home, the members of the Department of Classics at Dartmouth College have for ten years helped me learn more about the ancient world. In particular, Professors Jeremy Rutter, archaeology, and William Scott, Greek, have been patient with my questions; the misconceptions that remain are entirely my fault. Chrysanthi Bien's expert instruction in modern Greek helped me make my way through Greece one summer, which in turn enabled me to understand that land a little better.

Also at Dartmouth, Leslie Wellman, education director of the Hood Museum of Art, made it easy to try out new ideas with my students and encouraged me to use work in the Hood's collection for this book. Erling Heistad, a good friend and director of Dartmouth's Claflin Jewelry Workshop, has always been eager to lend a hand, whether it be casting sixty coins in an afternoon or photographing student pottery.

After years of writing articles and presenting workshops about the Norwich Odyssey Project, I was probably ready to write this book without being aware of it. Thanks go to Jack Wilde, who planted the seed, and to Philippa Stratton, who provided early encouragement at Heinemann. My current editor, Carolyn Coman, has been both welcoming and calm; working with her has been a pleasure. Thanks are due to Vicki Kasabian for her careful attention to detail and to Jenny Greenleaf for her elegant book design; from the beginning, I wanted this book to be more than words. I also appreciate the thorough copyediting of Linda Howe.

Writing a book is one task; getting it published is quite another. For assistance with the business side of publishing, I am indebted to Pam Bryant, Jere Calmes, Sonja Hakala, Harry Henderson, Peggy Sadler, Ruth Sylvester, and David Whitin.

I am fortunate to teach in a community that welcomes the kinds of activities described in this book. Many thanks are due to hundreds of Norwich families who have supported and extended my work over the years. I also acknowledge the support of the Norwich School Board, whose award of a sabbatical leave in 1988–89 let me study Greece and write several articles that reappear in different form in this book.

My students have been my best teachers. Year after year, I am fortunate to work with children who are eager to learn and willing to try something new. In particular, I thank those who granted permission to use their words, their writing, and their artwork in this book.

Thanks go to first-grade teacher Brigid Farrell, who shared my enthusiasm for Homer that summer in Georgetown and for many years thereafter. I've relied extensively on Brigid's memories for Chapter 8, as well as on recollections by first-grade teachers Terri Ashley, Laurie Ferris, Susan Nellen, and Cindy Pierce. None of us would be working together in Norwich without the continuing support of our principal, Milton Frye, whose vision of a good school keeps us centered.

Other colleagues at the Marion W. Cross School have given me the freedom and support over many years to try out my ideas. Peter Anderson, Tracy Goudy, and Susan Voake have worked especially closely on the Odyssey Project with our fifth graders. From Peter, I've learned the importance of documenting what happens in a classroom; his example and his assistance make it fun to build a multimedia collection of Odyssey materials. Tracy combines a continual willingness to try yet another new project with an unswerving commitment to high standards, both for herself and for her art students. Susan's enthusiasm for books is infectious, and she has assembled a teacher's dream collection in our school library.

Early drafts of the manuscript were improved by my sister, Amy Millstone, and by Beth Haney and Nancy Valtin of the Cross School faculty. Another colleague, Mary Ann Haagen, read through a later version and made valuable suggestions, as she has on many other pieces of my writing. My parents offered thoughtful comments on the entire manuscript, as well as last-minute proofreading.

My most helpful editor was my wife, Sheila Moran. In addition to her love and her ongoing appreciation of my Greek passion, she wields a red pen with grace and precision. Like E. B. White's Charlotte, she is a true friend and a good writer.

PREFACE

I never planned to be a teacher. As a child, inspired by images of white-coated men gazing intently into gleaming beakers and test tubes, I dreamed of being a research chemist. I spent hours in my basement laboratory, eagerly manufacturing distilled water for my mother's steam iron. Near-failing grades in college chemistry and linear algebra combined with new personal and political interests to ensure a change. I graduated from college in the late 1960s, impatient with detached academic discourse and aware of the many wrongs in American society that needed righting. Graduate school was out of the question and I did not even consider teaching as a profession. I wanted to be involved in changing the world, not explaining it. After working as a journalist, a political activist, and a printer in a large environmental organization, I came to New England in 1972 to visit friends for two weeks, enjoyed the taste of small-town life, and stayed on.

That spring, I found myself in an elementary school classroom and was surprised to discover that I liked what I saw. Gone were the desks in rows that I remembered so vividly from my own youth. Instead of regimented children I found lively individuals painting, reciting poetry, and solving math problems with brightly colored wooden rods and geometric shapes. The teacher, a man my age with shoulder-length hair, blue jeans, and a faded workshirt, had abandoned the traditional place of authority at the head of the classroom. His desk was off to one side, and he moved quietly from child to child, from individual to small group, questioning, listening, smiling, encouraging. It was the height of the "open classroom" movement in American education, and I was intrigued.

The following fall, I enrolled in what is now called the Upper Valley Teacher Training Program. I would spend the year as an intern working in combined second- and third-grade classrooms, with time off for seminars every other week. I would receive an aide's wages. At worst, I reasoned, I'd have an interesting year and then I could do something else. I remember sitting down to organize my first budget. Everything looked fine. Sharing a house with friends, I calculated that I could live comfortably on the $2,500 I would earn.

By the end of that internship, I was hooked. I had found my calling.

Over the summer, I found a job as a fourth-grade teacher, and like so many other beginning teachers, I was determined to make a difference. My classroom would be warm and welcoming—no tyranny of desks in rows, no regimentation, no authoritarian teacher presence. I spent most of the summer living in my classroom, going through twenty years of files and dusty shelves filled with outdated textbooks. When I wasn't actually in the room, I was busy thinking about school and building furniture.

I found a large wooden packing crate and decided it was the perfect base for a loft. I built sturdy two-by-four legs that would support the other end of a sheet of plywood. I painted the loft bright red and yellow, lined the inside of the crate with fabric, and sewed large pillows to furnish a comfortable nest. Children entering *my* room, I thought happily, would know at first glance that this was a different sort of room. Within such a stimulating environment, their own creativity would surely flourish. I borrowed a friend's pickup truck, drove triumphantly to school, backed up to the front steps, and located a large moving dolly.

"What's that?" asked my principal as I passed his office, gingerly maneuvering the crate down the sparkling hallway, freshly waxed and polished. "And where are you going with it?"

I explained carefully and eagerly.

"It won't fit through the door," he grinned, and followed me to my room. He was right. I looked at it from several angles and briefly considered removing the picture window from its metal frame. He walked away, shaking his head at my folly. I went home for a saw.

The rest of the summer passed without incident, and I was ready. I had planned that first day of school as only a first-year teacher plans, minute by minute. We'd start the day by sitting on the rug in a circle, children would introduce themselves, and I would share my vision for the year. The bell rang and children barged in, looking around in confusion.

"Which is my desk?"

"Where do I put my stuff?"

"What's *that*?"

I pointed to the loft. "That?" I smiled. "Sit down, and we'll talk about it. Put your jacket on the hooks for now." Everything was going fine, if a bit faster than I had anticipated.

"Here," said one girl, holding out a handful of coins. "Here's my lunch money."

"Here's mine," added her friend.

"Are you collecting lunch money now?" shouted a boy from across the room and he raced across the floor. "Wait for me!"

Lunch money?

Nobody had prepared me for this. At the school the year before, lunch money was handled by the cafeteria staff. These students clearly knew the routines better than I did. Ten minutes later, I had survived lunch money and recess milk money, those children paying for the day and those paying for the week, those paying full price and those with free or reduced-price meals. ("I know, I know," explained one girl patiently. "My Mom needs to fill out some papers that you give us at the end of the day, but we always get it free. You'll see.")

We made it through that first meeting, although the discussion never reached the ideal of full democratic participation I had envisioned. I was ready to send the students off to work when Brian raised his hand. "Uh . . . what do we call you?"

I'd been on a first-name basis with students during my intern year and saw no reason to stop; titles were unnecessary and undemocratic. "You can call me David, or Mr. Millstone, whichever you want," I replied easily.

"I don't think Mr. Carver will let you do that," he said.

"I'll talk to him," I said, suddenly realizing that there might be other perspectives to consider. "I'll let you know later this morning." By 10:30, my students knew. I was Mr. Millstone.

I stumbled through that first year, and the next two, with lots of help and with lots of overtime. I confirmed what teachers everywhere know, that twenty-four hours in a day is not enough to do everything that can be done for a group of children. I looked forward to Saturdays, when I could spend the entire day in my classroom without interruptions. Slowly, I learned how to be a teacher.

The hardest part was being so alone. During my internship year, I had worked closely with my supervising teachers and met frequently with a supportive advisor. The entire group of twenty interns met regularly for seminars and for mutual support. Suddenly, as a newly certified professional, I spent most of my hours behind a closed door with twenty-five children, with only rare visits from my principal, who was there for the obligatory supervision. In time, I started forming friendships with like-minded teachers on my hallway. Spurred by a course we were taking, another teacher and I started a program of peer supervision to get feedback from each other and to have another professional with whom we could discuss our students.

After three years in my own classroom, I teamed up with yet another teacher from down the hall. We both had been part of that informal school-within-a-school that was centered in our hall, each of us interested in alternatives to basal readers. Later on, the two of us joked that the main thing we knew about each other was that each of us hated administering standardized tests.

Team teaching was a wonderful experience. We worked hard for three years, harder than I had ever worked before, and the harder we worked, the more we enjoyed it. It was the phenomenon known as synergy, where one plus one equals three. One of us would come up with an idea, the other would take it further, and before we were through we had designed a program that neither of us on our own could have imagined. We agreed to meet all forty-five sets of parents for fall parent conferences, and we spent many weekends over supper planning our next round of activities. The team-teaching program, which we were allowed to start only after obtaining explicit written permission from each child's parents, soon enjoyed outspoken parental support. We wrote a grant and built a photography darkroom in one corner of the classroom; we took children on winter camping trips.

The better things got inside our classroom, the more isolated we became in our school. With the wisdom of hindsight, I realize that the energy we needed to build bridges with other teachers went solely into each other and into our own program. We were confident, impatient, and brash in our youthful excitement, and we probably scared away potential allies. In time, we started defining our room in opposition to those other classes—we were what they weren't—which left us further alienated from many other teachers. Inside the classroom, however, it was a time of tremendous excitement and personal and professional growth.

After six years of teaching third and fourth graders, I was ready for a change. It was clear that my colleague was looking for something new, and I did not relish staying in the school by myself after his departure. I called the principal of the elementary school in nearby Norwich, Vermont, and asked about job possibilities.

"Yes, it looks like we'll have a vacancy," he said. I was thrilled. He'd been at the school for six years after leaving a faculty position at Dartmouth College, and he had a great reputation. It would be wonderful to work with him and to be part of his school.

"What grade?" I was interested in older grades or younger grades, anything different.

"Upper grades, fifth and sixth," he said.

Norwich was departmentalized in the upper grades, I knew, with students moving from one subject area to another. That would be an interesting change in itself. In the staff development workshops my colleague and I led, there were always teachers who complained that they couldn't do the sorts of projects we described because they taught in departmentalized classrooms at the mercy of a forty-five-minute period. This might work out very well, I thought, a chance to see if that was a valid complaint.

I started thinking, very rapidly: "Okay. English . . . I can do that. Writing process . . . children's literature . . . poetry . . . chanting and songs. Math? Strategy games, geometry, basic arithmetic, problem of the week, Cuisenaire rods, and pattern blocks. No problem. Science? There's all the ESS units . . . tracks, structures, ice and snow. Scientific method and record-keeping. Three out of four . . . not bad."

I turned back to the phone. "What's the vacancy?"

"Social studies."

There was a long pause at my end. "Oh. Let me think about that, okay?"

A month later, I was hired as the social studies teacher in Norwich.

ITHACA

C. P. Cavafy

(translated from modern Greek by Rae Dalven)

When you start on your journey to Ithaca,
then pray that the road is long,
full of adventure, full of knowledge.
Do not fear the Lestrygonians
and the Cyclopes and the angry Poseidon.
You will never meet such as these on your path,
if your thoughts remain lofty, if a fine
emotion touches your body and your spirit.
You will never meet the Lestrygonians,
the Cyclopes and the fierce Poseidon,
if you do not carry them within your soul,
if your soul does not raise them up before you.

Then pray that the road is long.
That the summer mornings are many,
that you will enter ports seen for the first time
with such pleasure, with such joy!
Stop at Phoenician markets,
and purchase fine merchandise,
mother-of-pearl and corals, amber and ebony,
and pleasurable perfumes of all kinds,
buy as many pleasurable perfumes as you can;
visit hosts of Egyptian cities,
to learn and learn from those who have knowledge.

Always keep Ithaca fixed in your mind.
To arrive there is your ultimate goal.
But do not hurry the voyage at all.
It is better to let it last for long years;
and even to anchor at the isle when you are old,
rich with all that you have gained on the way,
not expecting that Ithaca will offer you riches.

Ithaca has given you the beautiful voyage.

Without her you would never have taken the road.
But she has nothing more to give you.

And if you find her poor, Ithaca has not defrauded you.
With the great wisdom you have gained, with so much experience,
you must surely have understood by then what Ithacas mean.

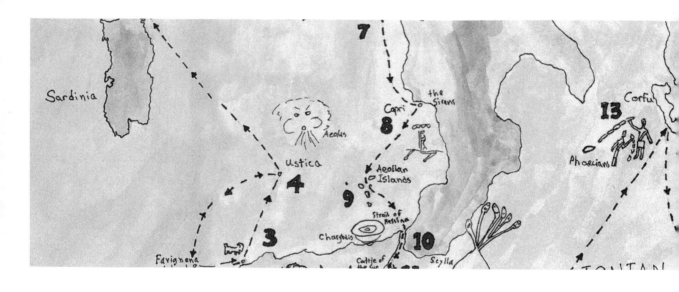

GETTING
STARTED

1 | GOTTA HAVE A HOOK . . .

A dark classroom, shades drawn and lights out, illuminated only by the flickering glow of three candles . . .

Fifty children, fifth graders, sitting and leaning and sprawling on a small rug in the meeting area of the Social Studies room, with another half-dozen teachers and parents dimly visible in the half-light . . .

A bearded young man with keen eyes, a guitar placed over one knee, his flickering shadow looming behind him on the wall, his gaze resting on the audience . . .

The storyteller waits for silence, then takes a breath. All eyes focus on him, a shadowy figure in the dim light. He strikes a chord on his guitar; we hear the cry of a gull. He begins:

"This is the tale of Odysseus, master of land ways, master of sea ways." He pauses.

"Darkness . . ." Children are in the belly of the Trojan Horse with Odysseus and his companions, and the children sitting on the rug move closer to the candles. "And silence . . . and the breathing of men closely held, so that it is not loud." A cough. "Silence! Choke on your cough if you need to, but make no sound!"

So we begin our study of Homer, listening to a modern bard bring new life to an ancient tale. Our fifth graders come to Homer's *Odyssey* as did the Greeks thousands of years ago, hearing the tale fresh from the lips of a stranger, a storyteller. I often read out loud to my students, and I could begin this unit by reading a good translation of Homer, but there is no substitute for a storyteller's presence. The storyteller in the classroom brings the necessary majesty and mystery to the tale.

This is the story of an interdisciplinary project that centers on our study of *The Odyssey.* It is the story of collaboration between fifth and first-grade teachers, and between older and younger students. From that darkened room, from that storyteller, emerge months of telling Homeric stories, reading, conducting research, studying the ancient world, writing, doing art work and drama. The storytelling, however, comes first and provides the initial spark and the fuel that sustains the collaborations.

Like many curriculum innovations, this project developed slowly, and I was as surprised as others by its success. Fifth graders now enter school in September asking, "Do we get to study *The Odyssey* this year?"

How did this project begin?

DESIGNING A CURRICULUM

Shortly after being hired as a fifth/sixth-grade social studies teacher, I met with my new principal. "Let's get down to details," I said. "What is the social studies curriculum in the fifth and sixth grades? Is there something specific I'm supposed to teach?"

"Geography and ancient civilizations in the fifth grade," he told me. "Sixth grade is American history, up to the Civil War."

"Any particular text I need to use?"

"There's one available for sixth, but no, you don't need to use it. See what you think."

I walked off slowly, thinking. Social Studies? What did that mean? I found an old topographic map and a new calligraphy pen, and I carefully lettered a sign for my classroom door:

David Millstone
5th and 6th grade Social Studies
People and Places

While the sixth-grade curriculum took shape easily, the fifth-grade focus was never as clear. Geography and ancient civilization? I had always been a lover of maps, so it was no surprise that I turned first to geography in implementing the curriculum. Children mapped the classroom in both metric and in English measurements. They mapped the playground. They mapped their bedrooms and they mapped their neighborhoods. We built rudimentary surveying tools and measured the hills and gullies behind our school, collecting and plotting data to create topographic maps and relief models of the varied landforms. One year, we examined a large tract of land owned by a local cooperative to determine how that land might best be used. Another year, we studied the nearby Connecticut River, and our work culminated in an overnight canoe trip. Students over the years wrote away to different states and culled information from the glossy packets that arrived for the ubiquitous state reports; they memorized states and capitals; they completed research on regions of the United States, folklore and food, forests and factories. In one form or another, geography dominated our work for most of the year.

I consistently turned the ancient civilization component of the curriculum over to one of my interns: "Take your pick—Greece, Rome,

Egypt, China, India . . . You choose. Develop a unit and teach it; you can take three or four weeks if you like. Let me know how I can help." A short unit of study on a specific ancient civilization was a convenient package for a teacher-in-training; my interns were able to try out their ideas and the fifth graders studied two ancient civilizations each year, one in the fall and one in the spring.

Greece was inevitably one of the civilizations they picked. One year, students acted out the Battle of Salamis on our playground, with the unwieldy Persian ships hemmed in and outmaneuvered by nimble Greek triremes. Another year, spurred by the class's interests and skill in map-reading, the intern located a detailed atlas of Greece in a nearby college library. Working from contour maps and charts showing temperature and rainfall, students predicted what kind of civilization might emerge in different locations. They looked at Corinth, for example, strategically located on the narrow isthmus, and correctly predicted that this would be a center of trade. Spurred by the popularity of "Trivial Pursuit," another intern helped students design their own "Greek Trivial Pursuit," and classes eagerly played and answered questions created by the students in the other homeroom. Each time, I listened to the intern's plans, made occasional suggestions, helped teach the unit as needed, and enjoyed watching my students engaged in the world of ancient peoples. I noted that each intern found a completely different way of approaching ancient Greece, and that the same activity was rarely repeated from year to year. It was clear that there were many valid approaches, but I had no particular interest in the subject myself.

That all changed the summer of 1984, when I was one of sixty elementary teachers from around the country selected to participate in a summer institute on Homer's *Odyssey,* funded by the National Endowment for the Humanities. I had read *The Odyssey* in college and remembered it fondly; indeed, several years after graduation, I took my worn paperback copy along on a winter camping trip with friends. While we huddled in our sleeping bags in a mountain lean-to, we read passages aloud around the fire, the hot Mediterranean sun warming us in the New England snow. What drew my attention to this particular institute was the peculiar juxtaposition of "Homer" and "elementary school." What a strange idea! I went off to Washington, D.C., questioning my sanity— leave rural New England and the green of my garden to spend July and early August sweltering in a southern city?

The trip was no mistake. I became totally absorbed in the subject. I dashed from breakfast to get a good seat for the 9 A.M. lectures, and more than once I found myself in the Georgetown library at midnight, annoyed because it was closing and I was in the middle of tracking down an obscure reference in an eighty-year-old *British Journal of Archaeology.* I returned to school that fall determined to find a way to bring Homer to my fifth graders.

As it happened, one of my Norwich colleagues was also a participant in that Odyssey Institute. (The NEH wanted to avoid sponsoring teachers from the same school, thinking that the summer activities would thereby reach a broader constituency and would have a wider impact. Brigid lived in Vermont, however, and I lived in New Hampshire, and it was only after we had each been accepted that the organizers realized that we taught in the same school.) After the summer ended, we wanted my fifth graders and her first graders to work together. More accurately, the two of us wanted to support each other in this new interest, so it seemed natural for our classes to work together. Storytelling was the key.

SEARCHING FOR A STORYTELLER

In one of his songs, Vermont musician Jon Gailmor tells the bittersweet story of his experiences in the big-time music industry. Despite his talent, his voice, and his relaxed stage presence, he learned that all decisions were based on one criterion—what would sell. His songs were too thoughtful, too sensitive. He received a recording contract with a major label, but was told that the success of the album depended not on those qualities, but rather on creating a catchy tune with a simple chorus: "Gotta have a hook to have a hit." In designing curriculum units, I knew that a similar principle applied; children need a lure to attract their interest and a hook to sustain their enthusiasm.

I left Georgetown that summer knowing that I wanted my students to encounter *The Odyssey* through storytelling. That decision was not based on thoughtful application of educational criteria. The truth is much simpler. "If storytelling worked for the ancient Greeks," I reasoned, "it's good enough for my students." By this time, I knew that the Homeric epics in written form represented generations of storytelling; most evidence suggests that the stories were at least five hundred years old by the time of Homer, if, indeed, there was such a person. Academic footnotes aside, these tales had been passed along by bards for a very long time. There had to be a power in the telling which could reach my students. Only one small detail remained—finding a storyteller familiar with *The Odyssey*.

That fall, I started asking around. I scoured storytelling catalogs. I looked through dusty workshop listings from old social studies conferences I had attended. I contacted a storytelling center at a university. I wrote letters and spent hours on the telephone. Surely there was someone who told tales from Homer.

I discovered that storytelling was undergoing a renaissance and there was no shortage of available stories: Native American legends and creation stories; tall tales and folk tales; fairy tales, classical and New Age; scary stories and healing stories; stories from literature (Dr. Seuss, Edgar Allan Poe, Lloyd Alexander); African stories, Irish stories, Jewish stories, Maine stories; stories told with puppets, with masks, with musical instruments . . . The variety was exciting but very few people dealt with Greek mythology at all, let alone the Homeric epics.

Then a letter arrived, signed "Odds Bodkin, talesman," and my hopes rose. Here was a storyteller from nearby New Hampshire who was familiar with the wily Odysseus, the cannibal Cyclops, the lovely enchantress Circe. He sent me his publicity packet full of rave reviews. We exchanged letters, spoke on the telephone, and agreed on dates and a price. I began to look forward to his visit.

Then doubts crept in. I had hired the man, sight unseen, or perhaps more to the point, tales unheard. Around this time, I spotted a press release in the local newspaper; Odds Bodkin would be telling tales at a nearby inn later in the week. I sat in a back corner at that performance— this is my confession—thinking that if he were no good I'd have to find some way out of our agreement. (Several years later—this was his confession—Odds admitted that at the time he wrote his first letter he had never told all of *The Odyssey.* However, like any talented artist eager to earn a commission, he researched the subject thoroughly, sounded confident, and was committed to thorough preparation once hired.)

Within minutes at that first storytelling session at the inn, I relaxed. Odds was a powerful teller of tales, a gifted musician, a master of sound effects and of character voices. He could be serious and he could be funny. The audience of adults and children sat motionless.

His visit to school a month later went as I had dreamed. For six sessions spread over three days, he mesmerized our fifth graders, spinning out his version of the ancient saga with a strong guitar accompaniment. My journal recorded several vignettes of children listening to those early tellings:

> *Before the Cyclops story, many kids had seated themselves right next to Odds, up close to the candles. I noticed them inching backward as the story progressed—as Polyphemus, he'd shout out his questions, aiming them at a child, who looked distinctly uncomfortable.*
>
> *Maya sitting in the front, a gleam in her eyes, half scared, half excited; and Amy sitting next to me, a finger half in her mouth, looking at me in a lull out of the corner of her eyes, smiling a little, both of them enjoying being scared there together . . .*
>
> *The girls sitting on the floor in the afternoon, close up to Odds, while the boys took the chairs and backed off, looking more aloof. Move extra chairs out of the way tomorrow? Several days later: boys complained that girls were rushing to get all the good seats and demanded equal time in front.*

After the success of that first year, of course we arranged for a repeat performance. Odds returned the next year and said earnestly, "I think you're going to like this year's version."

"This year's version? I liked last year's version just fine."

"I've made some changes," he added mysteriously. "You'll see."

Changes, indeed. Feeling that he had been unable to evoke the many female characters to his satisfaction, in the intervening year Odds had taught himself to play Celtic harp. Now he could change the instrumentation of different episodes, some benefiting from the power and varied tonalities of his guitar, others responding to the warmth and gentle repetition of plucked strings. We recorded that year's telling, and it became the basis for many such performances to come. Odds' telling that year set the standard for our introduction to *The Odyssey,* and before I realized it, we had established a tradition. It was the start of the Norwich Odyssey Project, now more than ten years old.

YOUNG CHILDREN TAKE THE LEAD

During the week the fifth graders were learning about the fall of Troy and the subsequent wanderings of Odysseus and his crew, the school's first graders received their own introduction to the classical world. A Norwich parent (and professional storyteller herself) told first graders the Apple of Discord, a story not found in Homer's epics that describes the mythological background of the Trojan War. She repeated her performance in later years; eventually, the first-grade teachers themselves began to tell their students about the events that form the background of that war.

After listening to the tale, children make their own comic strips of the story, practice telling it to each other, contribute character names to large classroom charts, and prepare to meet their older partners. (See Chapter 8, "Odysseus in First Grade," for more details of the first graders' preparations.)

The stage is now set, with two groups of children knowing complementary pieces of one of the oldest tales in Western literature; the first graders know the background of the Trojan War and the fifth graders know about the fall of Troy and the wanderings of Odysseus. We ask the younger children to tell their part first. Each first grader has a fifth-grade partner, chosen after the first- and fifth-grade teachers discuss potential partnerships. Perhaps there's a fifth grader who writes very slowly; he needs to be paired with a slow-talking and patient first grader. On the other hand, an exceptionally confident and capable and outgoing first grader needs a fast writer to keep up with the sheer volume of her words. We try to match personalities, too, providing strong role models for younger children and matching shy children with partners who will be sensitive to their silences.

The charge given the fifth graders? "You are a scribe for your partner. Your task is to write down exactly what they say, every word just as you hear it." Here are those instructions spelled out in detail in one year's journal:

"Some of you are probably nervous about this. That's understandable. You know that you're going down to the first-grade classroom in a few minutes, but you don't really understand what you're going to do there. Let me try to explain what's going to happen, what we expect of you, what you'll be doing, and then give you a chance to try it out for a few minutes. I think you'll have a better idea after we talk . . ."

I outlined what the first graders had learned and told them their mission was to write down exactly—well, almost exactly—what their partner dictated.

"Now, I said to copy exactly. That means, if your partner says something that you know is bad grammar, you write it down anyhow. Let's say they're dictating and they say, 'Zeus said, "I ain't gonna take that." ' That's what you write, even though it's wrong. It's not your job then to try to teach them English. You'll have a chance later on to make the story better. Just get it down.

"I said 'exactly' but you have to use your head. If they say, 'And then Zeus—no, I mean Paris—' you don't write 'And . . . then . . . Zeus—no . . . I . . . mean . . . Paris . . .' You're fifth graders. You'll have to make some hard decisions." The fifth graders grinned. "Now, you'll have some problems getting the right speed. With some kids, they'll talk and talk and talk and you just won't be able to keep up with them. What do you do? Stab your partners with a pencil to slow them down? [Laughter! They really are nervous.] No, of course not. You work out a system with your partner, you tell them politely that they're going too fast.

"And what about the shy ones? There'll be some kids who are terrified of you. After all, you're Big Kids, and most first graders know that Big Kids beat up Little Kids [more laughter]. You're going to have to be friendly, and supportive, and give them lots of help. You know: 'And then what happened? Good, now what happened next?' Comments like that.

"And some of you—probably lots of you—will have a partner who tells the story a word at a time, looking at you to make sure that each word gets copied faithfully. It sounds a little funny, but they like making sure.

"Remember, however you do it, you've got to make your partner feel comfortable. You may be nervous, but so are they, even more."

The kids were starting to relax. I sent them off in pairs to practice: *"One of you take dictation, the other one take down what they say. Remember to double space with your partners today! You'll need the room for making corrections and changes when we go back and edit. Okay, ready? Tell what happened when you woke up this morning."*

And the room filled quickly with the buzz that satisfies: "Alarm clock . . . my mother yelled . . . my little brother . . . cereal . . . ran to catch the bus . . ."

"Switch!" And they continued for another three minutes. "Okay, time to go. Anyone learn anything?"

"Yes. I can't read my writing when I write that fast. I'll have to tell them to slow down because if I don't . . ."

We always start by having the older children visit the younger children's classroom; it's a comfortable space for the first graders and being around all those small desks and chairs reminds the fifth graders just how much they've grown. What follows is a delightful afternoon for all. Children meet their partners, disappear into all corners, and the room buzzes. The younger children often take charge, since they're doing the talking: "Hephaestus made the apple . . . you know, the blacksmith god—he's over here if you can't spell him," and they lead the hard-working scribe to a large chart of proper names and point vaguely, confident that their older partner can locate the right word in the long and confusing list of Greek proper names. The older children, initially nervous, quickly relax as they are reminded of how much they've learned since they were in first grade, for even our weakest fifth graders can usually write better than their young partners. The fifth graders are full of compliments—"I can't believe how much you know!"—and the first graders bask in the attention. The teachers usually have little to do except watch and smile. We help out when a first grader gets stuck with a name or a detail and intervene on those rare occasions when someone is balky or uncooperative.

Thinking about the fifth graders' behavior in these partnerships, one first-grade teacher remarks, "I'm struck by their gentleness and caring. No adult could be so 'present' at that time. How often can I have such intimate and personal conversations with the first graders? Not very often! But I look around the room and see every first grader with someone paying total attention to them, someone to listen to them. The first graders feel genuinely appreciated; they feel they've made a lifetime connection." Another teacher describes the fifth graders' scribing as "a dream" in which the younger children have someone whose attention is totally focused on taking down their words.

The partnerships work at different speeds. Some first graders have finished all they have to say in fifteen minutes. Others fill an hour and still have more to tell; they schedule extra time during recess and lunch on the following days. That first afternoon, though, I enjoy watching the partners find something to do once they've finished their dictation. The first graders often ask their partner to read with them; other popular choices are playing simple games or drawing. A first-grade teacher recalled seeing two boys working intently over a piece of paper: "I asked Jared [a fifth grader] what he was doing, and he said he was teaching his partner how to write his name in cursive. 'That's what my partner taught me when I was in first grade,' he said proudly. I had the sense that he'd been waiting four years to pass along the gift."

That night, the older children carry home their scribbled drafts and print or type neat copies; later in the week, storytellers and scribes meet again. These meetings are editorial conferences. If the first graders can, they read their stories aloud; if they can't, the older partner does the reading. After years of participating in writing process conferences, the fifth graders know to begin with positive comments. One year, we wrote down fragments of conversations overheard during editing conferences:

5: Do you like the way it sounds?
1: Uh-huh.
5: Because we won't change anything unless you want to.
5: (To another first grader) I think what you said is good.
1: I think so, too.
5: Well, that's good. You want to have a good story, don't you? It's going to be put up in the hall for everyone to see.
1: Okay.
5: Now, what about this? I don't really understand this sentence.

FIGURE 1-1   *Fifth graders take dictation from first-grade partners*

Only gradually do they make suggestions for revisions. Concerned that he might be too heavy-handed in his editorial suggestions, one fifth-grade boy decides to make his point indirectly. He reads the offending section aloud, emphasizing the words that bother him: " '*And then* the three goddesses started arguing *and then* Athena grabbed the apple away from Hera *and then* she grabbed it back *and then* Zeus finally got tired of them fighting so he put the apple next to his throne.' Do you hear anything funny there that we could change?"

Faced with the same issue, a classmate takes a more direct approach with her partner: "I'm not writing 'and' or 'then'! I'm sick of 'and' and 'then'! We're starting a new sentence now, and we're not going to use 'and' or 'then'! Okay?" Despite that comment, the fifth-grade editors acknowledge that the final choice of words is up to the younger author and they leave with their scribbled copy. They have the rest of the week to produce a final version, which must be neatly printed or typed on computers, suitable for display. (The scribes are asked to avoid cursive handwriting because the first graders can't read it. When the stories are eventually displayed, we want the younger children to be able to read each other's work.)

During that week, the partners spend one more afternoon together, jointly illustrating their stories. Both first- and fifth-grade teachers take responsibility for providing different art materials—one classroom has a grab bag of fabric scraps and recycled odds and ends for collage, one features watercolors and crayons, another offers fingerpaints and Cray-Pas chalks, and several rooms provide colored pencils and markers. Children first meet as one large group to hear the guidelines:

> You and your partner will have the next hour and a half to produce an illustration for the story you wrote earlier this week. We want you to work together on the same picture rather than having each of you do a separate picture. You and your partner will need to decide which part of the story you want to illustrate, who's going to do the different parts of the whole picture, and what materials you're going to use for each part. We want you to use at least two different kinds of materials in your picture. Fifth graders, you're responsible for seeing that the picture has a title or a caption, as well as the names of both artists. We also need volunteers from the fifth grade who will help with cleanup in the collage room at the end of the afternoon.

After receiving instructions, children wander off with their partners, moving from room to room selecting different art materials as they go. Again, the fifth graders play a sympathetic and supportive role. A sophisticated fifth grader watches his partner dramatically change the look of the rugged stone castle the older boy had designed as Menelaus' home in Sparta. He rolls his eyes toward the teacher, but then turns to his first-grade partner: "You know, I really like those curtains. That may be my favorite part of the castle." (The teacher overhearing that conversation was impressed: "He kept a straight face throughout!") By the end of the week, visitors to the school can see neatly mounted illustrations and stories on display along many corridors, some fifty different versions of the same tale.

This week-long collaboration achieves several purposes. First of all, it establishes a friendly relationship between older and younger children. Even our most difficult fifth graders are on their best behavior working with the young ones; from some four hundred students over the years, I recall only one fifth grader who was unable to participate successfully in this activity. The first graders end up with an older friend, someone they can look up to. The older children, in turn, accept the responsibility of teaching the younger children, and they grow to enjoy the social contact. After the classroom mail is delivered one morning, one fifth-grade girl holds up a stack of papers and groans in mock despair: "Three more love letters from my partner! What am I going to do with that kid?" Fifth graders break into friendly conversation with their young partners and they become supportive older buddies. "Oh yeah, I remember when I was

FIGURE 1-2   The Ocean, *collage and painting by partners Eli Schned (first grade) and Marc Manganiello (fifth grade)*

in first grade," says one boy sagely. "I had a real hard time writing anything." His young partner, who is having that very problem, nods solemnly and they return to their work.

This quality of improved personal contacts between children in different grades was one of the unexpected benefits of working together. One other teacher and I simply wanted to find a way to work together, and our entire school reaped the rewards.

Finding ways for teachers to work together and ways that children can work with other children of different ages (or with adults) is one of the simplest and most far-reaching changes a school can make. Many schools pair older and younger children for reading aloud, and I have heard of other schools in which older children act as individual tutors. In our school, some teachers have expanded this model of studying the same subject at different grade levels to create a process in which older and younger children do science experiments together.

There is an added dimension when disparate classes as a whole collaborate on a major unit of study. Two excellent examples come from Quaker schools. At Brooklyn Friends School nearly fifteen years ago, the part-time music teacher also worked with residents in a nearby senior center. She organized her two groups of music students into a chorus. Children and seniors rehearsed their parts separately, then met each other and produced a joyous concert together. Similarly, a fourth-grade class from Germantown Friends School in Philadelphia joined forces with a residential center for children with severe cerebral palsy, most of whom were confined to wheelchairs and had difficulty speaking. The project? Producing a musical. In both cases, not only was there an impressive product at the end of the collaboration but children had learned a great deal about themselves and about others along the way. (In both cases, there are excellent films that document the process. *Close Harmony* won an Academy Award for documentary films and is available from Brooklyn Friends School, 375 Pearl Street, Brooklyn, NY 11201, telephone (718) 852-1029. *Something Magical,* which describes the Philadelphia collaboration, is available to the education market only from PBS Video, P.O. Box 791, Alexandria, VA 22313-0791, telephone (800) 328-7271.)

By the time our children get to fifth grade, many of them can still remember their partners from when they were in first grade. Even if the relationship is short-lived, it improves the quality of life in school. First-grade teachers report that their students talk proudly about "*my* fifth grader," that they no longer feel a distance from "the Big Kids," that they feel a warm connection with the upper grades in the school. First graders approach the bigger children on the playground, interrupting a game of four-square to tug on a sleeve and say, "Hi! How are you?"

The connection works both ways. The fifth graders, instead of being bothered by the interruption, make a great show of turning around, stopping the game, smiling, and returning the greeting. The connections last beyond the moment, too. One year, a sixth-grade boy was busy talking with his friends during the school's weekly assembly. Suddenly, he glanced at the stage and saw a small girl step forward with a recorder in her hand, ready to play a duet with a friend. "Shh!" he cried, waving his friends to silence. "That's my partner from last year." He listened intently while she played her short piece, applauded vigorously (and made sure his friends clapped), then continued to talk through the remaining performances by other children. Teachers nod when hearing this story; yes, we want him to show the same consideration for all the performers, but at least he felt a bond with one younger child.

As the Odyssey Project continues year after year, children become part of a sustained process instead of an isolated event. They discover different roles for themselves in a larger whole. They participate as first-grade storytellers, then four years later get to be the Big Kids taking dictation. Some find opportunities to use their Odyssey experiences in later years; several graduates of our elementary school returned when they were in high school to tell the stories they had learned in fifth grade. Children passing these benchmarks take pride in discovering their own growth and in helping others along the path. Fifth graders also discover a new goal, to get good enough so that they will be invited back when they are in high school.

Finally, the collaboration lays a foundation for storytelling later in the year, when fifth graders will teach *The Odyssey* to the first graders by telling episodes one at a time. Since the first graders have already told a story to their partners, it's only fair for the older children to repeat the favor. At that later date, the older children will be telling their story not just because a teacher expects it but because the younger children are looking forward to it.

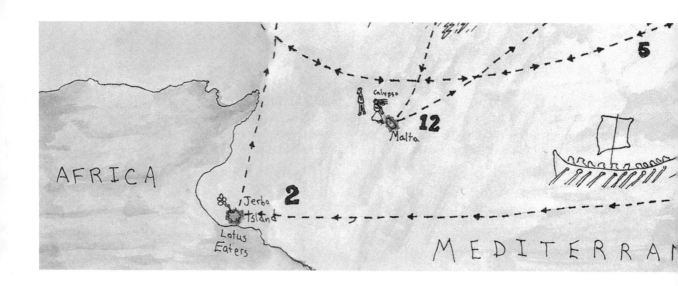

AFRICA

2

Jerba
Island

Lotus
Eaters

Calypso

12

Malta

5

MEDITERRAN

SOCIAL STUDIES ARE INTERDISCIPLINARY: A CLOSE LOOK

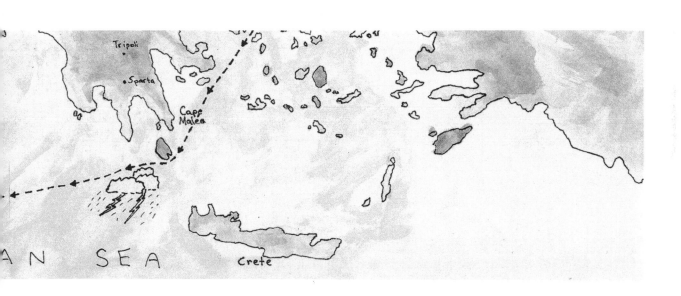

2 | "SO WHAT DO YOU DO BESIDES READ THE TEXT?"

Fifth graders hear *The Odyssey* unfold in epic detail. It is a complex tale, full of scores of unfamiliar proper names presented in nearly twenty episodes. In the months to come, if I speak about Charybdis, the powerful whirlpool, and my students think I'm referring to Circe, the sorceress who turns men into pigs, we're bound to have problems. Before we can move on to deeper discussions, we need to build a common working vocabulary.

One early technique used for this purpose is "debriefing," devised by my colleague, English teacher Peter Anderson. After each storytelling session, children reflect immediately on what they have just heard. We start by making four columns on the chalkboard or on large chart paper: characters, places, images, and emotions/ideas. Children take turns calling out contributions—"You know, that sea nymph who rescued him after he washed up on the beach!"—and a teacher writes in the appropriate names—"Oh, you mean Calypso."

Figure 2-1 is one such set of lists (from 1991). Students have just heard about Odysseus' adventures with the Lotus Eaters and with Polyphemus, the Cyclops.

The first two columns give children a chance to see the unfamiliar and unusual names written out in English, a visual reference for the spoken word. We also mention at this point that the original names are Greek and that there is more than one way to spell a Greek name in English; this list provides one common spelling of each name.

The "images" list contains the vivid pictures that will be of crucial importance later on when children go to tell their own versions of an episode. Adding to this list—turning pictures into words—somehow seems to fix the images more permanently in memory, just as this storehouse of pictures will help the words emerge when telling the story later on. In storytelling, pictures are conveyed in part through well-chosen words, and I remember one debriefing session years ago, in which children showed a keen appreciation for the language of the stories. In summoning pictures for the list, they even hung on to some of the phrases. One child suggested the "fat-bellied sails" and I wrote that down gleefully. "Do you remember another one with the same rhythm?" I asked. "The ___-___ ships?" "Black-hulled!" cried several students at once. Poetic language endures.

The final category, ideas and emotions, initially the hardest to fill, reminds me that these ten-year-olds get more from the story than a simple travelogue filled with monsters. This list hints at the complexity of the story as perceived by the listeners and reminds the teacher that the rich undertones of this adventure resonate with the young audience. How often in fifth grade does one day's story present an opportunity to discuss revulsion, anger, loneliness, and laughter?

This last list also takes us to surprising places. One entry in my teaching journal documents such a detour:

> *Today, looking for more ideas, Lisa tentatively offered: "Romance?" The kids can't bring themselves yet to use the word "love." They were again staying away from the mushier aspects of the story until Lisa nervously volunteered "Romance," which she had added to the morning list. Peter wrote it down, and I took a deep breath.*

Characters	Places	Images	Emotions/Ideas
Cyclops	Thrace	blood bubbling	pain
Polyphemus	Ismaros	dismembering the crewmen	revulsion
Nobody	Land of Lotus Eaters	dribbling wine and manflesh	anger
Laertes	Cyclops Island	racks of cheese	loneliness
(O's father)	small island nearby	smashing brains	laughter
Agamemnon		ripping mountains & throwing	happiness
Maron (priest)		Lotus Eaters feeding men	revenge
Lotus Eaters		turning spike in the eye	bliss
Cyclopes		men hiding under sheep	conceited
		Polyphemus yelling	sadness
		juicy grapes	crying
		dawn's rosy fingers	despair
		Polyphemus' hand	dazed
		Poly. first sees the men	drunk
		Poly. yelling "Nobody!"	astonished
		running with sheep to the ship	regret
		the pole hidden in manure pile	frightened
		red-hot tip of the spear	
		slaughtering sheep	
		Poly. talking to his ram	

FIGURE 2-1 *Four-column chart on the* Odyssey

*"Lisa, is there a difference between 'romance' and 'love' and if so,
which word is the one you want?" I asked. She mumbled, "Love," but
turned so red that it was impossible to get more out of her. The other
kids were giggling, whispering to each other. We had about ten minutes
of discussion on the difference—kids all agreed that "love" was the
right word for that column but had a hard time pinning down what the
difference was. It was the sort of discussion we'd be able to have easily
at the end of a year, when we knew each other better, but they just
weren't ready for that kind of seriousness yet. Someone shouted out,
"Romance is style." Both Peter and I were pushed to explain the difference, and we stumbled around a bit. I've been surprised at how much
I've thought about it since.*

The lists are displayed for several weeks in the classroom; some years,
when I am especially well organized, we distribute typed copies to each
student in the class, neatly three-hole-punched to fit into their notebook.
Children make good use of these lists in the activities that follow.

Early in the Norwich Odyssey Project, after the initial storytelling
each year, children typically spend three weeks going over the information in the stories, playing a series of games, and participating in other enjoyable activities. The purpose is not for students to learn these classical
names for their own sake, but rather for students to acquire background
for the work to be done later in our study. At the start, children feel overwhelmed by the sheer volume of names, but by the end of our review,
they have become adept at sorting them out.

Here is a brief description of some of those activities, presented in the
approximate order in which each is introduced. This list includes both
short and long projects; keep in mind that we don't complete every activity every year.

Draw favorite scenes: After each day's storytelling session, children are encouraged to draw scenes from the unfolding tale—not carefully polished artwork but their quick emotional responses to the story.
This sketching allows them to recall images and record details on paper.
Drawing also provides an emotional safety valve after some of the more
gruesome episodes. The completed drawings are so varied, the children
see that different people hear the same story differently, an issue that sur-
faces later on when we teach storytelling techniques (see Figures 2-2 and
2-3).

Summarize the story: Working together, with the teacher serving
as scribe at the chalkboard, children in the class draw up an outline of the
story as they remember it. After listing the major episodes, they number
them and then add supporting details. This collaborative effort is a valuable exercise, far more useful than simply looking at a teacher-prepared
list. These story outlines are transcribed, duplicated, and distributed

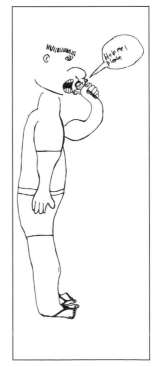

FIGURE 2-2
*Polyphemus devouring a
member of Odysseus'
crew (Ross McGee)*

along with the lists from the early debriefing sessions and my own sheets; carefully saved in each child's three-ring binder, they serve as useful references. Since the storytelling changes from year to year, the written materials change from year to year. Keeping a summary filed on the computer makes it easy to make appropriate revisions. By itself, the list would be of little use, but coming after such engaging tales, it serves as a helpful reminder of what happened when. Here is a typical summary of the story's highlights:

Apple of Discord

Judgment of Paris

Trojan War

assembling the chiefs
Odysseus feigning madness, Achilles hiding on Skyros
sacrifice of Iphigenia
fighting at Troy
quarrel between Agamemnon and Achilles
death of Patroklos
Achilles' return to battle
Achilles and Hector
Trojan Horse

Raid on the Ciconians

FIGURE 2-3   The Wedding Feast *(Elizabeth Spencer-Green)*

Land of the Lotus Eaters

Polyphemus, the Cyclops

Aeolus, King of the Winds

Laestrygonians

Circe

Land of the Dead

Sirens

Scylla and Charybdis

Cattle of the Sun

Calypso

Nausicaä and the Phaeacians

Return to Ithaca

meets Athena and becomes beggar

meets Eumaeus

meets Telemachus and reveals his identity

sees Argos, his dog

Eurykleia washes his feet

test of the bow

slaughter of the suitors

test of the bed

reunited with Penelope

In the early years of our project, children received a simple list of names showing correct spellings or, rather, one of many possible correct spellings. More recently, after many requests for a convenient reference chart, the list has come to look like Figure 2-4. There is one disadvantage in distributing these detailed lists: it removes a good project possibility many children have enjoyed—compiling a glossary of characters and places mentioned in the story. (See Appendix A for one outstanding example of such a student project, Fritz Krembs' "Dictionary of Homer.")

Cartoons: Each child draws a cartoon version—a simple storyboard—of the entire story. (We used to ask children to draw their comic strips at the end, but we have had more success in recent years asking them to add to the strip as each day's storytelling brings new adventures.) Each comic strip contains several dozen panels, so that every major episode is represented at least once. Again, the quality of the art work in this activity is not important—many children draw stick figures—and students are deliberately asked not to draw in detail. This exercise is intended to help children reconstruct the chronology of events, review the names of major characters and places, and think of important visual images for each episode.

Twenty Questions: The teacher, or a student, thinks of a character mentioned in the story, and the rest of the class tries to guess who it is. We

Characters and Places

Achilles: greatest fighter of Greek army

Aeolus: king of the winds

Agamemnon: commander of Greek army at Troy; brother of Menelaus; killed by his wife upon his return from the war

Ajax: largest and strongest of the Greeks

Alcinoös: (Alkinous, Alkinoös) Nausicaä's father, king of Phaeacians

Anticlea: mother of Odysseus

Antiphates: king of the Laestrygonians

Antinoös: leader of suitors; first to be killed (with the arrow in his throat)

Aphrodite: goddess of love & beauty, awarded the golden apple by Paris

Ares: god of war

Arete: Nausicaä's mother; queen of Phaeacians

Argus/Argos: Odysseus' dog

Athena: the grey-eyed goddess of wisdom, protector and friend of Odysseus

Calypso: goddess who loves Odysseus for 7 years; after Hermes tells her the will of Zeus, she helps Odysseus build his raft

Cassandra: priestess who could tell the future but no one believed her; warned against bringing horse into Troy

Charybdis: the whirlpool

Ciconians: people Odysseus raided immediately upon leaving Troy; horse men returned to kill six men in each ship

Circe: enchantress who turns O's men into pigs

Clytemnestra: wife of Agamemnon

Cyclops: another name for Polyphemus; Cyclopes is the name for his people

Elpenor: got drunk at Circe's, fell off roof & died; met O in Hades and asked for a proper burial

Eris: goddess of discord and strife

Eumaeus: the swineherd who remains faithful to Odysseus

Eurykleia: O's old nurse, who bathes his foot and recognizes him by the scar

Eurylochus: O's second-in-command; he did not enter Circe's house. He also appears in the episodes of Aeolus, the Sirens, and the Cattle of the Sun

Hades: brother of Zeus, lord of the land of the dead, which is also called Hades

Hector: greatest fighter in the Trojan army; son of the king and queen; brother of Paris; killed by Achilles and dragged behind a chariot around the walls of Troy

Hecuba: Queen of Troy

Helen: "most beautiful woman on earth"; "the face that launched a thousand ships"; married to Menelaus, but goes with Paris to Troy

Helios: god of the sun, whose cattle are killed by O's men on Thrinakia

Hephaestus: god of metal-working; married to Aphrodite; makes apple for Eris and later on makes new armor for Achilles

Hera: wife of Zeus, most powerful of the goddesses; wanted the golden apple

Hermes: messenger of the gods

Hyperion: another name for Helios

Ino: sea nymph who gives Odysseus her veil to help him to stay afloat

Iphigenia: daughter of Agamemnon and Clytemnestra, sacrificed to gain a fair wind for sailing to Troy

Laertes: father of Odysseus

Laestrygonians: giant cannibals who destroy 11 of Odysseus' 12 black-hulled ships

Laocoön: Trojan priest who warns against bringing Trojan Horse into the city; "I fear the Greeks bearing gifts!"

Leda: mother of Helen (and Clytemnestra)

Leukothea: see Ino

Lotus Eaters: whoever ate the lotus lost all thoughts of returning home; Odysseus nearly lost three of his men here

Maron: priest of Apollo who gives Odysseus the wine O later gives to Cyclops

Melanthius: shepherd in Ithaca who is mean to Odysseus upon his return

Menelaus: king of Sparta; husband of Helen, brother of Agamemnon

Nausicaä: princess of the Phaeacians; she welcomed Odysseus to her island and fell in love with him

Odysseus (note the spelling; you are responsible for spelling it correctly)

Paris: prince of Troy; brother of Hector; after giving the golden apple to Aphrodite, he takes Helen with him to Troy; with Apollo's help, shoots arrow into Achilles' heel

Patroklos: best friend of Achilles, killed by Hector in the Trojan War

FIGURE 2-4 *Characters and places in the* Odyssey

Characters and Places, *continued*

Peleus: husband of Thetis, father of Achilles

Penelope: wife of Odysseus and mother of Telemachus; she is under pressure to marry the suitors, but she postpones that decision by a clever trick. She pretends that she has to finish a piece of weaving, but then unweaves it at night.

Persephone: queen of the land of the dead

Phaeacians: seafaring people who finally take Odysseus back to Ithaca

Polyphemus: Cyclops; one-eyed giant; son of Poseidon, kills and eats six of O's men

Poseidon: god of the sea & brother of Zeus; angry with Odysseus after the blinding of Polyphemus

Priam: king of Troy; father of Paris

Scylla: six-headed monster who lives across the strait from Charybdis

Sirens: half bird, half woman, their singing lures men to their death

Teiresias: blind prophet whom Odysseus visits in the land of the dead

Telemachus: son of Odysseus

Thetis: sea nymph who marries Peleus; their wedding party is the scene of the Apple of Discord; mother of Achilles

Zeus: king and most powerful of all Olympian gods

Places:

Aegean Sea

Aeolia: floating island; home of Aeolus

Aiaia: home of Circe

Hades: land of the dead

Ionian Sea

Ismaros: home of Ciconians, in Thrace

Ithaca: home of Odysseus

Mediterranean Sea

Mycenae: home of Agamemnon

Ogygia: home of Calypso

Scheria: land of the Phaeacians

Sparta: home of Menelaus

Styx: river at entrance to Hades

Thrace: region in Greece, north of Troy

Thrinakia: island belonging to Helios

Troy

---

usually make this activity more challenging by insisting that questions can only be answered "yes" or "no," which encourages students to phrase their questions carefully. For example, children who ask, "Is it a god or a goddess?" are disconcerted when I answer, "Yes." They soon learn to be precise. This is a popular game for the start of a class or to fill out a few minutes at the end of a period.

Who am I?: This variation of "Twenty Questions" has an interesting twist. In "Twenty Questions," only one person knows the secret; here, everyone in the room knows the answer except the person who is it. Tape the name of an *Odyssey* character onto the back of a student volunteer, who turns around so the others can see the name. The volunteer then asks questions and chooses from the raised hands for a "yes" or "no" answer to her question. Students are encouraged to narrow the choices before guessing specific names. A typical session:

Am I immortal?
Did you say "a mortal" or "immortal"?
Immortal.

No.

Am I male?

Yes.

Did I fight during the Trojan War?

No.

Am I human?

Yes.

Did I meet Odysseus in one of his first several adventures?

No.

Did Odysseus see me in the land of the dead?

No.

Did I see Odysseus after he returned home to Ithaca?

Yes.

Am I related to Odysseus?

No.

Was I one of the suitors?

No.

Did I take care of animals?

Yes.

Am I Melanthius?

No.

Am I Eumaeus?

Yes. [Applause]

As the first question demonstrates, children soon learn to enunciate clearly. But even more than careful pronunciation, success requires careful thinking. Categories that seem clear-cut at first become fuzzy upon closer examination. Mortals and immortals are easy to separate, but how do we categorize nymphs? What attributes do they share? Charybdis was once a young woman; is she still mortal after she is turned into a whirlpool?

Answering these questions is complicated by alternate myths, which offer different explanations for the same phenomenon; Achilles' vulnerable heel is one well-known example. In one version of the story, his mother, Thetis, holds the infant over a fire to make him invulnerable but is stopped when Peleus, his mortal father, discovers what she is doing. In another story, Thetis dips her newborn baby in the waters of the River Styx, holding him by his heel and so leaving that part of his body vulnerable. Children who know both versions are startled when they learn that before reentering the Trojan War, Achilles waits for new armor to be made: "Why does he need armor and a shield if he can't be killed?"

Students become skilled at answering the question exactly as it is phrased, and the questioner needs to examine assumptions, as Jacob discovered in this excerpt from one game:

Am I a god?

No.

Am I human?

No.

I'm not a god and I'm not human. Hmm . . . [Looking puzzled] *Maybe I'm a monster. Are all monsters immortal?* [pause] *Am I immortal?*

No.

Am I a monster?

No.

So I'm not a god, I'm not a human, and I'm not a monster. That makes no sense . . . [Much later, with enthusiasm] *Oh, I know! Am I an object?*

No.

[Looking dejected] *So I'm not something like Odysseus' bow?*

Right.

[After twenty minutes of concerted questioning] *Am I an animal?*

Yes.

Am I Argos? [Odysseus' dog]

Yes! [enthusiastic applause]

If the volunteer is stuck, he may call on a classmate for a clue. That classmate has the responsibility of suggesting a legitimate question to ask, but not one that will give it away. The teacher can also vary the difficulty by choosing harder or easier characters depending on the volunteer. Children enjoy seeing a quiet girl with "Polyphemus" taped on her back, or a macho boy with "Aphrodite" on his, and the game allows children to laugh and work together. My journal recorded one day's session of this game:

> *One good part in both classes: as the child with the name tag walked around, it was clear that some watching kids obviously knew who the mystery character was, and others didn't. There was a lot of huddling, whispering, kids clumping together to share information. Maybe I can build on that. I think I'll ask them to work in groups of their choosing today. The task: make a list of the major episodes in the story and another list of gods and mortals mentioned. After doing that, we'll try playing the game again. Kids in both classes yesterday wanted to do more.*

When everyone is familiar with both the rules and a useful assortment of questions, we tape a name on everyone's back. Now, all the children are simultaneously trying to figure out their hidden names, but they may ask only two questions of one classmate and then must move on to someone else. Children eagerly wander around the room, asking and answering each other's questions until they correctly guess their secret identities. Then they rush up to the teacher, demand a new name, and re-enter the hubbub.

Riddles: This is a written variation on the previous two games. In our school, the activity originated when first graders attempted to stump fifth graders. The person with the riddle starts with a difficult clue, and follows with additional clues, each one giving away more information. By the time the last clue is reached, the audience should be able to guess the answer. My favorite first-grade riddle that year began, "I am everywhere in the story," and left us all baffled until the final clue, "I am wine-dark," at which point the fifth graders shouted out, "The sea!" My journal captured the day I first introduced riddle-writing:

Kids in my homeroom took the period to write "Who Am I" riddles, using as a model the ones that Brigid's first graders brought us last year. I asked for six to eight clues, beginning with hard ones and ending with one that would make it obvious. As an example, I listed clues that led to teacher Jim Tobin:

1) This person is a human being; 2) This person teaches at the Marion Cross School; 3) This person is male; 4) He does not teach fifth and sixth graders; 5) He plays the guitar; 6) He does not read Watership Down to his class; 7) He teaches second grade.

Kids started guessing on the second clue, but then slowed down. By the end, everyone knew who it was: "I knew that long ago!" The model made the assignment easy for them to understand.

They were slow in starting out, trying to figure out how to write clues. Then they'd come up with lots of clues but have trouble sequencing them. Lots of individual conferring about how to write tricky clues: "You don't have to say they lived on Ithaca at first. Why not say they lived on an island? That's a clue, sure, but it doesn't give away as much information. And here, instead of saying that Hermes gave me a warning, why not say they had a conversation with a god—that could be lots of people in lots of situations. The idea is not to give it away too soon. Okay?"

As time went on, kids started to get the hang of it. The assignment is a wonderful way of quizzing them on all the characters but in a more sophisticated way. Instead of my giving them tons of clues and them coming up with one name, this way they have to figure out all they know about the character and relate that information to what they know about all the other characters in the story. And because it's in a game format, it's fun, and a challenge, and kids enjoy doing it.

Here are three sample riddles. Try covering them and reading them a line at a time. (Caution! To answer, you need to be well-versed in Greek mythology. The bibliography offers suggestions for helping you refresh your memory on this subject.) Answers are found at the end.

1. I am immortal.
2. I am a male.
3. Odysseus never meets me in person.
4. I am very close to my animals.
5. They live on Thrinakia.
6. But I don't let anyone else touch them.
7. Odysseus spends months on my island without touching my cattle.
8. Odysseus' men disobey me and get bad luck.

(by Hillary)

I love Penelope, I try to string Odysseus' bow, I yell at a beggar, I am the first shot by Odysseus, and two streams of red come out of my throat.

(by Steve)

My daughter-in-law is Aphrodite.
My nephew is Triton.
I rescued my brothers and sisters from my dad.
I made someone let Odysseus go home.
I had my head split open when Athena was born.
My daughter is Athena, though I have other kids.
Who am I?

(by Graham)

(Answers: Helios; Antinoös; Zeus.)

Concentration: This is a literary variation of the well-known card game, sometimes called "Memory." Using three-by-five index cards, prepare a set of thirty to forty matching cards, for example, "Zeus" on one and "father of Athena" on another. Shuffle the cards and place them all face down on a table or rug; children take turns turning over two cards at a time, attempting to find matching pairs.

In the early years, I prepared different decks of cards—general *Odyssey* review, gods, characters from the Trojan War, mortals and monsters—and distributed them to interested students for play. More recently, students working in small groups have prepared their own clues and made up their own decks. The first method ensures that information in the clues is uniformly easy or difficult; the second method pushes children to examine specific wording, since each character can be described in many ways. Consider Penelope, for example. She could be "wife of Odysseus" or "mother of Telemachus," both easy clues. For more of a challenge, she could be "Eurykleia's mistress," "daughter-in-law of Laertes," or, harder still, "daughter-in-law of Antikleia." A clue could also say "She wove by day and unwove at night" or "She proposed two tests," the test of the bow and the test of the bed, which finally revealed

Odysseus' identity. Making Concentration cards, like making up riddles, pushes children to draw on all they know about a character.

Crossword puzzles:

Finding an appropriate character description is also important in completing a crossword puzzle. At a minimum, students try to solve a variety of *Odyssey* crosswords created by others; for several years, they also constructed their own puzzles before swapping them with classmates. Designing a crossword puzzle is not an easy task; I set aside more than a week for children to complete their own. In addition to writing clues that are not too hard and not too easy, counting squares on graph paper is a tedious task. Children frequently discover mistakes that need correcting, and many puzzles have to be re-drawn. Once a puzzle is tested and then completed in ink, the child asks the school secretary to make photocopies to share with other students and faculty.

Picture sequence:

Photocopy illustrations from different versions of *The Odyssey,* mount them on oaktag or poster board, and laminate them for repeated use. The challenge? "Arrange these pictures in the order that they happened in the story." With forty pictures spread out before them on the rug, small groups of children can easily spend an entire forty-five-minute class period sorting and discussing. Some pictures, showing men being turned into pigs or a ragged beggar effortlessly stringing a bow, are easy to place. Others require more careful discrimination, such as one picture of a storm-battered ship:

> "Where do you think this goes? Right after Polyphemus, when they were escaping from his cave?"
>
> "No, because the ship is damaged. And when Poly was throwing the boulders at Odysseus' ship, he missed both times. Remember? One landed just in front of the ship, and one landed right behind it. Besides, you can't see any islands in the picture, and at Polyphemus', you'd be able to see either his island or the other small island, where the rest of the ships were waiting. I think it's the storm after the bag of winds was opened."
>
> "No, that doesn't work, either. Odysseus still had all his ships then, so you'd see all twelve ships, not just one. He didn't lose the other eleven ships until the Laestrygonians."
>
> "Hey! Look at the lightning bolt in the corner!"
>
> "Yes! It's when Helios asks Zeus to destroy the ship, after the men kill the cattle of the sun. There's the mast floating in the water; that's the one that Odysseus hangs on when he escapes. We got it!"

Since certain episodes are described in more detail in Homer's tale, and since illustrators have their own favorite episodes, our collection includes a dozen pictures from the Polyphemus episode alone. This forces children to be even more precise, looking at minute details to place the picture correctly. This activity also leads children to notice discrepancies in the pictures; sometimes an artist includes details that do not follow the information given in the text. Which is correct? Looking carefully at pictures also adds to the student's visual storehouse, a stockpile of images which can be drawn on as needed.

Listen again: Many children want to hear the spoken stories more than once. With permission, we record the storyteller's presentations, sometimes on audiocassette and sometimes on video. Many children borrow these tapes to take home. Having taped versions lets children who were absent hear what they missed. Students have also enjoyed listening to a previous year's version from a given storyteller and comparing it to the version they heard. (The bibliography lists taped versions of *The Odyssey* that are commercially available.) Listening to the story on tape is a poor substitute for a flesh-and-blood storyteller, but even a taped story benefits students in tackling an unfamiliar text.

Read good translations aloud: Every day or two in the opening weeks of our study, I like to read selected passages orally. My favorite *Odyssey* is Robert Fitzgerald's translation, although I also read Richmond Lattimore's and, for comparison, occasional selections from other translators. Never mind that these books pay no attention to the controlled vocabulary so dear to the creators of basal reading series. It's important to let the sound of well-written, rhythmic English flow from your tongue; children will get the sense of what you're saying and will be enriched by their exposure to new words. Here, for example, is Homer's lyrical description of the island of the nymph Calypso, a passage full of vivid images the audience will feel even if they do not immediately understand all the words:

> Upon her hearthstone a great fire blazing
> scented the farthest shores with cedar smoke
> and smoke of thyme, and singing high and low
> in her sweet voice, before her loom a-weaving,
> she passed her golden shuttle to and fro.
> A deep wood grew outside, with summer leaves
> of alder and black poplar, pungent cypress.
> Ornate birds here rested their stretched wings—
> horned owls, falcons, cormorants—long-tongued
> beachcombing birds, and followers of the sea.
> Around the smoothwalled cave a crooking vine
> held purple clusters under ply of green;
> and four springs, bubbling up near one another
> shallow and clear, took channels here and there

through beds of violets and tender parsley.
Even a god who found this place
would gaze, and feel his heart beat with delight:
so Hermês did . . .

The Odyssey V, trans. Fitzgerald

Such a passage cries out for colorful illustrations. We distribute several descriptions like this and ask children to choose one and draw a detailed picture. This activity encourages them to read and reread the passage, strengthening their familiarity with this rich language.

Children often want to know if the version told to them is "correct," if the storyteller took liberties with the original. On one level it is an easy question, since each storyteller makes no pretense about staying completely faithful to the original. Each spoken version is unique. At the same time—and this is more difficult for ten-year-olds to comprehend—each English translation is different from the Greek original. (See Chapter 4, "Transforming Children into Storytellers," for further discussion of this point.) Instead of answering the question immediately, I ask students to select a favorite episode, and then I read that passage from a translation. We discover that while the storytellers often come up with their own wording, and sometimes with their own details, they generally remain true to the spirit of Homer's tale.

Take the blinding of Polyphemus, always a popular moment. Children sometimes ask if the version they heard is more gory than the original, whether the spoken tale was somehow embellished to make it more appealing to an audience of schoolchildren. We need do little more than consider Fitzgerald's version of that moment:

Now, by the gods, I drove my big hand spike
deep in the embers, charring it again,
and cheered my men along with battle talk
to keep their courage up: no quitting now.
The pike of olive, green though it had been,
reddened and glowed as if about to catch.
I drew it from the coals and my four fellows
gave me a hand, lugging it near the Kyklops
as more than natural force nerved them; straight
forward they sprinted, lifted it, and rammed it
deep in his crater eye, and I leaned on it
turning it as a shipwright turns a drill
in planking, having men below to swing
the two-handled strap that spins it in the groove.
So with our brand we bored that great eye socket
while blood ran out around the red hot bar.

Eyelid and lash were seared; the pierced ball
hissed broiling, and the roots popped.

The Odyssey IX, trans. Fitzgerald

No one hearing that passage will grow up thinking that the classics are boring. I love studying Homer with children because there is something for everyone. Blood and guts, action and adventure, romance and love, magic and monsters and mystery, courage and cowardice, honor and heroism—it's a rare child who cannot get interested in at least part of this story.

What about the violence in the Homeric epics? Is this material appropriate for ten- and eleven-year-olds? Should we be exposing children to such vivid descriptions, to such horrific situations?

This is not a question raised by children. To be sure, there are the groans and expressions of disgust during the Polyphemus episode, the occasional "Gross!" and the sick faces. But the violence in this tale is rooted in context. The gory details supplement the story; they are not the story by themselves. Indeed, children discussing an episode after a storytelling session frequently learn that their mental pictures differ markedly, that the scary parts are so effective precisely because so much is left to the imagination. In later readings, they are often struck by the spareness of many of the scenes. The episode of the cannibal Laestrygonians, for example, during which eleven of the twelve ships are destroyed and all the sailors killed, is one of the shortest in the entire *Odyssey*.

Later in the year, when we study classic Greek drama from the fifth century B.C., three hundred years after the composition of the Homeric epics, students learn that violent action takes place off stage. For example, in *Antigone* messengers bring news of the suicides of Antigone, Haemon, and queen Eurydice. Children acting in productions of Greek tragedies often express their admiration of the playwrights for leaving such brutal scenes to the imagination of the audience.

Review sheets and quizzes: After some three weeks of review, everyone takes a quiz on major *Odyssey* characters; before the quiz, they can look at samples from past years' exams. (See Figure 2-5 for one such quiz.) By the time of the test, the children are ready; the confusion of the early days has changed into an easy familiarity. Most fifth graders score in the 90's; those few children with low scores receive additional assistance and a chance to take a retest.

Why does this work? How are so many children able to feel comfortable with such unfamiliar material?

For effective learning to take place, says Dartmouth psychology professor G. Christian Jernstedt, some 20 percent of a learner's time should be spent meeting new material and 80 percent rehearsing that information. Sadly, many schools follow a model of nearly 100 percent new

FIGURE 2-5
*"Key Characters in the
Odyssey" quiz*

Key Characters in the Odyssey

Directions: Match each name from the list on the left with the correct description on the right. Write the letter of your choice in each space, as shown in the sample. **Some names may be used more than once; some names may not be used at all.**

A. Achilles	**E** Goddess who helped Odysseus throughout his journey.
B. Aeolus	___ She waited 19 years for her husband to return.
C. Agamemnon	___ Cannibals who destroyed 11 of Odysseus' 12 ships.
D. Ajax	___ Sea nymph who cared for Odysseus for seven years.
E. Athena	___ King of Mycenae; brother of Menelaus.
F. Calypso	___ She wove all day, then ripped out her weaving at night.
G. Charybdis	___ Son of Odysseus.
H. Circe	___ He hung onto a tree to avoid being sucked into a whirlpool.
I. Helen	___ Helen went with him to Troy.
J. Hector	___ King of the winds.
K. Helios	___ Six-headed monster who yipped from her home.
L. Hermes	___ He was furious that his cattle were killed.
M. Iphigenia	___ One-eyed monster tricked by Nobody.
N. Laestrygonians	___ Their beautiful singing killed men.
O. Lotus Eaters	___ God of the sea.
P. Menelaus	___ Enchantress who turned men into pigs.
Q. Nausicaä	___ Their drug made men forget their homes.
R. Odysseus	___ She sucked in the sea each day, making a whirlpool.
S. Paris	___ Princess who found Odysseus while doing her laundry.
T. Penelope	___ Father of Athena, and mightiest of the gods.
U. Polyphemus	___ Husband of Penelope, and son of Laertes.
V. Poseidon	___ Phaeacian princess who helped Odysseus.
W. Scylla	___ Father of Polyphemus, he hated Odysseus.
X. Sirens	___ He had to choose the winner of a golden apple.
Y. Telemachus	___ Most beautiful woman on earth.
Z. Zeus	

EXTRA CREDIT

Directions: Listed below are eleven characters from our story. Choose between one and five names and write a short identification of that person. Each name correctly identified is worth 2 points. *If you describe more than five characters, you will receive no extra credit points at all.* [This sentence is to encourage students to read directions. Children who lost extra credit points

continued next page

Key Characters in the Odyssey, *continued*

on this quiz reported to me as high school students that they still read directions carefully as a consequence of this experience.]

Alkinoös	Eurylochus
Antinoös	Hecuba
Cassandra	Laocoön
Elpenor	Priam
Eumaeus	Teiresias
Eurykleia	

material and 0 percent rehearsal. Think of the stereotypical course organized around daily lectures and nightly assignments in the textbook, the grim pedagogy of one fact after another. In such settings, students constantly encounter new information, with precious little time and intellectual engagement to let it all sink in. That's one reason why social studies in general—and history in particular—has such a dismal reputation and why it is consistently cited in student polls as the "least favorite" subject in American schools. Through these overlapping *Odyssey* activities, children have many opportunities to review the same material in different ways.

3 | INTEGRATING THE ARTS

*Limitation makes for power. The
strength of the genii comes from his
being confined in the bottle.*
—*Richard Wilbur*

Language is only one way of sharing information and emotions in human society. Art serves a similar function. The language skills of young children are rarely developed enough to enable them to fully express their emotions or their understanding, and a teacher does well to provide extensive opportunities for students to create art as part of their studies.

Building art projects into the curriculum is not new territory for me; I have known for years that emphasizing only reading and writing in an elementary classroom guarantees failure for many children who still have much to contribute in other media. This realization is not original; Sybil Marshall's *An Experiment in Education* (1963) is an excellent narrative of how, as an elementary teacher in England, she discovered methods for making art an integral part of her classroom. Just as children learn in diverse ways, they also prefer different ways of sharing what they have learned.

Encouraging—no, demanding that—children explore the visual arts in an elementary classroom also pushes everyone to explore new territory. The emotional reactions hidden inside the organization of a research paper may spill onto a page with watercolors; subtleties and small details that lurked inside a scribbled drawing may emerge fully formed in a clay sculpture. New materials present new possibilities and new challenges. Each completed project demonstrates a different facet of a child's understanding.

We have seen how children were encouraged to make their own drawings in response to the telling of the *Odyssey* stories. This chapter explores art projects that involve the whole class (individual art projects are profiled in Chapter 5).

POTTERY: AN ANCIENT ART COMES FIRST

The Homeric poems are believed to have been created around 750 B.C., in what classicists call the Archaic Period of ancient Greek history, the several hundred years before the height of classical Greek civilization in the fifth century B.C. In the same way that starting with storytelling had simply felt like the right thing to do, it also seemed appropriate to introduce children to an ancient art form.

When the Odyssey Project began, the school's art teacher, Connie Skewes, was a potter in her own right. In our second year, seeking to find ways to coordinate art classes with the social studies curriculum, she contacted several potter friends and asked them to throw more than forty pots, one for each student, in many different shapes of classical Greek pottery. Each child was given a pot to decorate, and another Norwich tradition was born.

A year later, with a change of personnel, our new art teacher had a problem. A fabric artist herself, she was reluctant to lean on the same volunteers for new pots, and the number of children had steadily increased. She turned to a local ceramics studio for assistance, and selected several small bowls and vases that had clean lines. The studio would pour as many copies as we needed at a reasonable price; furthermore, they could provide a clay that produced a pleasing reddish color when fired. After several years of searching for an attractive black finish, we finally settled on materials to complete our own red- and black-figured vases. Students use an underglaze called "One Stroke," which works as simply as its name suggests. It produces a luminous black to complement the orange of the clay. On top of the "One Stroke" children paint a transparent glaze, which adds lustre and allows the fired piece to hold water. In the early years, children simply painted black lines on the clay; more recently, they have been experimenting with scratched lines on a black background, which produces a dramatic effect (see Figures 3-1 and 3-2).

FIGURE 3-1
Nongeometric pottery: Polyphemus *(Sam Madeira)*

Students studied dozens of slides of Greek pottery, looked at numerous pictures of vases, and sketched different border designs before they started work on their pots. Their goal was to create an illustration using *The Odyssey* or *The Iliad* as a source of inspiration. Children were generally pleased with the results, and as the years went by, we noticed that younger siblings got excited when it came to be their turn. The art teacher would start to introduce the pottery project and she'd often be interrupted: "Oh, we have a vase like that my sister made when she was in fifth grade."

We finally realized just how much the pots meant to children the year we proposed a change. We were looking for something different, and instead of glazing pots, we asked students to design large medallions or small shields. There was a revolt in all three classes, and even polite students protested: "We've been waiting *years* to make pots in fifth grade. It's not fair." We placed a hurried order for small pots and gained a renewed understanding of the importance of tradition in children's lives.

FIGURE 3-2
Nongeometric pottery: Owl detail *(Sarah Torkelson)*

Of continuing concern, though, were those children who didn't like to draw. They found the pottery work frustrating. It didn't matter whether they were designing small vases or large medallions: creating images for their pots was a formidable task.

One summer, shortly before I left for a long-anticipated trip to Greece, our principal took me aside and handed me a check for two hundred dollars. "There's some money left in a curriculum account," he said. "You're going to be in a great position to get things that you can use in the *Odyssey* unit. Keep your eyes open for whatever seems appropriate. There's one condition, though."

"What's that?" I asked.

"You have to use part of the money to ship back what you buy," he said. "I don't want you lugging pottery and books all over Greece for the six weeks, even if it does save money." The small sum went a long way in that poor nation. My wife and I soon found that nearly every large town had a souvenir shop specializing in inexpensive replicas of ancient pots. We purchased half a dozen samples and mailed them home.

During the Homeric era, the Archaic Period, pots were decorated in what we now refer to as the Geometric style. The work is characterized by extensive rows of repeating designs, with only small areas set aside for representations of human activities. Human figures are a composite of simple geometric forms. Elizabeth Barber (1992) of Occidental College

FIGURE 3-3   *Greek* pyxis

has suggested that these figures are the work of craftsmen copying complex woven tapestries, which were the art forms that survived the chaos of the breakup of the earlier and richer Mycenaean kingdoms. With a brush and glaze, there is no inherent necessity to make human torsos so angular, she argues; later fifth-century masterpieces demonstrate clearly that human musculature can be shown in detail. But weavers are limited by the rectangular grid of warp and weft, resulting in simplified step-by-step triangles for the human torso and stick-figure legs and arms, the same shapes that appear on Geometric pots. Whatever their origin, the human figures on Geometric pottery are stick-figure art raised to a higher plane (see Figure 3-3). I suspected that many children, frustrated by their own drawing abilities, would love seeing examples of work they could copy.

That next year, children studied our growing collection of photographs of red- and black-figured vases and the more confident artists attempted their own designs in that flowing style. But the newly purchased reproductions were passed from hand to hand and examined closely; the bands of geometric designs struck a nearly universal chord. The effect was as I had hoped. Even the least skilled children could see that repeating a few simple shapes resulted in an attractive finished product. Some children started painting pots that consisted of little more than repeating designs, very much in the Geometric style (see Figures 3-4, 3-5, and 3-6).

Our experiences with pottery demonstrated again that limiting the range of choices encouraged children to produce better work than if they had been given freer assignments. It took me a long time to learn the lesson, repeated in many different forms, that structure enhances creativity.

FIGURE 3-4
Geometric vase with owl (Lynn McCormick)

FIGURE 3-5
Geometric vase (Nick Hall)

DIORAMAS: BUILDING SMALL WORLDS

Start with Homer's *Odyssey,* a tale of adventure on a grand scale, and look at it in detail. What happens when you examine it minutely or, more accurately, when you attempt to re-create it in miniature?

Children are fascinated by the world of the small. David Sobel (1993), a professor of education and environmental science at Antioch New England Graduate School, argues that children use hiding places like treehouses and forts as a social space in which they can discover themselves. Within a short time, they turn their attention to organizing the new society that will use the space and creating elaborate rituals as they figure out what the rules will be. They pay loving attention to building their special places and to creating their own social order, a microcosm of the larger society in which they live.

Students bring that same passion for detail to the *Odyssey* assignment in which they are asked to work in small groups to construct a diorama of a scene from the tale. I knew from past work with model-making that

FIGURE 3-6
Geometric vase with alternating animal motifs and other designs (Ceileigh Syme)

children would attempt to build on wildly different scales, using for their models anything from shoeboxes to a refrigerator carton. Therefore, for the diorama assignment I imposed two restrictions:

- Each group's diorama had to be built in a standard ten-ream paper box.
- Every human figure had to be built around a standard clothespin.

Again, I followed the principle of freedom within structure. I chose the paper boxes for many reasons—they were sturdy; their similar size would make storage easier; they came with lids, and there was no shortage of them, thanks to the school's photocopier, which regularly consumed vast quantities of paper. Why clothespins? With everyone working on the same scale, figures from one diorama would fit in any other. A giant such as Polyphemus would tower over the human figures instead of being the same size as an Odysseus in a neighboring scene.

We divided *The Odyssey* into twelve major installments, and each group of four or five children chose episodes by lot. In this way we were assured of a series of models to illustrate much of the story, rather than many projects representing one popular scene. Selecting episodes at random also meant that most children would be working with a different story than the one they were going to tell.

Before we could start building, we had to rearrange the room. We pushed several long tables into a row and filled them with supplies: One held felt and fabric, leather and lace, buttons and beads and bric-a-brac. There were boxes filled with wood scraps. There were erasers and stamp pads, tempera paints, wads of cotton, and hunks of modeling clay. One table held containers of sand and gravel, twigs and grasses, and the necessary clothespins and pipe cleaners. Several trays kept construction paper, wallpaper samples, and adhesive-backed gold and silver paper that had been recycled through a children's museum. Another table was fitted out as a small workshop, with glue, brads, hammers, saws, clamps, and that modern boon to classroom projects, the hot-melt glue gun. We covered the computers carefully with sheets and pushed them into a distant corner.

For a week the room was an absolute mess; I spoke to the custodians beforehand and asked them to do only minimal cleaning during that time. Indeed, at the end of several especially hectic days, I posted a "Do Not Clean" sign on the door, preferring to let the children face the consequences of the mess they had left behind the previous day.

The first time we built dioramas I expected students to talk to each other in their groups, to review their common episode, to argue over what particular moment in the adventure would be shown in their model. I expected that they would come up with an overall scheme and would then divide specific tasks among group members. I knew they would enjoy creating their miniature worlds, and I thought the project would provide a good review of the stories. But I had not anticipated how much new learning they would do as a result of this assignment.

Take, for example, human figures; every diorama needed half a dozen or more. How should they be dressed? We turned first to Homer, looking through full translations for as many details as we could find. Children started learning how to navigate that thick book: "It'll be in the Polyphemus section, Book IX, right after the Lotus Eaters." Out came the different illustrated editions of *The Odyssey* as children pored over pictures for fresh information. As they quickly discovered, different illustrators had different conceptions of appropriate clothing. Where else could they look? "The library," exclaimed one girl, and several more dashed out the door, returning ten minutes later lugging histories of costume and clothing. Meanwhile, one boy was rummaging through the books on the Greek shelf in the classroom library and discovered Peter Connolly's lavishly illustrated book *The Greek Armies,* filled with detailed pictures of shields and swords, helmets and body armor. Children making soldiers discarded white cloth and generic robes and reached for the box of leather scraps, shaping sturdy tunics instead. Similar investigations produced information about buildings, ships, and even the landscape of Mediterranean hillsides. This research heightened children's understanding of the stories they had heard, and those details inevitably reappeared in their own storytelling and writing.

MURALS: SEEING THE BIG PICTURE

If the dioramas heightened the fifth graders' appreciation for the minute details of the tale, working on a large mural reinforced the grand scale of the story, its "epicness." Students had made murals several times before in the Odyssey Project: two children had painted a series of large pictures on large paper and joined the sheets together. However, we had never attempted working as a class on the scale I now had in mind. I wanted to create something monumental.

Once again, I turned to Tracy Goudy, the art teacher, for help. I proposed several different possibilities—a giant version of the comic strips children had completed earlier, or a long strip of butcher paper running the entire length of the hallway, or a series of panels that would be fastened together one after another. Then Tracy said, "You know, it could be round."

I stared at her. "Round?"

"Round," she said, quickly sketching a circle on a piece of scrap paper. I smiled. That year, we had moved into a just-completed addition to the school. There was a large blank wall over the stairwell leading up to the fifth-grade hallway—a space crying out to be filled.

A few days later Tracy and I met after school in the multipurpose room. We laid out wide strips of brown paper, overlapped the edges, and glued one piece to another. Using string and a pencil as our compass, we marked off a circle twelve feet in diameter and cut along the line. The circle was enormous.

"There has to be a border," I said.

"Okay," she said. "They really liked doing borders on their pottery this year." We drew another circle about a foot in from the edge.

"Let's divide it into sections," I suggested. "Otherwise, we're going to have twenty-some kids in each class getting in each other's way." Thinking back to the dozen dioramas, we divided the circle into twelve wedge-shaped pieces.

"Those points in the middle are awkward," she said. "You can't really do much in that space."

"Let's put another circle in the center," I agreed. "We could have another set of border designs and leave the center blank. Let the kids figure out what to put there."

FIGURE 3-7   *Lotus Eaters*   FIGURE 3-8   *Polyphemus*   FIGURE 3-9   *Aeolus*

Twelve panels in all would allow each of the three classes to complete four, which meant that each group working at a given time could be spaced at a distance from its neighbors. (See Figures 3–7 through 3–12.)

Children completed the mural, from start to finish, in just over a week. On Monday in social studies I gave each class a pep talk. We visited the site and tried to imagine how it would look with the finished mural. We looked at a diagram of the mural, similar to the one shown above, and we discussed how the project would be organized. After we drew names to form the groups, there was a little time left in the period to start talking with group members. The following day in art class and in social studies, the groups started their sketches, frequently working on scrap paper the size of a finished panel. They also tested ideas for border designs. By Wednesday, they were drawing on the mural itself, both the major panel and the borders. (We had to rearrange the social studies room once again, pushing desks and tables to the corners to provide enough space for the mural to fit on the floor. Students also established new class rules, such as removing shoes before walking on the mural.) Early in the week, one of the groups decided that the border designs outside each section should reflect the scene being depicted, which gave the border makers a clearer focus. Artists retraced their lines in heavy black marker—Tracy provided an entire box of new markers. By Thursday, most of the panels were finished, but the mural as a whole looked flat. One of the groups started filling in areas of the sea so that alternate swells were solid black, and the idea caught on. Thursday afternoon, my homeroom class had permission from other groups to go around and fill in appropriate areas. Those massive black areas made the mural jump to life. We stood around the outside rim, admiring our work.

FIGURE 3-10   *Sirens*

FIGURE 3-11   *Calypso*

FIGURE 3-12   *Cattle of the Sun*

That left the center. I had no idea what would come of that. Each class selected a few representatives who would meet as a group to finish the project. They decided to add another border, the Greek meander, which would delineate the central circle. They divided the remaining area into thirds, with an even smaller circle in the center. In those four central panels they represented the four elements of the Greek universe: earth, air, fire, and water. Air was symbolized by a picture of Aeolus, king of the winds; fire, by Hephaestus, the blacksmith god; water by Poseidon, and earth by a map of mainland Greece and neighboring islands. The students' task was finished.

Hanging the mural in the stairwell was another major project involving improvised scaffolding, several ladders, and an equal number of adults. More than once, as I dangled high above the floor balancing duct tape and pushpins, I wondered if this whole project wasn't an insane idea. But we finally got the map mounted and taped it well. It made quite an impression on everyone. At the end of the year, we removed the mural to free the wall space for future projects. For the next few years, as younger children reached fifth grade, I was able to refer back to that mural and be greeted with a roomful of nods—they remembered.

The project built a wonderful sense of camaraderie and the fifth graders took noticeable pride in their accomplishment. In schools today, in our quest to make each child accountable and in our desire to individualize academic offerings to meet each child's needs, we fre-

FIGURE 3-13
The Odyssey *mural*

quently lose sight of the power that comes from feeling part of a group. Most children at this age are intensely social, and with clear expectations and some help in working together, they will strive to meet the challenge.

WORKING WITH A MUSEUM

One autumn, the Hood Museum of Art at nearby Dartmouth College mounted an exhibition centered on the Panathenaic Festival, the most important recurring event in ancient Athens. (About one-third of the days in ancient Athens were set aside for festivals, and the Panathenaic Festival, a sort of birthday party for Athena, was the most important of them all. It took place each year, and every fourth year it assumed even greater significance.) Normally, the fifth graders study ancient Greece in the spring, but we changed our schedule that year in order to take full advantage of the show. It was an unparalleled opportunity.

Conventional wisdom dictates careful preparation before taking children to a museum, and most of the time, I agree. Our introduction to *The Odyssey,* however, had been a leap directly into the story. There was time enough for explanation and interpretation after the initial encounter. I decided to follow a similar pattern with the museum show. We booked visiting time in the small galleries and arranged the schedule to allow each fifth-grade class more than an hour alone. I specifically asked that we *not* be given the standard tour. I wanted my students to come to the show with fresh eyes, to look and see whatever they could, without preconceived notions of what they "should" observe.

Children had three basic assignments on that introductory visit:

- Walk around and look at anything you want in the exhibit.
- Explore the information displayed on the computers.
- Spend most of your time drawing, and concentrate on one or two pots.

After the initial burst of excitement, as children rushed to the touch-screen computer and gazed with awe at dozens of amphoras, the gallery grew quiet. They settled down to their drawing; many spent a full forty-five minutes staring intently at one piece, meticulously copying designs onto their drawing pads.

The entire show had been inspired by a single large piece (see Figure 3-14) in the Dartmouth collection, which was joined by many similar pots for this exhibition. These large amphoras had been commissioned by the Athenian government as prizes for the Panathenaic athletic contests. Depending on the event, the winner received a number of prize amphoras filled with olive oil, a valuable commodity in the ancient world. The vases had a special shape, and they were always decorated with a large figure of Athena on one side and the appropriate athletic competition on the other. Interestingly, most of the sports illustrations of ancient Greek athletics in general, and the Olympics in particular, that fill our textbooks come not from the Olympic games, where the only prize was a wreath, but from the Panathenaic Games. There, the city-state sponsored the special production of the prize amphoras, in part to advertise the wealth of Athens in faraway regions. The athletic events pictured provide classicists today with an important source of information about early athletic competitions.

Back at school after our gallery visit, instead of hearing a short lecture, children shared their observations in answer to a series of questions:

FIGURE 3-14
*Panathenaic vase with
Athena*

- What were the athletic contests in the Panathenaic Festival that you saw depicted on the pots?
- What objects had Greek letters on them?
- How is Athena depicted?
- What is one piece of information you learned from the computer program?

Everyone had seen different objects and everyone had seen the same objects. The children argued about what had been depicted on certain pots, referring to their drawings and to the item number. Most important, each child was able to contribute to the growing body of pooled knowledge. That body of shared knowledge, and the visceral impact of dozens of Greek amphoras, became the starting point for our study of classical Greece that year.

In the months that followed, children created their own artwork in Greek style. Nearly half our students worked in collaborative groups to produce large coil-built amphoras inspired by the Greek models on display (see Figures 3-15 and 3-16). With instruction from a local master weaver, other students worked together on large vertical looms, producing their own version of the woven *peplos* presented to the cult statue of Athena (Figure 3-17). Everyone made wax models of coins, tiny sculptures that were then cast in bronze at Dartmouth's jewelry workshop (see Figures 3-18, 3-19, and 3-20). In the same way that the Homeric stories inspire students, so did the opportunity to see actual objects from 2,500 years ago. The museum show opened new doors into the ancient world.

FIGURE 3-15
*Stamnos amphora
(Cyrus Cross, Dylan
Brown, Phil Goelet,
Josh Hill, Hugh Karol,
Worth Parker, Geoff
Vitt)*

FIGURE 3-17   *Peplos woven for Athena*

FIGURE 3-16
*Stamnos amphora (Nick
Colacchio, Rachel
Collier, Jenna McRee,
Jamie Sachs, Aaron
Sheldon, Nick Vincent)*

FIGURE 3-18
Turtle (John Thorne-Thomsen)

FIGURE 3-19
Owl (Molly Turco)

FIGURE 3-20
Dots around rim (Andrew Larkin)

When I started out as a teacher, I was responsible for all subjects; this is often called a "self-contained" classroom. In Norwich, I had primary responsibility for one subject, social studies; this was a "departmentalized" classroom. Although I had always enjoyed teaching all subjects, one of the unexpected pleasures in a departmentalized schedule was being able to conduct a lesson twice, once for each section of fifth grade. Beforehand, I imagined that it would be boring, but I discovered that I liked the opportunity of refining a lesson the second time through. I could try one way of presenting information, and if it didn't work, modify my plans for the second class. Since I usually have teaching interns working with me, this coincidentally provided an ideal environment in which they could hone their own teaching skills. I could teach a lesson to one class and my intern could try the same thing with the second class. Sometimes we would switch the order, letting the intern try out an idea first and then watch to see how I did it. Many times the intern would teach both sections, and would learn that each class has its own chemistry; a lesson that went extremely well with one class might flop with a different class. Instead of waiting another year, we could experiment the same day and find a better way of helping children learn.

As our school grew, the two sections of fifth-grade social studies became three. The third time through a lesson, it was sometimes hard to remember what I had just said and what I was remembering from a previous period. (On those days, I thought sympathetically about high school teachers who meet many sections of the same class.) It grew increasingly difficult, with our constantly changing schedule, to keep all three sections in step with each other; despite my best efforts, there would inevitably be a fire drill or similar event that only affected one class.

The solution was as obvious as it was slow in coming: Not every class has to cover the same material in the same way. That year, each class tackled a completely different art project connected with *The Odyssey*. One class built a large mobile of important characters from the *Odyssey* to hang from the upper-grade balcony, each student picking a name from a hat. They sketched the final figures on foam-core matboard and then applied liberal amounts of paint, wool, yarn, cloth, glitter, and other accessories. After the mobile was assembled and hung, each student contributed a paragraph description of his or her character to be included in a large chart hanging on the wall, a key for other classes to read as they looked at the mobile.

A second class created a "video filmstrip" based on a series of drawings in the style of red- and black-figured vase paintings. After they had done the usual preliminary sketches, students made a good drawing on white paper, each student selecting a major episode or an important moment in a particularly long episode. We photocopied each drawing and the children quickly colored several different versions, comparing the look of black figures on a red background to red figures on a black background. Then they painted their final picture as they wished. We filmed each picture with the school's video camera, with the artist standing by to provide narration for that part of the story.

Children enjoyed the process, and I know that it can be successfully implemented. In the PBS series *The Civil War* and his later history of baseball, for example, filmmaker Ken Burns skillfully demonstrates the power of a camera moving slowly over a still image. Our finished film, however, was less successful. Each illustration was on camera for too long, and despite the extreme closeups, there was rarely enough detail to hold the viewer's attention. The next time we try this, instead of attempting to cover the entire *Odyssey* we'll pick one episode only and break it into twenty discrete moments; each child can illustrate that particular moment. Less breadth, more depth, better film.

The third class that year, my homeroom, worked under the direction of the teaching intern. Their assignment? In small groups, construct a board game based on *The Odyssey*. This project took three weeks and yielded several outstanding games, each very different from the others. Children delighted in creating their own games and in playing those made by their classmates. Creating board games is an easy and effective way to review nearly any substantial body of material.

One consistent lesson emerges from these diverse projects, whether miniature dioramas or the grand mural: Give children an *ambitious* yet *appealing* task, provide a *structure* so everyone knows what is expected, help them break the overall job into *discrete parts,* and stand back. The results will be impressive.

4 | TRANSFORMING CHILDREN INTO STORYTELLERS

Sing in me, Muse, and through me tell
the story of that man skilled in all ways
of contending . . . Of these adventures,
Muse, daughter of Zeus, tell us in our
time, lift the great song again.

The Odyssey I, trans. Fitzgerald

Several years before my *Odyssey* fascination began, I was given a valuable lesson that helped me discover the power of storytelling in a classroom. I had asked my teaching intern, Jo Valens, to prepare a lesson on Columbus for our sixth graders, who were studying American history. Jo had been

trained as a Waldorf teacher, and some weeks later, she told me that she planned to tell a story about Columbus. I was doubtful about her chances for success, but decided to give her lots of rope, quietly rehearsing the speech that I would deliver afterward on Why This Wouldn't Work.

"Do you want me to watch, to give you some feedback?"

"No," she said. "I think that this first time I'd like to be alone with the children. Maybe later."

At the end of class, Jo said she needed more time, that things were taking longer than she had expected.

"How did it go?"

"I think they're fine," she said, and that was all.

The next day, I was startled to discover a group of the most difficult boys in the sixth grade racing down the hall, eager to be the first to reach the classroom.

"What's the rush?" I asked, as I sent them back down the hall to walk.

"She's telling the rest of the Columbus story today, and we want to get a good seat!" Something unusual was going on.

I followed them into the room—Jo nodded that it was okay—and observed several things during the period. First of all, students were paying unusually close attention to her story. Second, she included all the facts I considered essential. The difference in presentation originated in Jo's mind; she saw herself as a storyteller rather than a lecturer. At that moment, I knew that I wanted to incorporate storytelling into my classroom.

This chapter will examine the storytelling process in detail and the decision to expand the role of storytelling in my classes. How did we start? Why listen to stories anyhow? Why ask children to tell them? And once that decision has been made, how do fifth graders become storytellers?

An incident from the first year of the Odyssey Project reinforced my earlier desire to explore storytelling in school. I had asked for volunteers to tell the first graders an episode from Homer, and only one child had raised his hand. I think it fair to say that he was a boy who had met with few successes in school. In a class of academically oriented children, he was slow to learn what we had to teach; surrounded by skillful readers and writers, he was neither. But he had absolutely no qualms about telling a story. He went to the first-grade room and delivered an excellent version of the story of Aeolus, king of the winds. He remained true to the basic thrust of the story, and it was clear from his animated telling that he was caught up in his tale.

In that one afternoon, he moved to the center of attention. His classmates crowded around him upon his return from the first grade classroom: "How did you start? Weren't you nervous? How did you remember what to say next?" I decided then to require that everyone tell a story from Homer. I wanted to validate his success, and I wanted the other children to experience the thrill of successfully learning a tale and passing it on. Having good storytelling models was a crucial part of the process.

For the project's first four years, Odds Bodkin came as a storyteller-in-residence and shared his *Odyssey* tales with us. His first week's residency was funded in part by the local Friends of the Schools. In subsequent years, partial funding came from the state Council on the Arts, and as the years passed, we were able to build money into the budget to cover his rising fees.

Even in the early years, however, we never relied totally on one storyteller. I had learned about Anne Bodman, a storyteller then living in Ithaca, New York. Anne had a special fondness for the homecoming of Odysseus and had collaborated with a group of other New York storytellers to present different Homeric episodes, each person telling one. She had released her own taped version of the story, and we listened to parts of her telling as an alternative. One year, just before his visit, Odds had lost his voice, and we were unable to reschedule a mutually convenient time. Children learned the story by listening to tapes that year, tapes of his past performances and tapes from other sources.

We also listened to an elaborate production of *The Odyssey* that was broadcast on public radio. While the storytelling moved more or less in a straight line, from the fall of Troy through the return of Odysseus, this radio version followed Homer's chronology, which begins in the middle of Odysseus' travels and tells the earlier adventures through a series of flashbacks. That structure, jumping back and forth, made it harder to follow, but the major difference was that here, different actors were reading their lines. None of us felt that it had the same impact as the straight tellings. No matter what complaints students made about a taped storyteller compared to a live performance, I never found one who preferred the radio play. That was another clue that confirmed the power of storytelling.

THE LURE OF STORIES

After a period of minimalism in modern literature, we now enjoy a new phase of literary storytelling. As one critic writes, "contemporary fiction seems crowded these days with raconteurs and anecdotalists, would-be novelists, old-fashioned spinners of yarns and plain un-reconstructed liars" (Kakutani 1989). Readers as well as writers continue to enjoy "old-fashioned" stories, as noted child psychiatrist Robert Coles (1987) reports in this account of reading literature with men and women at the Harvard Business School:

> When coupled with continuing practical experiences . . . stories, I believe, can work their magic on the heart—and help one resist the ever present temptation of the intellect to distance anything and everything from itself through endless generalizations. Yes, we used our heads in that course. But mostly we sat back and let those stories get to us, prompt us to remember past times and wonder anew about the future.

Notice Coles' use of the word "magic," which underscores the nature of the forces at work. These authors are discussing the power of stories as literature, as written documents. But as another author has commented, "Despite the implications of its name, literature does not seem to have been the invention of literate people" (Berkeley Peabody, quoted in Egan [1987], 450). If written stories have a richness and a fascination for the reader, then spoken stories seem to operate at an even more fundamental level of consciousness.

When Odds Bodkin tells stories, he typically requests a darkened room in which he places his wax-encrusted candelabra. Telling stories by candlelight is an effective theatrical device, but Odds says it also appeals to some primal instinct in the listeners, summoning echoes of people long ago crouching around the ceremonial fire to listen to a story. Telling stories is surely an ancient art that predates the written word; even our earliest literary works, such as *Gilgamesh* (which can be dated from Sumerian tablets to as early as 2,600 B.C., nearly two thousand years before Homer), are thought to grow out of an even more ancient oral tradition. This reflects the relatively recent appearance of writing in human society; for countless millennia, people spoke without writing.

Anthropologists and folklorists alike have documented the persistence of storytelling traditions in nonliterate cultures. (See, for example, Bruce Chatwin's *The Songlines* for a discussion of the role of stories in the lives of the aboriginal people of Australia, or the classic work on the research leading to the conclusion that Homer did not merely recite, he composed orally, Albert Lord's *The Singer of Tales*.) Walter Ong (1982), a major voice in these discussions, argues that humans are naturally oral learners, and that the development of oral language skills should accompany silent reading and other studies in the language arts.

One scholar with an intense interest in both storytelling and the development of children's oral language skills is Kieran Egan, an education professor at Simon Fraser University in British Columbia. In a singularly rich article published several years ago, Egan looks at the thinking skills developed in traditional oral cultures, examines the intellectual development of young children in modern literate societies, and speculates how those children's oral skills might be put to use in our twentieth-century classrooms:

> We should consider children when they come to school as already in possession of some features of orality that are *bon à penser* [good for thinking with]. Their ability to think and learn is, in general, sophisticated, but structured according to norms significantly different from those of literate adult cultures. Two corollaries follow. First, clear understanding of children's orality is essential if we are to make what we want to teach engaging and meaningful; second, orality entails valuable forms of thought that need to be developed as the foundation for a sophisticated literacy and Western rationality. If we see the educational task as simply to put literacy in place, we risk undermining the very foundations on which a rich literacy must rest. Stimulating children's imaginations, metaphoric fluency, and narrative sophistication can become more prominent aims of early education. . . . The fullest achievement of literacy requires the fullest achievement of oral capabilities as well. (Egan 1987, 469)

Most elementary teachers already know the value of reading aloud to their students; among other things, it is frequently the calmest moment in the day. (A note on language: "reading aloud" is usually shortened to "story" on my daily lesson plan and in my conversations with children.) Educational writers agree that this is an important part of the day. James Britton's classic *Language and Learning* has a thoughtful discussion of the learning that accompanies read-aloud time. Many parents tell me that read-aloud stories are among their children's best memories. Similarly, many adults who have long forgotten countless hours in elementary classrooms remember clearly a particular teacher reading aloud. Susan Stamberg, a host of National Public Radio's "All Things Considered," once described her memories of a fifth-grade teacher who stood on a desk each day to declaim the next installment from Homer.

If reading stories aloud is useful for the listener, then telling stories brings additional life to the tale. With young children, the reading and telling sometimes benefit from visual props. Several years ago, I visited the kindergarten classroom of a Philadelphia colleague from the Odyssey Institute, Peg Perlmutter, and watched her make effective use of a tool I remembered from my own years in the primary grades, the flannelboard. Peg showed me her flannelboard pieces for dozens of stories. The best figures she has commissioned from local artists, and for many stories, she has two sets—one that she uses when telling a story, and another less delicate set that children may use in their free play. On the day I visited, Peg read a beautifully illustrated version of the myth of Daedalus and Icarus, and as she spoke, she moved small wooden characters around a simple labyrinth to perform the story. Children eagerly made that story their own during free play, moving the figures and telling the story over again to themselves. Peg also uses puppets to tell a story, and children re-create the story with props provided by the teacher.

Flannelboards are no longer in vogue as a tool for teaching language arts. What about other popular methods of language instruction? Certainly the whole language approach follows the philosophy described here, with its emphasis on chanting and singing and rhythmic poetry, using techniques that draw on children's deep inner resources in much the same way oral cultures do:

> This process of enthralling the audience, of impressing upon them the reality of the story, is a central feature of education in oral cultures. Their social institutions are sustained in large part by sound, by what the spoken or sung word can do to commit individuals to particular beliefs, expectations, roles, and behaviors. Thus the techniques of fixing the crucial patterns of belief in the memory—rhyme, rhythm, formula, story, and so on—are vitally important. Education in oral cultures is largely a matter of constantly immersing the young in enchanting patterns of sound until their minds resonate to them, until they become in tune with the institutions of their culture. (Egan 1987, 451)

EACH TELLER IS UNIQUE

During the 1988–89 school year, I was on sabbatical leave from my classroom. The following September, at our Parents' Night, I suspected that I might change my approach to the *Odyssey* unit. A father, who had a daughter in one of my classes—her older sister had been a student of mine several years before—raised his hand after listening to my description of the year, and asked who was going to tell *The Odyssey*. I explained that Odds was probably coming back, as he had for years; indeed, having him start the unit was part of our tradition, one that children were no doubt anticipating.

He disagreed: "You've just returned from a year of studying this material. I like listening to you describe your plans. It's clear that you have a deep love for this story. Why don't you consider telling it yourself?"

I could not shake the man's question from my mind. I knew I was not ready to undertake telling a story of that magnitude; my own storytelling experience was limited. Although I had been helping children develop their own storytelling skills, it took me an additional five years before I summoned up the courage myself. During a year when I taught third grade, as part of a unit on tall tales an intern had challenged children to tell at least one whopper to earn a seat on the class's Liars' Bench. Toward the end of the year, I accepted the challenge myself and learned one story to tell. "Owl" was a tale I had heard twice before; it comes from a collection of Haitian folktales called *The Magic Orange Tree*. I told that story once at an adult storytelling swap session, once to my class, and once at the school's weekly assembly program. I was alternately nervous, exhausted, and pleased.

Now, as the months went by and I did not call Odds to make the usual arrangements for his visit, I realized that I was leaning toward making a change in the routine. We had always worked with one storyteller at the start of the unit, but I found myself thinking more and more about inviting many storytellers.

In the past, some children had had difficulty making the leap from student to storyteller. How much of that difficulty, I wondered, came from thinking that in order to tell a story well they needed to be able to mimic Odds Bodkin's style, to retain dozens of character voices, play different instruments, and create vivid sound effects? If some children were able to tell stories well using Odds as their sole model, how might their work improve if they had a variety of models on which to base their own telling? Would other children find it easier to create their own style of telling if they could select elements from different styles?

That year, instead of having one visitor to the school to tell stories, we had eleven. The following year, with a few changes in personnel, we had seven storytellers. The list of storytellers during those two years was wide-ranging:

Rod Alexander	actor and director
Becca Ashley	high school student
William Cook	English professor
Linda Costello	second-grade teacher
Laurence Davies	English professor
Brigid Farrell	first-grade teacher

Laurie Ferris	first-grade teacher
Milton Frye	school principal
Jim Hunt	high school English teacher
Larry Kelly	parent and attorney
David Millstone	fifth-grade social studies teacher
Mary Sinclair	professional storyteller
Jim Tatum	classics professor
Jo Valens	Waldorf kindergarten teacher
Judy Witters	parent and professional storyteller

Some of the adults read translations of the story and added their own comments. Our principal, Milton Frye, for example, read excerpts from the same story using different translations and then spoke about language and meaning, while Rod Alexander read a story from one translation and demonstrated the importance of enunciation. The storytellers each brought a different approach. Judy Witters became Circe and told the story from her point of view. Jim Hunt drew an exaggerated map of the Mediterranean before launching into a casual and humorous telling. Jo Valens brought a harp to set the mood and a staff on which Odysseus leaned as he spoke. Laurence Davies invited children to participate in the story with appropriate sound effects, and used a cap to differentiate between Odysseus the beggar and Odysseus the strong hero. His colleague, Bill Cook, drew on an easel while he talked and acted out the tale. Other tellers simply sat and spoke.

The language and tone used by each storyteller varied dramatically and children responded differently to the style and language of each. For example, consider the opening moments of three different tellings. What pictures do you see? Where does your mind start to wander? Where does each opening take you?

1. This is the tale of Odysseus, master of land ways, master of sea ways . . .

Darkness, and silence, and the breathing of men closely held so that it is not loud.

[cough]

"Silence, you! Silence!"

"But . . . but Captain, I have to—"

"Silence! Choke on your cough if you must but make no sounds."

Odysseus of Ithaca lay in the wooden belly of a horse, near the sea, and he looked at his men as the light rose slowly from the east above the great city of Troy. A thin thread of light came through the tightly joined planks of wood that formed the belly of the great wooden horse. And Odysseus thought to himself . . .

(Odds Bodkin)

2. Oh goddess, Muse, sing in me, breathe through me the story of Odysseus, the wanderer, the bold and wily warrior, and of proud Penelope, his match in wit and wisdom, who awaited him at home for twenty long years.

Once, long ago, more than three thousand years before our time, on the island of Ithaca off the west coast of Greece, lived a king called Odysseus. Since then, we have called him Odysseus, Ulysses, the sacker of cities, destroyer of armies, the man skilled in all ways of contending, of fighting. Put him in a footrace, a discus hurling contest, arm-wrestling—he was a hard man to beat. But his real excellence lay in using his mind, and that is why Athena, the goddess of wisdom, especially loved him and favored him. Put him in a dangerous situation where another man would first draw his sword, Odysseus would draw on his wits.

(Anne Bodman)

3. I'll tell you a story, but please don't ever forget this isn't the whole story. If you want to hear the whole story, you'll have to listen all the rest of your life.

Long ago there was a mighty war, the Trojan War, and it raged for ten years, neither side a clear victor, until the great Greek prince Odysseus found a way to win the war, through trickery and deception. And that's a wonderful story, but it's another story, and our time is short and this story is long. This story is about the journey of Odysseus, back home to the shores of Ithaca.

For the Greeks, all creativity, all inspiration came as a gift from the Muse:

Tell us, oh Muse, of this great man Odysseus, a man who like so many others we know today seemed to be never at a loss.

Tell us of this man, so masterful in the ways of the world, and yet a stranger to the inner realms, the realms of the soul.

Tell us of this man of many potentials who had done everything, seen everything, and in his intellect, at least, understood everything . . . and yet, nothing at all.

Tell us of the pains he suffered on the wide sea. And Muse, tell us too of Athena, the goddess of creativity and skill and the high arts of civilization, the goddess who guided Odysseus home and assisted him in his victory over his enemies.

And Muse, never let us forget what lies hidden behind any victory—the loss and the anguish and the bloodshed.

Of these adventures, oh Muse, lift the great song again, tell us again in our time.

(Mary Sinclair)

After we had listened to all the storytellers that year, I asked the fifth graders to evaluate them. What criteria should they use? Here are the lists that three different fifth-grade classes drew up one year to answer the questions, How can you judge a storyteller? and What are the qualities you would look for?

Homeroom #1	Homeroom #2	Homeroom #3
how clearly they speak	character voices	Do they make sense?
voices for different people	really knows story	Can you understand them?
doesn't drag the story on	loudness / softness	They make the story
acting—not boring	speak to audience	interesting, exciting?
description—vivid images	act out characters	voices
knowledge of story	forgetfulness, hesitation	loud voice
tone—appropriately funny	descriptions, details	clear speech
or serious	seeing it in your mind	props
action	speaking clearly	details—visual images
use of props	style—how they tell	emphasize key parts
		movement

The lists were similar, which in itself pleased the children a great deal. I, too, was pleased by their comments. It is rare that we give children an opportunity to evaluate each other's work, let alone the work of adults. Their choice of categories and their short evaluations of different storytellers demonstrated how seriously they took the assignment:

> Bill Cook has a way of telling stories that nobody could match. Something that helped me understand the story were the pictures he drew. Other things that helped me were facial expressions and different voices. To me it was like he really got into the story and became part of it.   (Emily)

> I really liked the way Becca Ashley told her story. She used different sounds in her voice. For example when she was talking as Odysseus she made her voice sound really sad because Odysseus wanted to go home and when she talked as different townspeople it was like there was all different people doing the different voices.   (Kara)

> I really like the way Jo Valens told her story. The way she used her harp made it sound so beautiful and also the words she used at the end made it sound as terrible as it really was.   (Matilda)

> Mary Sinclair seemed mystical in her dress and I really liked the way she paused between important phrases to let it sink in.   (Shawn)

> Jim Tatum told us a story in Greek about Polyphemus. It was neat how the pitch of his voice went up and down speaking

Greek. After he said some in Greek he translated it. I liked the sound in Greek of the blood gurgling out of the eye.   (Peter)

As I had hoped, when the children themselves were finally ready to tell their stories six weeks later, they found the criteria a useful reference; after all, the list was their own. In offering critiques of their peers, they referred to their list.

After two years of bringing in many storytellers, we went back to the one storyteller model. Mary Sinclair presented her version of the story and returned a month later to direct storytelling workshops for students. For the next two years, I told most of the story myself, and relied on taped versions and a few visitors to provide different voices and styles of telling. Obviously, we are still experimenting. I would like to be able to report that one way—working with one storyteller or with a variety of individuals—is clearly superior, but there are advantages to each.

One teller brings a unified vision to the telling, a clarity and sense of purpose. The teller has a strong mental image of Odysseus and the other characters, an idea of how each character talks and moves, a sense of how everyone fits into the larger story. One teller also builds a relationship with the audience and provides continuity. Children are immersed in one style and start to notice that the teller makes repeated use of certain effects or of a particular stock phrase (such as the familiar Homeric epithets "rosy-fingered Dawn," "wine-dark sea," and "grey-eyed Athena"). Finally, a single storyteller brings a certain power to the telling, a sense that the story inhabits the teller. Children are awestruck in the presence of someone who is able to tell the whole Homeric story, and that wonder affects them in unknown ways. Arranging for a single storyteller to visit school is also more direct, less complicated.

Having many storytellers *does* have the effect I initially sought of providing a variety of models children can use in their own tellings. When Odds Bodkin was the only storyteller, for example, all the fifth graders telling stories sat, as Odds did. After hearing many storytellers, children began to bring in props, moved about the room, involved their audience, showed maps, tried out different tones of voice, wore costumes . . . In short, they drew from a wider repertoire of storytelling techniques.

Which is better, one storyteller or many? One good teller probably does a better job of passing along the story but limits the range of the storytelling that will result. With many storytellers, children might lose some of the initial story but experience a wide variety of storytelling styles. In any event, having flesh-and-blood storytellers is better than listening to recorded stories, and listening first to the stories on tape is better than just reading the book.

From our discussions comparing storytellers and from our early work with first graders on the Apple of Discord episode, the fifth graders realize that the same story can be told in different ways. The proof—the many first-grade stories and collaborative illustrations—is hanging on the walls of the school; each version is unique. The challenge now is to bring that awareness to their next task, to learn one episode from Homer well enough to teach it to the first graders. These preparations take weeks.

"WHICH TEXT DO YOU USE?"

The question, "Which text do you use?" ranks right next to "What do you do besides read the text?" in many teachers' minds, although I find that these two questions are usually asked by high school teachers or college classicists. Elementary teachers do not appear to be as wedded to the notion of using a particular text.

In Norwich, we use no one text. Instead of twenty-five copies of one book, a standard reference all children will use, I prefer to have one copy of twenty-five different versions, ranging from comics through full translations. (See the annotated bibliography for a list of the different editions of Homer we use in our study.) In the same way that each storyteller has a unique style, so does each translation, each written version of Homer bring a different set of information to the careful reader. Take, for example, the blinding of Polyphemus, which we encountered in the translation by Robert Fitzgerald in Chapter 2. Here are four other versions of that same moment.

> They seized the beam of olive, sharp at the end, and leaned on it
> into the eye, while I from above leaning my weight on it
> twirled it, like a man with a brace-and-bit who bores into
> a ship timber, and his men from underneath, grasping
> the strap on either side whirl it, and it bites resolutely deeper.
> So seizing the fire-point-hardened timber we twirled it
> in his eye, and the blood boiled around the hot point, so that
> the blast and scorch of the burning ball singed all his eyebrows
> and eyelids, and the fire made the roots of his eye crackle.
>
> *The Odyssey of Homer,* trans. Richmond Lattimore

> I gave him wine again, and when he had taken the third bowl he sank backwards with his face upturned, and sleep came upon him. Then I, with four companions, took that beam of olive wood, now made into a hard and pointed stake, and thrust it into the ashes of the fire. When the pointed end began to glow we drew it out of the flame. Then I and my companions laid hold on the great stake and, dashing at the Cyclops, thrust it into his eye. He raised a terrible cry that made the rocks ring and we dashed away into the recesses of the cave.
>
> Padraic Colum, *The Children's Homer*

Then Ulysses rolled a boulder next to the giant's head and climbed on it, so that he was looking down into the eye. It was lidless and misted with sleep—big as a furnace door and glowing softly like a banked fire. Ulysses looked at his men. They had done what he said, broken into two parties, one group at each ear. He lifted his white-hot sword.

"Now!" he cried.

Driving down with both hands, and all the strength of his back and shoulders, and all his rage and all his fear, Ulysses stabbed the glowing spike into the giant's eye.

Bernard Evslin, *The Adventure of Ulysses*

That evening, after the Cyclops had eaten, I offered him a taste of some very strong wine I had brought with me. He took it and drank it in one gulp. "Give me more," he roared, "and tell me your name!" Then I replied, "My name is Noman." When he had finished all the wine, he fell asleep and began snoring loudly.

Then we brought out the sharpened pole and buried the point in the fire. When it was glowing, we held it above the monster's head, and plunged it deep into his eye. It hissed as we drove the pole deeper and deeper. The Cyclops awoke, screaming and clutching his eye. We fled to the darkest corners and hid.

I. M. Richardson, *Odysseus and the Cyclops*

Children frequently read half a dozen versions of Homer, concentrating on the episode that most interests them. They begin to notice the differences, and they want answers. Why should one story differ from another? Why does Evslin have Odysseus alone driving a sword into the Cyclops' eye? Colum never mentions the hiss of the eyeball; did it happen? Richardson's story is shortened; does that matter?[1]

In any case, I remind students, their job is not to retell Homer word for word, but rather to present the story in their own words. Each of our adult storytellers makes it clear that theirs is but one interpretation of the story, and we urge the fifth graders to find their own version, one that feels true. There is time in high school and college for textual analysis. I

---

[1]Some students, drawing on their own experiences in French class, understand how the same Greek phrase might be translated differently. Since we're working from English translations at best, and since English retellings are even further removed from the source, there are bound to be variations among the different versions. For those children who persist, who want to know "exactly what Homer says," we work backward. We arrange the different versions, especially the full translations, in a circle, like the rim of a wheel. We can imagine Homer's Greek lying at the center, changed slightly in each English version. On rare occasions, a student has wanted to know even more. I get out my Greek *Odyssey*, a Greek-English dictionary, and a well-thumbed Greek grammar; we painstakingly work our way through a few lines.

want children to know this story well, and I hope that by knowing it they will come to love it.

THE STORY CHOOSES THE TELLER

In a typical year, after working with *The Odyssey* for three weeks, children are ready to select one episode as their specialty. By this time, they have heard the entire story, and they have completed many introductory activities. They have heard additional translations of the story read aloud to them, and they have spent several days browsing through different editions of Homer, mulling over this choice. They know they have to learn one adventure well enough to tell it to the first graders, and they know they should pick a tale they really want to tell.

Although the actual procedure for choosing stories has evolved along with the rest of the unit, one rule has remained firm from the beginning—no child is required to tell a particular episode.

"But what if everyone wants to tell Polyphemus?" a student asks.

"Then we're going to have a lot of Polyphemus stories," I reply. "But I doubt that will happen."

It never has. I simply write on the chalkboard the names of all the different adventures and explain the procedure we will follow:

These are the different adventures which we've been studying. There are some that are much shorter than others, and some that are much longer. Take the Homecoming, for example. That might end up being separated into several shorter episodes. You'll notice that the Trojan War is one choice, but that, too, can be divided into many parts if we have a lot of people signing up.

Think about the different stories, and think about which ones you want to tell. Don't worry about getting all the episodes covered; it will work out fine. Concentrate on figuring out which one you want to tell. You don't need to know why you want to tell a particular story—just let your hunches guide you. This is a strange process and I don't pretend to understand it, but if there's a particular story that's appealing to you, that's the one you should probably tell. I think that the story chooses you, and if it decides that you're the right person to keep it alive, then you should do it.

Everyone will sign up, then we'll all look at the list and see what's there. Everyone will get a chance to change his or her mind, as often as you want, until everyone is set with a story that he or she wants to tell.

It's a fascinating process, one that I enjoy watching. Depending on the storytellers in a particular year, and depending on the personality of the children, certain episodes are clear favorites in the first round. We look at the list and discover that eight names are signed up for Polyphemus and none for certain other episodes. But there are always children who have many tales they want to tell, and they're eager to switch to a less crowded space. There are also children who want to do a tale that no one else is doing, and they wait to fill in the blank spaces. The children who have their heart set on one particular adventure always get to keep the one they want. Children have a few more days in which to change their mind, and then they are committed to learning that episode.

PICTURES IN YOUR MIND

After children have read half a dozen different versions of their story, they are ready to start preparing for their telling. Imagination is the key to successful storytelling, and imagination works through pictures.

Storyteller Odds Bodkin believes that children's imagination is stunted by too much television. Before beginning his tale one year with a group of children, he reminded them of their responsibility for creating the story:

> When you watch TV or go to the movies, the pictures are all there for you on the screen. All you have to do is look at them. Remember that as you listen to stories, in your imagination the stories must grow. If you make pictures in your minds for each of the characters I describe, each of the places, then it will be like looking at a movie of your own creation. If you don't imagine, then my words will echo off these walls and you will sit there, like a mushroom.

Several other storytellers have told me that they don't memorize the plot of a story; they work, not from words, but from a series of images. Odds once described the experience by saying that he had a movie projector inside his brain beaming pictures to the inside of his forehead; all he had to do was look there from time to time and describe the movie he saw.

Here are some techniques that have been successful in developing children's storytelling skills. I learned them by attending workshops with different storytellers (and heartily recommend that experience for teachers wishing to broaden their repertoire of teaching techniques).

Comic strips: We begin with a simple drawing exercise:

> Make a comic strip of your episode, just like the cartoons we did earlier that were based on the whole story. This time, though, you're concentrating on your own episode. Take that story and break it into little pieces, like frames in a movie. We're going to make a storyboard of the episode, but instead of worrying about the actual words, I want you to think about the pictures.

The comics are an easy first step, a chance for children to clarify whether or not they know the basic order of events. If not, there are the many versions around to refresh their memory. Once they have made this visual outline of the tale, it's time to investigate the story in more depth, to fill in the details.

Guided imagery: Children find a quiet space in the room, either sitting on chairs or stretching out on the carpet with a pillow. I turn off the lights and ask the children to review their episode silently and find one central moment:

> Close your eyes if that makes it easier to concentrate. Don't worry about your neighbors; they'll be busy with their own story. The more you can concentrate on your story, the clearer the pictures will be for you, and the clearer the pictures are, the easier it will be for you to describe what you see when you go to tell your tale.
>
> You're going to make yourself invisible and enter your scene. You can see everything and everyone, but they can't see you. Start by looking down on the scene as though you are a bird with sharp eyesight. Get a general overview of what it looks like.

At this point, I'm trying to ease children into their story. I sit in a corner of the room, talking quietly, with long pauses to allow children to relax. I try to follow a story episode myself, giving instructions and then looking inward for a few moments.

> Decide what time of day it is. Is it day or night? If you're inside, look around for a crack of light under the door. And if it's daytime, when in the day is it? Noon? Early morning or late afternoon? Are there long shadows? What's the temperature? Is the wind blowing?

We slowly walk through the picture, from bird's-eye view to worm's-eye, from distance to closeups and back again.

> What do you see? What's off in the far distance? And what's a little closer? Are there any trees? Move around a little, turn to the side and find out what you can see behind them. And now look down, right under your feet, what's there? Look over to the right now . . . slowly . . . and then quickly to the left, in case something's sneaking up on you.
>
> What can you hear? Listen . . . listen . . . Turn your head to one side, so you can hear better. Sounds of the sea? Of people, talking or breathing? Animal sounds?
>
> And walk around, with bare feet. What does it feel like under your feet? Is it the same over there, or over there? Rock underfoot, or sand, or maybe dirt, or rough wood?

I encourage children to pay attention to smells and sounds, textures and colors, to look at the body language of their characters, to examine the character's eyes. They freeze the action in their minds and look at the details of that stopped scene. The process typically takes fifteen or twenty minutes.

The first time I tried this technique, I was pleasantly surprised to find that what had been so helpful for me in storytelling workshops also seemed to work for my students. I opened my own eyes and noticed that most of the kids were in fact sitting with eyes closed. They really were involved—no snickers, no giggling, no complaints. Storyteller Judy Witters says the trick to storytelling is to believe in the story you're telling, and all the rest follows.

Revisiting the scene: After the guided imagery, I ask children to walk around the room without talking, to get the body engaged after sitting so still and to give active individuals a chance to move before settling down again. I then ask children to change their gait:

> Imagine you're a baby, just taking your first steps . . . and now you're an old woman making your way home . . . Be an athlete coming home after winning an athletic competition, proud but trying hard not to show it . . . and now you're a giant twelve feet tall, bringing home a load of logs to put on your fire . . . Pick any one of the gods or goddesses on Mt. Olympus, and move the way that person does . . . Be an important character in the episode you were just studying, and move the way that character moves.

While I'm giving these directions, I'm moving around the room in the manner I describe. This gives children an opportunity to see their teacher in unusual poses, provides a model for anyone who wants to copy, and makes it safe for children to take the risk of looking foolish. We are creating a space in which children can be silly, but it is a powerful and controlled silliness that will work for them rather than simply cause a commotion. This activity helps create a community of risk-takers.

> Now, stop right there. Turn to the person closest to you, boy or girl, and pair up with that person. Find a place in the room where the two of you can work and sit down. Decide which one of you is going to be a 1 and who's a 2. Okay? Ones, your job now is to describe the scene you were studying just a few minutes ago. Don't tell your story, just describe that scene in detail.

I cut off that telling after a minute or two, before children run out of pictures.

> Okay? Everyone who was listening, your job now is to tell the speaker the parts of the description that you could see clearly. This

doesn't have to be long—just let them know where their description was really clear to you.

The listener provides feedback, the roles shift, and the second partner gets a chance to describe her own scene. Then—and this part is strange and exciting—children continue their wanderings and do the same thing over again: find a partner, describe the scene, get feedback, and listen to a partner. That instant replay, going through the same description, is a powerful experience; children often discover that their image is now more clearly fixed in mind. The oral description flows more easily; children are more confident of themselves and their words; the *ums* and *uhs* and stammers are less of a problem the second and third time around. By the third time through, I let each teller have two or three minutes, and they continue with their telling beyond description into the story itself. By the end of the guided imagery session, everyone has had a taste of being a storyteller. What remains is to polish the performance.

Theatre games: Any adult involved in community theater has gone through a variety of activities designed to warm up the body and the voice, to get actors to work with each other, to prepare for a performance. Children love to try out those activities; they provide a welcome change of pace in the school day, and children benefit from them in the same way adults do. Each activity invites the class to take a risk together, and each offers the individual a chance to try something new. We never know who will be affected by a particular activity; rather, we offer a variety of games and hope that something will catch each person's attention. Inevitably, one game that seems stupid to one child will be another's favorite.

• *Pass the Clap*

Arrange everyone standing in a large circle. One person starts by facing her neighbor. Both children clap hands, trying to time their claps so that we hear the sound of only one clap. The second person turns to the next person in the circle and they try for two claps sounding as one, and on again, around the circle, faster and faster. Children have to look at each other and work together. It's a lively icebreaker, and gets everyone in the mood to try out something new, like Skeleton.

• *Skeleton*

"Imagine the muscles of your back slowly becoming unhooked. You bend forward, sinking down over your feet, exhaling and making little 'bluh bluh bluh' sounds as your breath goes out. Now your skeleton starts to get reconnected, and you rise like a marionette being slowly lifted by its head string. Your lungs fill with air and you end up standing straight and tall, feeling the air in your diaphragm. Try making some sounds with this full load of fresh air. Try making some *loud* sounds." Children love this opportunity to explore making sounds, and we work our way through different sound effects that might be incorporated into their telling—the roars and screams of a blinded Cyclops, the howl of storm winds, the magical sound a god makes when appearing before a mortal. No one has to incorporate sound effects into a story, but this is a safe way to try out sounds to find out which ones might work. One year, fifth-grader Molly described spending an entire day thinking about different ways of saying the swish of the arrow that Odysseus shot through the twelve axe heads.

• *Speaking in different character voices*

This is one of the harder challenges our storytellers face. It means finding an appropriate voice in the first place, then staying consistently in character as you switch from person to person. Many storytellers find that if they can put themselves into each character's body, the voice follows more easily. During her residency, storyteller Mary Sinclair asked children to rearrange the cells in their body from human into protoplasm, into lizard and chicken and monkey, into one of the monsters, and ultimately, into a speaking character from their scene. Sometimes we do this sitting around in a circle in the class meeting area, just working on the face; sometimes, depending on the class and the mood that day, we have children squirming and hopping all over the room. Once you've contorted your face and body into that of your character, you almost inevitably find a different voice.

• *Characters*

The adventure that Homer describes is but one part of the life of each character in *The Odyssey*. Children move into corners of the room, away from distractions, and in their imaginations explore the place where that character sleeps. Then, pairing with another classmate, they take turns showing and describing that space to their partner, who listens with eyes closed. Again, imagery is key, getting children comfortable with pictures and away from the notion that they must memorize their story.

• *Story variations*

Despite all the models, despite everything I say, there are always children who are certain that there is one—and only one—correct way to tell the story. One enjoyable activity to counteract this widespread belief is to take a tiny fragment of anyone's story and ask everyone in the class to present it. One year, a boy volunteered a line from his version of the Trojan War in which Achilles was scornfully listing his enemies. One after another, twenty-three children strode into the center of the meeting area and spoke: "That Trojan runt, Paris!" They did it straight, they did it with gestures, they did it looking at the audience, they did it shouting and ranting and laughing. By the time we were through, we had heard the phrase well over a hundred times, and each time was unique. Even the staunchest believer in The One Right Way had a hard time choosing.

• *Enunciation exercises*

These offer an opportunity to say really silly phrases, which emphasize the same consonant or vowel sounds. It's a chance for children to bring out their own tongue-twisters and to learn new phrases that force them to stretch their jaws, limber up their tongues, become aware of their breath.

G.I. JOE, LIZARDS, AND STUFFED ANIMALS

There are homework assignments for storytelling, of course. We start simply:

> Write a letter from the main character in your episode to you. Let the character tell you one or two things about him or herself that you didn't know. Don't worry whether it's right or wrong; you won't be graded on that. Let your imagination flow and really *be* that character writing the letter.

This simple writing assignment unleashes a flood of words. Some children concentrate on description, putting on paper the images they have heard and seen in their minds. Here, for example, is part of Caroline's letter from the sea nymph Calypso describing her island:

> My cave is on a small rise in the middle of the island. Growing up the sides of my cave are grape vines, heavily laden with bright purple grapes. I cannot wait to pick them—they seem almost as if they are breaking the vine with their immense size. Toward the left of the cave there are four fountains of various sizes. The water which overflows from them runs down the rise, where it splits up into three separate streams. Two of the streams run through a soft meadow which appears from above to be an ocean green, dotted here and there with beautiful violets and soft parsley. To the left of the meadows stands a forest, growing thick with black alder, poplar and my favorite, the fragrant cypress . . .

Some episodes leave a deep impression, and children rush to explain the motivations of their character. Here is an excerpt from Ceileigh's letter from Circe the enchantress:

> I looked into their warm eyes, the amount of emotions was astonishing, but more than love or sorrow or hunger I saw greed. I led them to my feasting table and then dashed to get my sorceress stick. I once saw them as sloppy grunting greedy men. I then saw them as sloppy grunting greedy pigs.

Ceileigh's classmate, Rosey, chose the same episode as her focus, and in this excerpt (a sentence of Faulknerian complexity), she describes the moment of transformation:

And every moment they act more and more like unmannerly swine, or some other unfathomable beast that I happen to have a preference to that day, and then I walk around the greatly crafted table at which they are seated, and tap each and every one of them on the shoulder with my evil wand, and suddenly the room is filled with the odor of reeking beasts who have not washed for an uncountable number of months, the sounds of what ever un-comprehensional sound might leave his snout, while chairs, dishes and what ever else is in his path, clatters to the floor grinding the sand and dirt into the beautifully polished stones which glimmer and gleam in the sunlight.

How to explain the violent deeds found in this epic tale? Blythe's letter lets the Sirens provide their own justification:

Our name, the Sirens, comes from the sounds of our voices, as they turn from beautiful, flowing sounds, to shrieks when we tear apart the flesh of all the unfortunate men who happen to pass by our island. No one has ever passed our island unharmed. We may seem to you like horrible, merciless creatures, but what else are we to eat on a desolate island with water as far as our eyes can see? If you have any recommendations, please contact us, and we will accept them with pleasure.

This letter-writing assignment allows children to explore the inner lives of the characters they have met in the story; it encourages them to think about those characters as real people. In David's letter, Agamemnon is in the land of the dead, remembering his murder at the hands of his wife, Clytemnestra, "and that snake Aigísthos" (David had been reading the Fitzgerald translation, and enjoyed the look of Fitzgerald's spellings for the Greek names). Agamemnon continues, "But let's not dwell on such matters," and describes the death of Achilles:

I was not the best fighter, though good. I fought and saw brave men of both sides go down. And it was awful; the stench, dead and rotting bodies, and blood, always blood. I remember the time Akhilleus went down, Akhilleus the best of all Akhaians in pure skill of fighting. He took an arrow in his heel, his only vulnerable spot. Odysseus was the first to reach him, brave cunning Odysseus. How I miss him, that great man. I arrived next with some comrades, but we were helpless. As the Trojan archers tried desperately to shoot us from the wall. We watched as Akhilleus lay writhing on the field, blood pouring from his wound, soaking the grass around him a deep red. That was one of the worst days for all the Akhaians.

This assignment lets children turn images into written words. Later homework assignments ask children to tell their story out loud, but not to another human being at first. Tell it to inanimate objects, I urge, or to animals. Several days later, tell it standing in front of a mirror. Try telling it in your room in the dark, or, with parents' consent, by candlelight. And when you're starting to feel comfortable with the story, tell it to a brother or sister, a parent, a friend.

Where do students practice their storytelling? How do they develop the confidence that allows each of them to get up in front of an audience of first graders and tell a tale from Homer? One year, I asked my students where they found a practice audience:

- "My little brother and sister."
- "My mom when she was cooking dinner, but she couldn't really follow it so I told my dad instead."
- "I told my grandparents when they came over one weekend. They were impressed."
- "I told it to my cat one afternoon on my bed."
- "I just said it over and over to myself before I went to sleep at night."
- "I went into the bathroom and locked the door and looked at myself in the mirror and told it. It was hard."
- "I told it to my brother's G.I. Joe collection."
- "My brother's pet lizard."
- "I lined up all my stuffed animals on the rug in my room, like a real audience would be, and I told it to them."
- "I told it to my horse when I was mucking out the stable."

After all this practice, there are always children who are ready to tell their story to their classmates. We listen and offer a critique, concentrating on the things the person has done well. Only after listening to a long string of positive comments does the teller call on a few raised hands for suggested improvements. Note that the teller, not the teacher, chooses who will offer suggestions. The teller may choose only good friends, from whom criticism is easier to take, or he may pick a child in the class who is not in his own social circle, opening himself up to the possibility of a blunt response. Some children always have suggestions but rarely positive comments. They usually notice after a short time that they get called on only rarely, and in an effort to be recognized, they start noticing and commenting on positive aspects of the telling.

At the end of the storytelling work, we sometimes draw up a list of guidelines, the condensed wisdom of all that the children have learned about how to tell a story. These guidelines are similar to those early lists the children drafted when they were evaluating different storytellers. Now, there is certainty in their voices as they make formal what had only been hunches before. Here is one such list of ten rules, which fifth graders in 1987 compiled:

1. Speak loudly and clearly; don't mumble.
2. Know your story; be able to tell it without saying "uhh . . ."
3. Imagine that you're there, in the place you're describing; have a picture in your head.
4. Include sound effects.
5. Change your voice for different characters.
6. Describe scenes well.
7. Practice.
   A. Practice telling your story to parents, pets, stuffed animals, brothers and sisters.
   B. Practice with people you know—they're harder than strangers.
   C. Tell it first to a critical audience, people who already know *The Odyssey*—the first graders will be easier.
   D. Tape yourself and listen back to it.
8. Know the first words you'll say. (And maybe know the last words, too.)
9. Take your time.
10. Make eye contact with the audience.

This list is not something I figured out to guide students' public speaking. It represents the collective wisdom of the students, who'd had many opportunities to practice and to speculate on what made their storytelling better. How often do we ask children to think about what they learned and how they learned it? To synthesize rules to help others? To reflect on their accomplishments?

Whenever possible, we give each child an opportunity to tell his or her story to the other fifth graders before telling it to the first graders. Fifth graders frequently dread telling it to their entire class, although after the fact they usually appreciate the boost in confidence they received. This audience of peers is certainly the most difficult of all, and it makes the subsequent telling to first graders much easier.

Fifth graders spend a full month teaching Homer to the younger children, taking turns telling their tales. Rather than follow Homer's flashback structure, we arrange the stories chronologically; then, one by one, the older children visit the first-grade classrooms. The schedule is arranged to fit the convenience of the first-grade teachers; each fifth grader knows that it is his or her responsibility to keep track of the schedule, to make the necessary arrangements to be excused from class at the right time, and to make up any missed work. Some years, with smaller classes, it was possible for me to sneak away to listen to most of these tellings. Now, with some sixty fifth graders it becomes increasingly difficult. I rely more and more on the descriptions of first-grade teachers as well as the students' own description of how it went. While several children are off telling stories, the other fifth graders are busy, working on group artwork (such as that described in Chapter 3), or starting work on individual *Odyssey* projects (described in Chapter 5).

For the first graders, each day simply brings the next installment in an exciting epic. (See Chapter 8 for a more detailed look at the first graders' activities.) Often there are several older children who have learned the same episode; this gives listeners an opportunity to hear the tale told in different styles.

The fifth graders' storytelling styles vary widely. Some tellers rely on singing or dramatic voice characterizations; others concentrate on sights or sounds. Borrowing from Odds Bodkin's opening, Cyi tells much of his tale in a whisper, Odysseus speaking softly to his men inside the belly of the Trojan Horse. Drawing on Mary Sinclair's facial contortions, Laurie shows us Polyphemus splattering sailors against cave walls and then stuffing them into his mouth. Taking a cue from Judy Witters' version of Circe, Heather S. tells her story from Circe's point of view and asks her audience to participate by making grunting noises when the men are changed into swine. I see her still, gesturing with her fingertips at precisely the right moment: "And then she added just a *drop* of poison to the wine." Remembering the theatrics of Laurence Davies and Bill Cook, Molly brings an old piece of cloth to her telling and she dashes back and forth energetically, first acting out Odysseus the bent beggar and, casting off the improvised cloak in one grand gesture, Odysseus the returning hero.

Yes, we have our share of humdrum storytellers, but each year brings fresh surprises. At the time I was writing this book I thought I had heard all possible variations of the Cyclops story. Then it was Jason's turn. He announced that he had a serious version and a silly one; his classmates (and teacher) asked for the silly one. He shrugged, as if to say, "You asked for it," and started chanting a mock-serious invocation to the storytelling Muse. His tale included Polyphemus shaving, sitting down to read the paper, grabbing two men and dunking them in his morning coffee. It was, not surprisingly, a hit with the first graders as well.

The best stories include images and words with lasting power, pieces of the tale that surprise even the teller. Heather W. includes information on a white scarf "because it just feels important to have it there," and after days of thought Becca decides to use the word "betrothed" in her story of Nausicaä "because it's an unusual word. I didn't even know what it meant at first, but without it the story just sounds plain, like something is missing."

Learning the skill of storytelling opens many doors to the fifth graders. In addition to their young audiences, there were parents and siblings to be entertained, as well as cousins and relatives and family friends over for supper. Years ago, Jeff's version of Polyphemus won him a 4-H state championship for public speaking and a trip to the huge Eastern States Farm Exposition in Massachusetts, where visitors encountered dairy cattle, prize rams, jams and jellies, and one very gory recitation from Homer. Heather W. and Mike took their stories to Lesley College in Cambridge and told them in front of more than a hundred teachers at a Saturday workshop. Siri told her version of Achilles to teachers at a Greek workshop at the Dartmouth College art museum, and a dozen other children told tales to teachers at different summer institutes sponsored by the Classical Association of New England. Sara, Lydia, Greg, and Robbie took their tales to the University of Vermont, where they held 750 high school Latin students spellbound in a gym during a presentation at Vermont Latin Day. These forums, in addition to the Parents' Nights at school, are a way of "publishing" children's stories, which is as important for these oral tales as it is for the written ones.

For the older children, the *Odyssey* storytelling is challenging, pleasurable, serious work. Over the three months, they demonstrate increasing mastery of a complex subject, and they are justly proud of their accomplishments. They seek fresh audiences for their newly learned tales; as Mark explains, "Once you've learned it, you just want to go around and tell the story to everybody you know."

STORIES SPEAK TO THE HEART

Storytelling is a powerful vehicle for passing along important information to students. Perhaps the boldest position concerning education and stories is that of Kieran Egan (1989), who proposes a new teaching methodology with storytelling as the central method of instruction in most subject areas. I would be content just to see more teachers using storytelling techniques more of the time.

Learning to tell a story is not easy. I know this from personal experience and I understand teachers who are afraid to take that leap. But I have also learned that it is not as hard as it would seem. I have discovered that an audience, comprised of children or adults, is forgiving and supportive of a storyteller's efforts when there is a personal connection between teller and listeners. I am not yet comfortable enough to step on a stage before twenty strangers to tell a tale, but I know that each time I start to tell a story the children in my class listen more intently. Perhaps "story" is signalled by a change in my tone of voice or my body language or the vocabulary I select; perhaps "story" is signalled by the lack of any barrier—book, overhead, worksheet—between me and my students. However the change is marked, children quickly settle into position for careful listening. They offer praise afterward and helpful suggestions, and I have slowly come to realize that my own inhibitions are a bigger stumbling block than my lack of storytelling expertise.

But why push children to tell stories? Why is it important to take that additional step?

As we have seen, preparing a story to tell is an exceptionally effective way of learning the information in that story. How often teachers are reminded of the truism, "You don't really know it until you have to teach it to someone else." Norwich fifth graders thrive on this challenge, learning their tales because the younger children are depending on them.

As with any activity that is out of the ordinary, storytelling allows different children to shine. The talented storytellers each year always include some surprises, children who have not stood out before. Similarly, there are children who breeze through the paper and pencil tasks in school, the reading and the writing, but who experience considerable difficulty learning to tell a tale. Indeed, I am happy to provide equal opportunity for all students to learn to deal with frustration. Coping with difficulties, learning to ask for help from each other, developing perseverance in the face of adversity—these are all skills worth learning in elementary school.

Children who tell stories develop confidence in their ability to speak in public. We all know that the language arts consist of four areas—reading, writing, listening, and speaking—but we spend little time in the upper grades teaching children how to speak effectively. To be sure, many classrooms have a sharing time, an equivalent of "Show and Tell" in the lower grades, but too often we seem to think that children will develop their oral skills through osmosis. In fact, as the year unfolds, the talkers tend to talk more and the listeners tend to listen more. Taking time to teach speaking and listening skills is a way of equalizing these abilities.

The Norwich fifth graders have few doubts about the value of learning to tell stories, although they all stress how hard it is. Students one year included these responses in a class discussion that happened to be recorded:

- "You can tell a story and not make it boring. You learn to get your point across. It's better to tell a story than to read a book out loud. You have your hands free, and you can make movements, make voices. You don't have something between you and the person who's listening." (Rachel)
- "You'll know how to speak well when you're older." (Andy)
- "It's a good way to entertain people." (Molly)
- "You can grow up to tell stories better to your own kids." (Angela)
- "You can pass the story along to other kids." (Matt)
- "It gives you more imagination compared to watching TV." (Sean)

That last comment goes to the core of the matter. Storytelling is a powerful way of unlocking the imagination. Remember that word "magic" used by Robert Coles? A story bypasses the rational intellect. A story awakens that sense of wonder without which there can be little learning. When we learn something permanently, we say we "learned it by heart." Unlike textbooks and worksheets, unlike computer-assisted drills, unlike all those commercially packaged, validated and endorsed, teacher-proof instructional materials, a story moves directly from the ear to the heart.

5 | BUILDING A COMMUNITY OF SCHOLARS

I expect my students to think and to learn. Children, especially, learn when they are actively engaged. In working with a subject as complex and significant as Homeric Greece, there is a temptation to pour all the facts into them, as if they were empty vessels—to lecture. Unfortunately, even the most well-organized and dynamic lectures will not create a community of scholars. How does such a community develop?

In the early stages of our *Odyssey* study, everyone in the class is carrying out the same assignments or going through the same activities at the same time. But each student is unique. At some point, it is important for each student to take individual responsibility for his or her learning. Independent *Odyssey* projects are one way to provide that opportunity.

Independent projects can be a waste of time or they can be one of the most valuable learning experiences of the year. What makes the difference is how seriously students approach the work. That, I believe, is determined largely by the teacher's initial presentation of the assignment:

> In a few minutes, I'm going to give you a sheet of suggestions for your independent *Odyssey* projects, which you're going to work on for the next three weeks. This is a major piece of work, and you're going to be expected to do most of it at home, outside of class. Before I give you the list of projects, I want to talk a little bit about what I expect.

That's the warm-up, the part of my speech where I tell them what I'm going to tell them. (Teachers are familiar with this much-used technique: "First I'll tell you what I'm going to tell you, then I'll tell it to you, then I'll summarize by reminding you what I've told you, and then I'll check your understanding by asking you to tell me what I've told you.") This introduction cues students to start to pay attention. I don't like to put the most important information at the very beginning of a class period; many children need a few minutes to settle down. The next part of my typical introduction helps focus their attention:

> Now, most of you went to this school as fourth graders, and many of you have been here for longer than that. Chances are, you've seen *Odyssey* projects from other years on display, either on tables in the upstairs lobby or outside the office. Does anyone remember them?

This produces a flurry of hands as children share their memories of projects they've seen in other years. At this point, there are always students who start calling out, "I know what I want to do!" Of course, my response is, "Not yet. We'll get to that." I want to get everyone excited about the idea of the project, so I usually extend the process of recalling as long as I can. "Have you seen other projects?" is a good start; it gets children remembering the vivid displays of work they've seen already. (Each year, the younger students looking at *Odyssey* projects are impressed by the fifth graders' work; the sixth graders, the oldest children in the school, reminisce fondly about the superior quality of projects in the old days, back when they were in fifth grade.) Asking about past years' displays is also a way of subtly reminding the fifth graders that their work, too, will be shown to the rest of the school.

> How many of you have older brothers or sisters? Can you tell us what you remember about their project?

Students can often describe in detail the work they recall from earlier years. Other children, new to the school or the oldest child in a family, start to get the idea—these projects are special and not to be taken lightly. It's time for the main message:

> Now, before I actually hand out the sheet of project suggestions, and before we talk about the schedule and when everything is due, I need to tell you one important thing.
>
> This assignment, this Odyssey project, can be either an incredible pain or a wonderful opportunity. It can be something you really don't like, or it can be something you have a great time doing. You can make this into Another-Boring-Homework-Assignment-I-Have-To-Do, or you can think about it as Wow!-You-Won't-Believe-What-I-Get-To-Do! It's up to you.
>
> Here's what I mean. When you get the list of suggested projects—and notice, these are only suggestions—you're going to see that there is a lot of variety. There are all kinds of projects listed. Almost everything on the list is something that a fifth grader in the past has really enjoyed doing. The trick is to pick a project that you really want to do.

Let's say that what you really love to do is to write. You'll notice that there are some projects that give you a chance to do a lot of writing. Or maybe you love to draw, but every time you pick up your colored pencils in the evening, your parents say, "Don't you have some homework to do?" Here's your chance. You can pick a project that requires a lot of drawing, smile sweetly, and say, "I'm working on my social studies project." Maybe you like to build things, or to sew, or to make models—you'll find some project ideas that will let you do that. You can work with computers, or you can make a video. You'll see when you get the list.

By now, students are eager to look at the list. Not yet. I know that once I pass out the papers, my audience disappears. I need to mention a few other details first:

You will have a few days in class to get started on your project, mostly to do research, but you'll do almost all of the actual work at home. Depending on the project you choose, you may need some help from other people. Let's say you're going to be using some special tools; maybe you're going to need help with a saw or with a sewing machine. You have to make sure that a parent will be available when you need help.

You'll notice that at the bottom of this cover letter, there's a place for a parent signature. That's to make sure that your folks know what you're up to, so they can help you with your schedule. Maybe your parent has a business trip coming up that you don't know about. Maybe you're going to visit your grandparents next weekend but they haven't told you about it yet. Maybe you have a big ski meet or a basketball tournament or a gymnastics competition; maybe you're in a piano recital. You need to look at your schedule and your family's schedule. That's why you have to show this letter to your parents.

One other thing: the project is due in less than three weeks. I know, that's not a lot of time. It means that you must get started quickly. There simply isn't much time to fool around. It's going to be a lot of work, but you won't have other social studies homework during this time. Your project is your homework.

At this point, we distribute copies of the cover letter, not the actual list of suggested projects. Before we reach the exciting part, children need to understand the schedule they will be following. Figure 5-1 shows a typical letter.

This cover letter, addressed to the students but really aimed at their parents, is an important part of this assignment. It summarizes what I tell children in class about the assignment and lets parents know when everything is due. The parent signature at the bottom is crucial; children know that if they don't bring back a signed slip, I will call their parents. Yes, this can be time-consuming; some years, as many as one-fourth of the students fail to bring back signed slips and I spend hours on the telephone

FIGURE 5-1
Schedule for the Odyssey Project

Schedule for *Odyssey* Projects

You have heard nearly twenty episodes based on ancient stories from Homer. You have reviewed many characters and you have a list of dozens of names to help you remember who's who. You have started reading many different versions of *The Odyssey*, learning how different translators and authors have described the scenes.

In **Social Studies**, you are doing a series of activities to help you remember the story better. You have also picked one particular episode which will be your specialty. This story is one you will be telling later this month to first graders. In **English**, you will be working with a small group to write a play based on an *Odyssey* episode; this may or may not be the same as the episode you're learning to tell.

Now it's time for you to select an independent project that you will work on for the next two and a half weeks. This is a major assignment; we are looking for a finished product that reflects serious study and many hours of work. Choose wisely.

Listed on the attached page are some project suggestions. You will have some class time to work on your project, especially in the early planning stages, but most of the work will be done at home. In most cases, you will be working on your own, although there are a few projects that will require the cooperation of several people. Your parents and other adults may give you some assistance as needed. However, most adults have busy schedules; make sure they know ahead of time that you want their help.

Schedule:

Tuesday or Wednesday, March 22–23: Receive this list of suggested projects. Discuss the possibilities with others in your family. Look at your family calendar and set aside time if others will need to help you.

Thursday and Friday, March 24–25: Talk to teachers if you have questions, and make your choices. In class, start research and planning.

Over weekend, March 25–27: Continue research; visit other libraries; start rough sketches and drafts; gather necessary supplies.

Friday, April 1: Half-way progress report in class. What have you finished so far? What do you still have left to do?

Over weekend, April 1–3: Continue work on rough and final versions of project.

Friday, April 8	Final projects are due on either of these days. Use the
Monday, April 11	Monday date if you need extra time over the weekend.

Parents: Please sign this and return it by Friday, March 25, so I know that you know about this assignment. Your child may need some assistance in choosing an appropriate project, and in budgeting time wisely. Thanks for your assistance.

_____   _____

child's name   parent's signature after school or in the evening. But few things are as important to good re-lationships with parents as this simple detail, letting them know when a particular assignment is due and telling them what is expected. Most parents are eager to help children with schoolwork, but teachers sometimes fail to let them know what they can do to help. I believe that children should be held responsible for their own work, but at the same time I know that many ten- and eleven-year-olds are just not organized enough to carry out long-term assignments on their own. By communicating with parents, we all benefit.

After distributing this letter, I make a big show of finding a calendar. (Note that we still have not looked at the actual list of projects.) With everyone looking on, we go through the schedule step-by-step. Children now have a visual picture of where we are in the month and when their work is due. Having such a specific schedule cuts two ways. There is little doubt that most children (and adults) work better with a deadline. On the other hand, when children tackle a major project, they sometimes cannot accurately predict how long it will take, and even whether it is feasible. I can advise children to scale back their plans if necessary, but my goal is that each child stretch his or her abilities to the fullest, and I don't want to subvert an ambitious attempt. In the end, children receive a double message: yes, there is a due date, and yes, there might be some flexibility:

> If you get started on something ambitious, and you're working seri-ously on it, and you work and you work, and you find that it's going to take longer than you thought, I'm going to have to relax a little and not bug you about deadlines. I'd rather have it come in a few days late and be done well, than rushed through at the last minute just to finish it up. That's just not fair. So I'll try to be understanding if your work honestly takes longer than you expected.

Instead of having one due date, flexibility is aided by letting projects come in on a series of days; typically, I'll pick a Friday and the following Monday as due dates. In that way, if a project goes longer than expected, the child can take advantage of the extra weekend and still get full credit. Early finishers will have the satisfaction of being among the first to bring their work for display.

It's almost time to pass out the project list; children are getting wiggly. There are just a few other questions to anticipate:

> Someone always wants to know, can I work with my friends? There are lots of projects during the year that let you work in groups: you know that. These projects, though, are mostly aimed at having peo-ple work on their own.
>
> There *are* a few projects here that require more than one person. Say you want to paint a mural that will cover the length of the class-room—given the time you have, that's not something that one per-son could do well, and you'd need to work with a partner. So there

are some projects where you might be working with someone else, but if that's what you want to do, you have to talk to me before you choose your project. I need to be convinced that both of you are equally interested in doing it; I want to avoid a situation where one person is working hard and another is just coasting. And no more than two people, with this exception. If you're making a video, you will probably need other people to act in it. In that case, you'd have to plan the video and arrange for someone to shoot it. Some of your friends could act in it, but they'd also be responsible for completing their own projects. Any questions?

There are usually a few questions, but not many. Children want to see that list. One last reminder:

Remember, we're not going to sign up for projects today. Even if you think you know what you're going to do, you need to take the list home and talk it over with your parents. We will actually sign up tomorrow or the next day.

With ten or fifteen minutes left in the period, I distribute the lists. They vary each year. Some years, for example, everyone in one class created a board game. Other years, everyone worked on a diorama, or created a puppet and helped write a puppet play. In those years, board games or dioramas or puppet plays would not appear on the independent project list. Here is a representative sample of activities over the years.

SUGGESTED *ODYSSEY* PROJECTS

Cartoons: Draw a series of comics based on an episode in *The Odyssey*. This could be a series of short strips, like those in the funny pages of a newspaper, or it could be a long series, like a comic book. If you complete your final version in black ink, we can make copies to share. [See Figure 5-2.]

Writing an epic: *The Odyssey* is an epic poem, a long set of verses on a heroic theme. Take part of the story and turn it into poetry. Your verses do not need to rhyme, although they may if you wish. An epic tells a story in a special, larger-than-life manner, using vivid language.

Mural: Working with a friend or in a small group, design and draw a large mural showing scenes from the travels of Odysseus. You may use paints or colored chalks or Cray-Pas for this project. Try to pick scenes that are especially appropriate for such a large scale.

Trading cards: Prepare a set of trading cards—similar to baseball cards—based on major characters of *The Iliad* and *The Odyssey*. You may include gods, mortals, and monsters. Each card might include a picture of the character, a summary of why he or she is famous, and even some statistics.

Quilt: Make a quilt (or a fabric wall-hanging) that tells an *Odyssey* story. You might make a series of squares with crayon drawings that have been ironed into the fabric, or perhaps glue felt pieces to make a colorful collage. You could show one scene or a series of scenes.

FIGURE 5-2
Excerpt from Odyssey *comic book (Nathanael Jensen)*

Timeline: Make an illustrated timeline, showing when things happened in the story. You could start with the end of the Trojan War, and then look at the wanderings of Odysseus for the next ten years, or you could start when the Greeks left for Troy. Suggested scale: 1 foot = 1 year.

Ships: After doing reading and research, make a series of pictures or a model of an ancient Greek ship. You might do one of Odysseus' twelve black-hulled ships, or perhaps the raft that he built when leaving Calypso's island. Your drawings or model should be as accurate as possible. [See Figures 5-3 and 5-4.]

French storybook: With additional help as needed, dictate, write, and illustrate a story in French about the adventures of Odysseus. [French is part of our school's curriculum, starting in fourth grade.] Write the story simply, for a young reader in France. For special vocabulary, ask Mme Kelly for assistance.

FIGURE 5-3   *Model ship (Ethan Babcock)*

Computer quiz: We have a computer program called *Ask*It,* which quizzes users and keeps track of their score. You could program it to ask questions about characters and episodes in *The Odyssey.*

Board game: Design and construct a board game based on the travels and adventures of Odysseus. You'll need to make the board, playing pieces, cards, and a sheet with the rules. Test-play your game before you make the final version. [See Figure 5-5.]

The Shield of Achilles: Perhaps the most famous description of any object in all of Homer is found in *The Iliad,* Book XVIII, starting at line 478 and continuing to the end of the book. At this point, the poet describes in great detail the armor that Hephaestus made for Achilles. Read this description in several different translations and draw your own detailed picture of this shield.

Stories: Take one episode and write a version of it suitable for first or second graders. Illustrate your story and bind it carefully as a children's book.

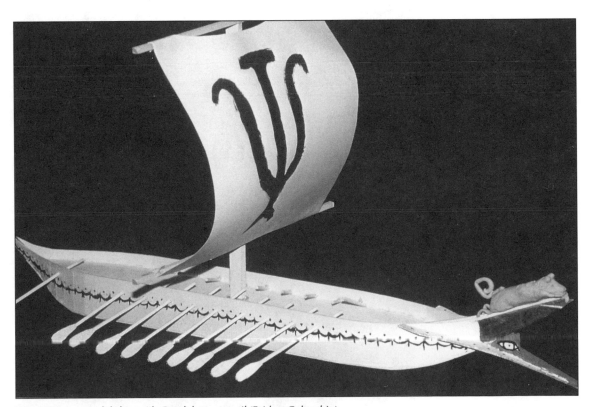

FIGURE 5-4   *Model ship with Greek letter on sail (Bridget Colacchio)*

Trojan Horse: Build a model of the Trojan Horse. The model might be solid, or it could be hollow, concealing Odysseus and his soldiers inside. In past years, students have used cardboard, balsa wood, clay, wood, wax, soap . . . it's up to you. You will need to supply your own materials. [See Figure 5-6.]

Battle scene: After doing appropriate research on armor and weapons from this period of history, draw a scene or build a model of a particular battle from the Trojan War. What about Achilles and Hector fighting

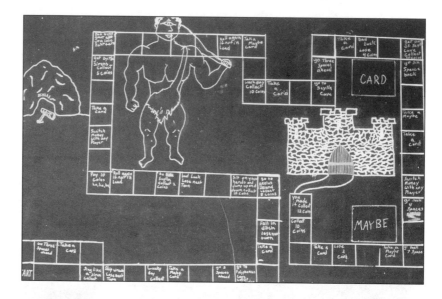

FIGURE 5-5
Board game
(Tiffany Willey)

FIGURE 5-6
Model of the Trojan Horse
(Shawn Nord)

in front of the walls of Troy? In preparation, you'll want to read versions of *The Iliad.*

Building a Community | **85**
of Scholars

Puppetry: Make several puppets and use them to perform a favorite scene from *The Odyssey.* (You will find that hand puppets are easier to make and to operate than marionettes.) Several people might work together on this, since it's hard for one person to operate many different puppets at once.

Map of the travels: Make a map showing the wanderings of Odysseus. For more than 2,000 years, people have been arguing about where in the Mediterranean Sea Odysseus might actually have traveled. There are several books and articles that you will find useful in your research.

Jewelry: In a famous scene in Book XIX of *The Odyssey,* Odysseus, disguised as a beggar, meets Penelope and tells her that he once met her husband, years ago. He describes in detail a golden pin that fastened Odysseus' tunic. After studying ancient Greek jewelry, design and make your own version of that brooch. Several local jewelers might be willing to help you with your piece.

Sewing: Design and sew a stuffed creature from the wanderings of Odysseus. What about a six-headed Scylla, or a Polyphemus with one eye, or a cuddly Poseidon?

Videotape: Write a storyboard of one episode, find some willing actors, locate a video camera, and film your own version of one of Odysseus' adventures. Be careful: it might snow in the middle of your production!

Animation: If you really like to draw and have great patience, you might make an animated cartoon of an *Odyssey* adventure. You will need to make several hundred drawings, and then film them with a special camera. (Warning: this is an incredibly time-consuming project and will require special permission and an extended deadline.)

Posters: Make a set of posters of the heroes, the gods, or selected episodes from *The Odyssey.* Try to organize your posters around one theme. You might use watercolors, poster paints, or collage.

Diorama: Build a model of one of the scenes from *The Iliad* or *The Odyssey.* You'll want to take one specific moment in the story and construct a model showing that scene. A standard paper box (ten-ream size) is the largest acceptable size for this project.

Sirens' song: Each complete translation of *The Odyssey* will contain the words to the song the Sirens sang to Odysseus. Take one of those versions, one you really like—or write your own in modern language—and compose a tune to go with the words. Perform your composition either live or on tape; perhaps you can record a group of people singing the Sirens' song!

Diary: Pick a character in the story (or make one up) and write a journal as if you were that person. What did the Trojan War look like from the point of view of a child living in Troy? What was it like to be a member of the crew on Odysseus' ship? How did Polyphemus normally spend his days?

Odyssey mobile: Design and build a large mobile of different characters from *The Odyssey*. If two people work together on this project and make a large mobile, we could hang it in the lobby by the yellow balcony.

Your choice: You may have another idea for a project. Discuss it with Mr. Millstone and get permission and suggestions *before* getting started. [See Figure 5-7.]

FIGURE 5-7 *Odyssey maze (Blythe Adler)*

Having this list of suggested projects is more than merely helpful. Left on their own to "do a project on *The Odyssey*," many children will flounder. Some will have no idea where to start, while others will come up with something impractical. However, a list like this one, which has guided fifth graders in years past, bridges the gap between dream and reality. It is a structured way to stimulate the imagination. Students know that these ideas will work, and it is a rare child indeed who finds nothing of interest among these possibilities.

THE IMPORTANCE OF CHOICE

That last item on the list, "your choice," is important for two reasons. First, students need to know that their ideas are welcome, that the list is a starting point rather than a closed set. Even if they choose one of the ideas already spelled out—and most students do pick a suggestion from the list—it is worthwhile for them to know that their own ideas will be considered seriously.

Second, students *do* come up with their own ideas, and they inevitably go beyond my own sense of what is possible. For example, I have a vivid memory of Seth coming up to me the day after receiving the list: "I have an idea for something that I want to do for my project, but I don't know if it's okay. I want to make an animated cartoon."

I managed to keep my jaw from dropping and I feigned reluctance. "It might be a possibility," I said. I had made a few short cartoons in workshops, and they were incredibly time-consuming. "Tell me more."

"Well, I took a course in animation last year at my old school. We learned how to make them and I think I could do one on my own. I thought about doing a Claymation movie, but I think I'll keep it simple. I'll make a lot of drawings and film them one at a time. There's one problem, though."

"What's that?"

"I wouldn't be able to get it finished in three weeks. I'd need more time."

I played hard to get. We talked for a few minutes and it became obvious that Seth had thought carefully about his project. He was a responsible student to begin with, and I had few doubts about his abilities. Slowly, I allowed him to convince me. Two and a half months later, he borrowed the school's movie camera and shot his film. Running time of the cartoon? Less than one minute. Number of drawings necessary? More than four hundred. It was well worth the wait. I added "animated cartoon" to the list, and sure enough, four years later, another student tackled it as a project.

Sometimes the best ideas come from students thinking about the "your choice" option. Cabot looked at the list one year and finally decided to do a series of *Odyssey* posters. "I wasn't sure about posters," he confided. "I was thinking about maybe doing a set of trading cards." Trading cards! Why hadn't I thought of that? I rushed to my computer, called up the "Odyssey Projects" file, and added "trading cards" to the list of suggestions already in place for the following year. That year, trading cards were the single most popular project for boys and girls alike.

Once I have distributed the list, I give children several days to choose their project. Some need time to meet with their families and to choose among many tempting possibilities. Others return to school the next day all fired up with their idea only to discover unforeseen difficulties as they start their research. Perhaps what seemed like a great idea is no longer as exciting, and they need to change. After a short grace period, though, they are expected to stick with their choice.

The next days in class are dedicated to research, both individual and in small groups. There are always projects that attract a wide following, although the "popular projects" have changed over the years. Creating a model Trojan Horse was the most popular project for many years; this is largely a work of the imagination. (Homer tells us little about the actual fall of Troy. The best classical source for the Trojan Horse is Vergil's *Aeneid*, Book II, in which Aeneas, the defeated Trojan, recounts in detail the treachery of the Greeks. Is there a historical basis for the Trojan Horse? Children reading Peter Connolly [1986] discover that it may be a literary device to represent a covered battering ram used to destroy the walls of Troy.) Since we have no archaeological remains and the literary evidence is sketchy, each illustrator has a different idea of how the horse looked. Students polish their own vision and choose a medium in which to build their model. (See Figure 5-8.)

Several project choices require extensive research on specialized topics. My intern and I meet with children frequently during these days, distributing materials, helping children locate information, answering questions, and helping to narrow grandiose schemes into feasible projects. Building a model ship, for example, became a more popular choice in recent years, although building a good ship demands extraordinary patience and precision. It also requires a certain amount of guesswork, since even trained archaeologists debate the nature of Homeric ships. Over the years, I have assembled a packet of information, complete with translated excerpts from Homer, pictures of ancient seal rings, modern renderings, and *National Geographic* articles on wrecked Bronze Age ships. Similarly, children trying to re-create the route that a historical Odysseus might actually have sailed receive a packet with summaries of Homer's descriptions of the places visited and references to modern accounts of adventurers who have their own theories about the geography of *The Odyssey*.

Such specialized research seminars provide an opportunity to explore a narrow topic in all its complexity. I described details of one such session early in the history of our project:

The high point for me today came when I sat down with Kian and Heather and Mark, all of whom were planning a project connected with mapping Odysseus' route. I had given them photocopies of Tim Severin's [1986] article in National Geographic *and Ernle Bradford's [1968] piece. On the meeting area rug we spread out a large map of Greece, the* National Geographic *map of the historic Mediterranean, copies of the articles, and a few copies of* The Odyssey.

"You're trying to figure out the route of a person named Odysseus, as described by Homer in The Odyssey. *We don't even know for sure that there* was *a person named Homer, or if there was a person named Odysseus. So if this task seems difficult or confusing or frustrating to you, well, it should, because it's not an easy task. Keep that in mind as you work."*

I went through their task, step-by-step. They needed to read the accounts of two different authors who have each sailed around the Mediterranean Sea trying to retrace the route of Odysseus.

"Each man has found where he thinks Odysseus really went. The problem is that each has found a different route! There are some places they agree on, sure, but most of the locations that one says are places where Odysseus stopped are different from the other one's locations. Here, look at their maps."

FIGURE 5-8
Model of the Trojan Horse
(Matt Mazur)

The differences in the maps, obvious at first glance, are startling. Tim Severin's Argo route hugs the Greek islands. Ernle Bradford's route swings far to the west, and includes islands west of Italy. The kids stuck with me, heads bent intently over the maps.

"So what you need to do is read the articles, follow each man's arguments, and see what makes sense. You might produce your own map based on one or the other of these, or you might try to show both routes. Maybe you'll be able to come up with a route of your own, one that combines pieces of each man's theory."

We spent the entire period looking at maps and reading Homer, the students absolutely engrossed in the problem. I joked to my wife that night that I had been running a graduate seminar in Odyssey navigation.

Not every topic requires a research seminar. Students working on their own use this research time to look through our class library with a sharper focus than before, taking notes, looking at pictures, making sketches, absorbing information.

After their initial research, students complete the actual work on each project at home. But there is one other important component that takes place at school, and that is the interim report. After ten days, I ask children to describe what they have completed to date and what remains. Most children have been hard at work, and they are eager to give a blow-by-blow account of their progress. Each year, however, there are always a few children who are slow to get started, despite all the structure built into the assignment. Listening to their peers provides a dash of reality.

"Uh-oh," I can see some children thinking as we move around the circle, "if everyone else is so far along, I'd better get started." After children have given detailed descriptions of what they have accomplished, it is easy to spot the procrastinators: "Well, I've been doing a lot of reading and thinking about what it's going to look like and talking to people and planning things out"—this usually accompanied by a look of earnest concentration—"and I'm almost ready to get started on my rough draft." Such students dash home that night and finally get to work.

LEARN SOMETHING OF SUBSTANCE

It is clear by now that my "lectures" serve more to shape students' working habits than to impart content. I do believe, however, that it is important for children to learn something of substance of that long-ago world inhabited by Homer's heroic figures. By saying "something of substance," though, I am not saying that all of them should learn the same things.

When I started the project, I originally wanted children to come to love *The Odyssey* as much as I did, but I quickly realized that this was an impractical goal. Instead, I decided to encourage them to become familiar with Homer's epic in as much detail as possible, hoping that affection would follow knowledge. But beyond that core familiarity with the story, just what should children know?

From my own coursework at the Odyssey Institute, I was familiar with the broad issues embodied in what classicists label "the Homeric question." Was there a Homer? If so, when did he live? How were the epics composed, orally or in writing? Were *The Iliad* and *The Odyssey* both composed by the same author? How reliable a guide is Homer in understanding early Greek history? Do the epics describe life in Bronze Age Greece, the time of the stories, or that of a Greece some five centuries later, the time of the poet? (For a brief discussion of these issues, see the introduction and first chapter of C. G. Thomas, *Homer's History: Mycenaean or Dark Age?*) If scholars cannot agree, surely these topics are too complex for children.

But here lies an important idea for children to learn: for many historical issues, there are no clear answers, only intriguing questions with sets of evidence to support different explanations.

There is no doubt that my own enthusiasm is contagious. The more I know about these arcane topics, the better I'm able to share their complexity with my students. This can be a powerful moment, having a teacher admit that there are questions over which adults disagree and being invited to enter the realms of scholarship—as apprentices to be sure, but invited nonetheless.

At some point during our study of *The Odyssey,* I mention the lengthy effort to decode Linear B, the written language of those early Greeks, the Mycenaeans. I tell students that the man who finally cracked the code, Michael Ventris, started his studies as a teenager and continued them as an amateur while he earned his living as an architect. "And Linear A," I continue, "which we think might be the language of the ancient Minoan people, is still undeciphered. Maybe one of the people in this room will be the person who finally solves that mystery." Archaeology is one academic discipline where amateurs have made many of the great discoveries.

I want my students to strengthen their amateur status. I want each child to develop an individual passion, to experience the thrill of intellectual exploration, and to contribute to the community's knowledge.

In addition to discussing topics with the others in their group, the young scholars share their research findings with others in the class. One child might be building a diorama depicting a particular battle scene from Homer. He is concentrating his research on weapons and armor, eager to show warriors correctly outfitted in Bronze Age regalia. Then he realizes that he needs to put a model ship in one corner of the scene and seeks out a friend who is building a ship to learn what he can of ancient ship design. He also discovers that he wants to include several women figures on the edge of the scene and talks with another classmate, who is studying the history of clothing. At our daily class meeting, children swap information, and I direct some requests for information to students in other home-rooms. Each child becomes a specialist with knowledge to share, and because we are united by our common understanding of *The Odyssey*, each person's specialty can be appreciated by all.

WHAT ABOUT THE PARENTS?

"Is it fair," some ask, "to expect children to do so much work at home on this major project? Some parents will give extra help, perhaps too much help. And what about those children who don't have a parent who can give the extra assistance? Aren't they being penalized?" Many colleagues, whom I respect, make a point of keeping lengthy assignments confined to the classroom to minimize parental influence.

This is an important point. Such questions have caused me to change the number of such assignments over the year and to reexamine this practice. Yes, some children work entirely on their own and bring a project to school, only to discover with dismay that a classmate, with adult help, has produced something more polished; I recall several such cases in the past ten years. A few others, having little parental presence or supervision, have been unable to get started at all; the deadline appears and they have nothing to show for their time. In those cases, yes, it would have been better to insist that all work be done in school, where it could be monitored more carefully.

Over the years, however, with the experience we have gained from such incidents, we have been more successful in coordinating long-term assignments with the many adults who play supportive roles in school, such as Chapter I teachers, learning specialists, personal-care aides, tutors, and the guidance counselor. By the time this independent project comes along, we have had months to notice a child who has difficulty completing homework assignments and sometimes flag that child for special help during the project. One of the finest models of the Trojan Horse was completed recently by a boy working exclusively at school with a tutor; he took extraordinary pride in his accomplishment and was eager to bring his mother to school to view the finished piece on display.

On the other hand, there is nothing wrong in working with a parent; indeed, many children find that working with a relative on their project is what made it special. Like many communities today, our town contains families that are stretched for time and adults who lead busy lives. Sometimes it takes a child's special project to get the adults to slow down. Over the years I've heard many warm stories, from children and adults alike, about the time spent together on a detailed project: carving in a wood-shop, learning to use a sewing machine, building and painting, editing and rewriting. Bridget described the pleasure she got from spending so much time with her father, a busy surgeon; Greg spent hours building a model ship with his grandfather, learning techniques that the older man had used when he was a boy and building models was his hobby. Aaron's mother liked to paint, and he spent hours with her learning how to make a color wheel and eagerly preparing preliminary paintings before starting his final version.

Projects do not receive letter grades, so parental help plays no role in helping the student earn a better grade. After so much effort, children take well-deserved pride in their work, which is worth more to me (and to their parents) than an external evaluation. The project itself stands as proof of their efforts, and since all projects are put on display for both students and parents, there is no need to compare one project with another. (Chapter 9 discusses evaluation at greater length.) I am generous with comments, oral or written, letting children know what I like about their work and what I think could be better. Children are not working for a grade; they are working to satisfy their own creative instincts. Parents, too, are given a window through which to watch their child at work and to provide as much assistance as they feel is needed.

Part of the reason for my initial cover letter when students start their projects is precisely to let parents provide meaningful assistance, rather than find themselves in the awkward position of being called at the last minute to rescue a child overwhelmed by an assignment. Most parents are eager to help their child learn to allocate time, to take a complex task and break it into manageable pieces. In this instance, Homer and the project provide the motivation, the classroom provides the academic background and some organization, and the home provides the follow-through and personal support. Over the years, this collaboration has produced some extraordinary work.

ALLOW YOURSELF TO BE SURPRISED

The first day *Odyssey* projects are due is one of my favorite days of the school year. We clear countertops and wall space in anticipation. The first projects to appear are a delightful stimulant for the whole class. Children arrive before school, sometimes carrying huge bags with padding to protect their delicate work. There's barely time to unwrap and admire one child's project before the next child comes through the door. As other students arrive at school, they turn eagerly to examine the work on display. Children dash from one homeroom to another, bringing their friends to look and admire. Within a few days, scores of great endeavors created in homes all over town are brought together in one dazzling display of talent and effort. Children take pride (concealed with modesty) in their own work and pride (announced with great clamor) in each other's achievements. The completion of the fifth-grade *Odyssey* projects is a monument to all we have learned in the past months, a celebration of the story and of the young learners who are giving that ancient tale new life. We always schedule an Open House shortly after the projects are completed to provide an opportunity for the greater fifth-grade community to celebrate their achievements.

Creating an independent project becomes a consuming task that brings children intense satisfaction. Take one year, when a single project suggestion had long-lasting effects. Half a dozen boys in my class that year were avid baseball card collectors, spending many recesses swapping cards and comparing their collections. I was not surprised that they made different sets of *Odyssey* cards, complete with special bonus cards, rare editions, and unusual "misprints," which commanded a higher price in their fictional trading card world. Many also created price guides, listing not only their own cards but those of rival companies. Given their knowledge and their interest in the card business, that could have been expected. What I could not have anticipated, though, was that for the next three months, long after the projects had been turned in and displayed, these boys continued to make *Odyssey* trading cards and to swap them, launching new companies and new series.

For some children, the work they do on this assignment represents the high point of the year and in some cases, of their elementary school career. Stated simply, each year someone brings in a project so lovingly crafted, so detailed, so extraordinary that I know the Odyssey Project has made a difference in that child's life.

When I first started thinking about this book, I expected that this would be the easiest part, sharing stories about the actual projects of actual children. But finding the appropriate words is difficult. Here are three snapshots:

Becca was concerned that all the versions of *The Odyssey* were aimed at older readers. She decided to retell the Polyphemus episode in language suitable for second graders. She wrote a lengthy text and illustrated it with stunning watercolors. My knees got weak when she handed me the finished book; I started crying when I came to her final picture showing Polyphemus throwing the rock at Odysseus' ship, while Poseidon, a shadowy and menacing ghost, looms in the distance.

Kyle had been in my class when I taught third grade. I knew he was a gifted artist, so I wasn't surprised when he decided to make a statue of Poseidon. He spent his research time looking for every picture he could find, and for odd bits of information as well. Poseidon was god of the sea, he knew, and god of horses, he soon learned. But what did his own horses look like? And how many pulled his chariot through the sea? I was thrilled when I finally saw the clay sculpture. At the Open House later in the week, I mentioned my pleasure to Kyle's mother. "That's the third one he made," she said. "He had two others before it, but he wasn't satisfied. They looked fine to me, but he kept changing the number of horses, and the way they looked, until he got it the way he wanted it."

Simon announced that he was going to do an oil painting, which was only a small surprise, since I knew that both his parents were artists. He asked for little help and gave only the barest details in his interim report. When he brought in his finished piece, I knew by the way he walked that he was proud of it, and with good reason. It is a powerful painting, unusual in its abstraction. The colors of the sea and sky, the spray driven by the wind and the lurking figure of Poseidon watching from the ocean depths all combine to reveal the power of this storm. I asked him how he managed to create such a work. "I've sailed on the ocean," he said. "It can be pretty scary."

The good projects come not just from the so-called gifted and talented; every teacher can cite examples of a few exceptional children. What continues to amaze me is that so many children get excited by their projects and produce outstanding work, year after year, class after class.

If we set high standards, children will work to meet those expectations. By encouraging children to take responsibility for their own learning, and by allowing them to choose the manner in which they will share what they have learned, we make it possible for them to leap ahead. Children create projects that astound adults, even those of us who have been pushing them to do what they've just done. At such moments, the Muses smile.

6 | WHAT ABOUT WRITING?

What a strange machine man is.
You put in bread, radishes and
wine, and out come laughter, sighs
and dreams.

—*Nikos Kazantzakis*

First students understand the story through listening to storytellers, reading extensively, and creating artwork. Then they write, and they write a lot. As in any classroom, the quality of my students' writing ranges widely. The Odyssey Project, however, stimulates all students to write, and different writing assignments present fresh challenges. In this chapter, I present several samples of good fifth-grade writing. They are representative of what can emerge when every student is given an opportunity to excel. Education is, after all, the art of the possible.

HISTORICAL FICTION: CREATING A BELIEVABLE WORLD

For those children who like to write, their first lengthy *Odyssey* composition comes as an independent project, after more than a month of other activities. Sonia was such a child. Like a dozen other children, she had been in my third-grade class two years earlier. I knew then that she was an avid reader and a gifted writer, so I was not surprised when she decided to write the diary of a child living through the Trojan War.

A few children had attempted a similar project in earlier years, but I had been disappointed by those efforts. The stories were flat and lacked grounding in an identifiable setting. This time, before she started, Sonia and I discussed historical fiction. In addition to creating believable characters, I argued, to make her story convincing she had to create a world filled with accurate details.

Homer tells us little about life in Troy; the focus of *The Iliad* is more on the Greeks than on the Trojans, and more on the battlefield than on domestic and urban life. We have other sources of information, however. Archaeologists starting with Heinrich Schliemann have dug at Troy and at other Bronze Age sites, and many fine books for children on those topics have appeared in recent years. Troy was involved in an extensive trading network with other cities of the eastern Mediterranean, and many artifacts of daily life might mimic those of other settlements. Sonia immersed herself in books and articles explaining day-to-day life in the Bronze Age. She realized that she could borrow details about furniture, jewelry, architecture, and cooking and adapt them to her Trojan setting, melding her research and her imagination with fragments from Homer's tale.

> My name is Electra. I've lived in Troy all my life. My father fights in the Trojan War. I was only five when the Trojan War started. The war has lasted for five years so far. I'll never forget the time I first saw Helen. I had just gone to the well at the northeast corner of the city. Helen was so beautiful I nearly dropped the clay vessel full of water I was carrying. She looked very foreign, not like she had come from Troy at all. She had very long hair; it was in several braids and she wore so much gold jewelry I thought even Queen Hecuba herself could be jealous of Helen. I would never have guessed then that she would cause a war.
>
> There are rumors that Helen brought with her a treasure that only King Priam, Paris, and Helen know about. People say that the treasure is what the Greeks are really after. My friend, who is a servant to Queen Hecuba, said that when the royal family had a banquet for Paris and Helen, she dropped a platter of food she was holding; Helen was that beautiful. After my friend had dropped the platter and was banished from the banquet hall, she overheard King Priam saying to Paris, "So, you have the treasure," and Paris answered, "Yes, Father."

The particular challenge of historical fiction is in incorporating historical details into the writing. The writer has to blend new information smoothly into a conventional narrative. Sonia's "Trojan Journal" works because she succeeds in making that faraway world of Troy come to life. Through nine journal entries, she blends references to Aegean trade networks with the mundane details of the evening meal, listing Mycenae, Tiryns, and Pylos in the same casual manner as lentils, beans, and chick peas. She takes an ordinary person, places her in a distant setting—long ago and far away—and lets us feel what it might have been like to live there.

EPIC POETRY: WRITING LARGER THAN LIFE

Ten-year-olds who attempt to write epic poetry must concern themselves not only with research and story-making but also with imitating a specialized literary form; they can tell the same story but they must do so in a particular style. For young authors struggling to make sense of an unfamiliar literary form, there is no substitute for studying other examples of the genre and imitating them. I remember fondly one story from the first year of the Norwich Odyssey Project, more than ten years ago. Jessica liked our work with *The Odyssey,* but she was annoyed that we weren't spending time on *The Iliad* as well. She read different versions of that story, borrowing books from the classroom library, and then decided to write her own version of *The Iliad* as an epic. Her father told me that when they were in the community library, Jessica begged him to sign out the Richmond Lattimore translation; her library card would only allow her to take books from the children's room.

"Jessica, your bed is already covered with four or five different versions of the story," he told her. "Why do you need this one?"

"I need to see how he translates the section about Achilles and his horses . . ."

Jessica got her book. Here is an excerpt taken from "The Death of Patroklos," Part 4 of the long poem she composed:

> The Greeks and the Trojans
> Fought over his body.
> The Trojans thought,
> "Let the Greeks slay us all together
> Then have them get the body of Patroklos."
> The Greeks thought,
> "Let the Earth open up and swallow us all
> Then let the Trojans get the body of Patroklos."
> And Hector stripped him of his arms,
> And put them on himself.
> And up on high Olympus,
> Zeus looked upon Hector and said,
> "Those arms will cost him dearly!"
>
> Meanwhile,
> Antilokos arrived at Achilles' tent.
> His eyes were full of tears as he said,
> "O Achilles! Patroklos is dead,
> And the Greeks and Trojans fight over his body!"
> Achilles fell to the ground,
> And took dust and poured it upon his hair,
> And wept and mourned.
> And Antilokos wept,
> But while he wept he held Achilles' hands,
> So that he would not draw his sword
> And slay his own throat,
> So great was his grief.
>
> And his mother heard him,
> And came to him.
> "O Achilles," she said,
> "Why do you weep?"

Achilles said,
"My dear companion is dead,
And I shall have no joy in my life
Other than the joy of slaying Hector."
His mother was sorrowful, and she said,
"You will not live long. Soon you, too,
Will be slain by Paris and Apollo."

At the battlefield,
The two immortal horses
Stood apart from the battle,
For they loved Patroklos,
And they knew he was dead.
They stood there with their proud heads low,
And their long manes trailing in the dust.
The tears flowed from their eyes,
And they would not obey the commands of their driver.
Then Zeus spoke to them:
"O immortal horses,
Why did I give you to Peleus?
Why do you have to suffer with men?
Those arms will cost Hector his life."

And the horses felt better,
And they obeyed their driver as before.

Jessica's writing was influenced by the many different editions she read. Years later, another student writer fell under the spell of a single translator. My favorite *Odyssey* translation is that of Robert Fitzgerald, and I keep a copy, annotated and well-worn, close at hand during our study. Chris borrowed it to read one morning and was struck by the look of the type on the page, especially the notion of starting a line halfway across the page. Captivated, he ended up writing several episodes in that style. This is an excerpt from his poem about the Land of the Dead:

As the ship sailed on,
the fog grew thicker,
the wind stronger
the sky darker. . . .
As the gull flew on,
as the ocean tilted,
they entered the land
where Sisyphus rolls the rock,
where Tantalus tries to drink,
and where Cerberus guards the River.
And so they set forth,
into the Land of the Dead,

to do what Odysseus
and Circe before him
had said.
                    And as they herded the sheep,
they looked with their weary eyes
at the dark Land of the Dead.
The shadows surrounded them
and engulfed them in their darkness.
They huddled together
and they lit the fire,
while their leader dug,
dug deep with his sword,
dug a trench.
                    Odysseus slit their throats,
and commanded his men:
    "Men, skin these beasts,
first the ram,
then the ewe,
and burn them.
Burn them on your fires.
Burn them until there is nothing!"
    And they followed his orders,
and as they burned them, the Shades came
searching for the source of the blood.
They advanced to the pit, but
the sight of Odysseus,
Odysseus the warrior,
Odysseus the king,
waving his sword
made them retreat.
Even though
swords could not hurt them,
as they are dead,
they drew back.
Back into the shadows.

    Now, some might argue that these two samples are not really epic po-
etry, that a ten-year-old is not capable of sustaining the complexity and
the emotional depth demanded by an epic. I'd rather not pursue the argument. In both these examples, it is clear that a student fell in love with a
literary form and successfully appropriated it for her or his own purposes.
Reading the poems again for the first time in several years as I type them
into this manuscript, I'm struck by how much the young writers have
been influenced by storytelling. Look at how many of Jessica's lines start
with "And . . ." Look at Chris' short lines, and his frequent use of repeating phrases: "and they lit the fire, / while their leader dug, / dug deep with

his sword, / dug a trench." These students are continuing an epic tradition, not the literary form of Vergil's *Aeneid,* but the vigorous oral tradition that produced Homer's epics, which they have experienced for themselves. What a powerful model it provides for their own writing!

WRITING AND STORYTELLING: THE BRAIDED STRAND

Storytelling also has an impact on students' writing in other ways. Although most children tell a different version of their tale each time, as do most of our adult storytellers, some refine their telling so much that it becomes a memorized script. Several children have created written versions of their spoken tales where the two forms of literature support each other. In some cases the written version leads to a strong spoken performance, while in other cases the spoken performance becomes so ingrained that it is easy to transfer onto paper.

Siri Daulaire was one of those children. Like Jessica many years before, she fell under the spell of *The Iliad.* Siri's grandparents are the authors of the finest collection of Greek mythology for children, *d'Aulaires' Book of Greek Myths.* Rereading their book with her newly discovered passion for Homeric stories, Siri felt there was a gap and decided to fill it. She explained her thinking in a brief preface: "The d'Aulaires left some myths and stories out of their book because it was a children's book, and if they put everything in the book it would be about 500 pages long. If you gave a child a 500 page long book, the child would say, 'I will read it later,' and never get to it."

Siri takes a serious episode from the Homeric tales, Achilles and the Trojan War, and slowly develops the story. We see the careful setting of the scene, the fight between Achilles and Agamemnon, the taking of Briseis, one action leading inevitably to the next. We learn early on, as Agamemnon does not—"But he was wrong, fatally wrong"—that his quarrel with Achilles will have grave consequences. The gods play out their designated roles and we see how they toy with the mortals, all building up to the moment when Achilles finally kills his enemy. Siri's writing, like her storytelling, conveys the utter contempt in Achilles' voice as he addresses the dead body of Hector:

> Hector staggered forward and fell to the ground with the cloak of death around him. Achilles then said to Hector, "So. You are dead. You thought nothing of me, Achilles, when you killed Patroclus, my dearest friend, or when you stripped his body of my armor. You thought nothing of me then, but you will think of me now and forever as you descend to Hades in the land of the dead."
>
> With that, Achilles picked up Hector's heels and drove holes through them with an arrow. Then Achilles strung leather thongs

through the holes and tied the thongs to the back of his chariot. Still crazy with rage, he rode around the walls of Troy, dragging Hector along behind, through the dirt and the dust, right before the eyes of Hector's parents, who had begged him not to do battle on that ill-fated night. Even the gods were shocked at this breach of honor. Achilles would pay dearly.

Despite her young age, Siri presents a picture of men at war with the weighty seriousness it deserves.

If this scene of death on the battlefield captures an emotional peak in *The Iliad,* what do we make of the fantastic adventures of Odysseus on his return home? What tone is appropriate in describing a confrontation between a tired hero and the alluring Sirens? Sonia found her answer by borrowing a technique from one of our storytellers. When Judy Witters relates the story of Circe, she turns Homer on edge and tells the tale from Circe's point of view. Similarly, Sonia lets a Siren tell us her tale. Again, the written and spoken versions of the story mirror each other:

> Only a few ships sail by our island. When a ship does we sing beautiful songs of knowledge, glory, beauty and whatever a man would wish for. The sailors can never resist us and row their ships toward our island. When they try to dock their ship it smashes against the sharp rocks at the edge of the islands, and it breaks into millions of pieces, leaving the sailors helpless. We retrieve the sailors who haven't managed to swim to one of the islands and bring them to shore ourselves. Once all the sailors are collected we divide them up among us. My sister Leucosia always gets the juiciest, fattest, most delicious sailor. I'm usually stuck with the small, salty, tough sailors . . .

The young author takes liberties with Homer's tale, but the Greeks had no one codified source for their mythology, and Sonia is continuing an old custom, selecting from different traditions to fit her purposes. Certainly she is charting new ground as her story moves from the familiar to the new, ending up with fresh-fried sailor and tourists on Capri. At this point in our study, that's exactly what I hope for, when students know a work of literature so well that they can begin to improvise around it.

PUPPET PLAYS: WORDS INTO ACTION

The Odyssey Project now involves some 120 first and fifth graders, but it is worth remembering that at the start, more than ten years ago, we were just two teachers—fifth grade and first grade—and a story.

The project expanded the following year into the classroom of the upper-grade English teacher, Peter Anderson, who had been away on sabbatical leave. From his own background in theatre and from years of directing the annual sixth-grade play, Peter knew the power of performance, taking words and bringing them to life on a stage. He was excited by our description of the unit, and agreed to coordinate his fifth-grade English classes with social studies. Traditionally, Peter's fifth graders built puppets in the spring and faced the daunting challenge of writing plays that included parts for all the puppet creations. This led to unusual cast lists and complicated dramas that bordered on Theatre of the Absurd, as students struggled to devise parts and plots for their disparate characters.

Peter recognized the advantages of having all the students working around a common theme. He continued the English unit, "Puppets and Playwriting," but now stipulated that all puppets must be based on characters from our Greek studies. Mortals, gods, and monsters were all acceptable. He listened patiently to the predictable complaints—"It's not fair! The other classes got to do whatever they wanted!"—and quietly pointed out later that the playwriting went more smoothly. Since all the puppets shared a Homeric lineage, they belonged together.

For many years, Peter's students followed a formal process of designing the puppets, which included identifying physical characteristics and drawing detailed front and side views before beginning the actual construction. To make life easier in the classroom, it helped to have all puppets made in the same style, although that style changed from year to year. (Hand puppets are easiest to build, but an ambitious teacher might try marionettes.) The students built the head by spreading six layers of papier-mâché over a balloon. They painted it, added wool or yarn with a glue gun for hair, and sewed an appropriate costume. This process took about three weeks (see Figures 6-1 and 6-2).

In later years, another fifth-grade English teacher felt uncomfortable with the time and mess involved in puppet construction, but she liked the idea of using *Odyssey* stories in a playwriting unit. Her students created Readers' Theatre productions instead of puppet plays. In either case, the playwriting process works much the same.

Children typically write collaborative plays in groups of four to six. To avoid quarrels over who will write juicy episodes, they draw one from a hat. The playwriting begins—no puppets at this stage—when children talk their way through the episode. As they retell their shared story, they add details to each other's tales. They begin to focus more on dialogue and stage directions and less on narration. After several days of planning, they take each episode and break it into smaller scenes, which they write individually or in small groups. Some students, much taken by dramatic form, write entire plays on their own. Here is a passage from Scene IV of Sonia's "The Land of the Midnight Sun," a play about the cannibal Laestrygonians:

Laestragonian Queen: Oh you poor little ducklings. Of course you'll want food. One minute while I summon my husband. *(Laestragonian Queen makes a piercing whistle and yells to a servant)* Servant, you lazy lout! Go fetch my husband from the town meeting.

Eurylochus: *(Whispering in Pilotes' ear)* Why her arms alone are as big as the pillars were on the temple to Athena in Troy!

Pilotes: *(Shaking with fear)* Shouldn't we try to leave? If her daughter is so much bigger than us, and the Laestragonian Queen is so much bigger than her daughter, imagine how big her husband will be!

Laestragonian Queen: *(Glaring at the sailors)* There's no need to whisper, my dears.

Laestragonian Princess: *(Whining)* Mother! Father never lets us have a bonfire to roast the sailors. We always have to eat them RAW. Ca . . .

Laestragonian Queen: *(Turning pale and sounding flustered, while the sailors watch in horror)* My dear sailors, don't listen to a word my daughter says. She has an overactive imagination and tends to . . . well . . . make things up.

Laestragonian Princess: *(Whining)* Mother! I do not have an overactive imagination. Anyway, I think it's time we brought up the subject of spices. You never let me put spices on the sailors, and I think it's plain unfair. Just because . . .

Laestragonian Queen: *(Picks up fan and fans her face; she is also swaying, as if about to swoon)* Please, please! We'll discuss it later. Please, please!

FIGURE 6-1　*Laestrygonian queen with Barbie doll earrings (Kate Robbie)*

FIGURE 6-2　*Laestrygonian king (Sarah Kerekes)*

Playwriting benefits greatly from the presence of word processing and computers in the classroom; as each child finishes entering her lines, she moves aside for the next student. A simple keyboard command at the end of class produces neatly typed scripts that can be taken home and revised for the following day's session.

By the time they've reached fifth grade, most students in our school have acted in many skits, short improvised pieces presented at the weekly assembly. In a few cases, they've worked with more formal scripts of short plays and learned lines. But for nearly everyone, this is their first experience of actually writing a play. There are new conventions to learn: setting, stage directions, minimal narration, and the daunting necessity of constant dialogue. Add to this the dynamics of working in a group to produce anything, and you have a worthy challenge.

Once they have written a script, children need ample time to rehearse and revise their production before presenting it to classmates, younger children, and parents. Theatre, like writing, benefits from publication—in this case, public performance. It is simply part of the process.

REWRITING HOMER IN YOUR OWN WORDS

The assignment itself is short, and comes in two parts.

"Take one episode from Homer . . ." Which episode to choose? Here's how I typically explain the options:

> In the past, some people wrote the story they were learning to tell and others decided to do a different story from the one they were telling. There may be an episode that you have become interested in over the past few weeks. You may be thinking, "Well, I've been working on telling the Laestrygonians for a while now, but I'm really getting interested in the Phaeacians. Maybe I could write about the Phaeacians." Pick any episode you want to write about.

While some students move in the course of their *Odyssey* studies from episode to episode, others select the same episode for many activities. In this case, a student might begin by painting a picture or building a model of that scene; this involves reading and research, and helps the child visualize details. As he moves on to practice telling the story, he develops character voices and sound effects. He hears the story read aloud in translation, with well-wrought English phrases. He discovers that each medium imposes its own restrictions; verbal sound effects are hard to transfer to the printed page and long passages of narration must be replaced by dialogue for a successful puppet play. Now it's time to return to that most familiar of literary forms, a story.

"**. . . and tell it in your own words.**" The first question is that omnipresent concern of schoolchildren about writing: how long does it have to be?

> We are concerned primarily with quality in this assignment. Your story does not have to be long. Two well-written pages are better than six or eight pages in which you ramble on and on.

Children are given a week or two to complete this assignment. I set aside hours of class time in Social Studies or English for writing, for conferences, for rewriting and more conferences, and for typing final copies.

Many of the choices a writer usually faces are narrowed or already settled:

- What to write about? There are only a limited number of adventures.
- What will I call my characters? Homer has already named them.
- What's the setting? That's already defined.
- What's the plot? Polyphemus cannot invite Odysseus to sit around the banquet table chatting amiably about bygone days. The men on Odysseus' ship must put wax in their ears. The crew has to kill the cattle of the sun. Odysseus cannot die at sea. The suitors cannot slaughter the returning hero. The action is already established.

What remains? Point of view, clarity of vision, narrative structure, dialogue, word selection—all those lofty aspects of writing that we rarely have time to explore with students because we are so busy cutting through the undergrowth trying to create a basic trail.

Because the assignment puts children under such tight constraints and because they now reap the benefits of all their earlier *Odyssey* work, these stories are often the best writing I see from my students in the entire year. Freed from having to choose among so many options, the writer's energy flows into expressing the story in the best words possible.

Some children take a light-hearted approach to their tales. Others demonstrate a sophisticated control of language as they milk an episode for all the humor they can. Here are the opening paragraphs of "Read the Menu Before You Eat the Food, A Modern Comedy of the Laestrygonians." Sara, the author, is both a skilled writer and a soccer enthusiast.

> The Cornell Soccer team, led by head coach Odie Seeus, played the USC Trojans in the NCAA Championship. It was a real battle, going into several over-times. Despite losing the best player with a ruptured achilles tendon, Cornell scored the winning goal with a fake and a shot by Joe Woodenhorse.
>
> The NCAA Championship Tournament is a single elimination 12-team competition. After defeating the USC Trojans, Cornell went on to win the championship with wins in the next two games. Odie Seeus told the sports writers, "We were lucky to defeat the

University of Polyphemus with a no-look shot," he said sheepishly, "and we just got past Lotus College although three of my players played like they were on drugs. It was a great tournament, but I will be happy to return home to Ithaca and my wife Penelope."

Trying to find an appropriate tone for the Olympian gods is always a difficult task. In her version of the Circe episode, Lorna successfully captures a sense of nobility and power without falling into stilted language:

> "Don't bow to me, Odysseus, for the god who sent me is greater than I," Hermes said. "Athena sent me. She watches over you and your quest. I was told to tell you that Circe, the witch that lives here, wishes to turn every traveler to swine. She has done this to your men."
>
> Hermes pulled a black root from the ground that only the gods can pull easily.
>
> "Eat this, and when she offers you wine, sip it and hold your sword to her throat. Make her swear never to do magic again. She will give you important information," Hermes said to Odysseus.
>
> "I will do as you say, great Hermes, and thank great Athena too."

Mastering the language of Olympians is not the only challenge for young writers. These stories offer many opportunities to explore the heroic voice of mortals. Here, for example, is an excerpt from David's version of "The Homecoming," describing the moment just after Odysseus has successfully passed Penelope's test of the bow. The writing shows the influence of the stories he has heard and his own wide reading:

> And Odysseus, son of noble Laertes, notched another arrow for yet another target. That target was Antinoös, most vile of the suitors. Antinoös was just raising his golden goblet to take a drink of Odysseus' fine wine, and no thought of death had entered him, when Odysseus, master of land ways, master of sea ways, let fly the arrow and it caught Antinoös just below the chin. Antinoös fell over, his life blood jetting out his nostrils, upsetting the chair and kicking the table over, too. Blood mixed with food was all over the floor. It was disgusting to describe. Then Eurymachus, one of the suitors, said, "Stranger, you make so bold to kill the best man in seaswept Ithaca. This will not go unnoticed. We shall feed you to the vultures and dogs and let your flesh lie where it may."
>
> And Odysseus, who had suffered many hardships, looked down upon the suitors and said, "Dogs, you thought I would never come home, did you? Yes, it is true. I am Odysseus. I have suffered many hardships, lost all my men, while you have tried to marry my wife, fondle the maids, mishandled my son

Telemachus, and eaten up my food and indulged yourselves in
my wine. You will now pay for this."

Just as students experiment with different points of view in their storytelling, they also try out first-person narratives in their writing. Here is an
excerpt from Ethan's story about Odysseus and the sea nymph, Calypso:

Calypso said that she would let me go after I was healed, but I
soon learned that she would keep me longer for she had fallen in
love with me. Everyday, after I was healed, I would take a chair
down to the beach and there I would sit looking out across the
water. My heart ached for Ithaca and tears streamed down my
face. Meanwhile Calypso would sit in her enchanted grove weaving on her loom and singing in her beautiful voice.

NEWSPAPER SATIRE: ODYSSEUS FOUND IN LOVE NEST!

How long can we expect ten-year-olds to study a topic before they get
tired of it? How much is enough? How much is too much?

Our study of the ancient Greek world typically takes some six
months, and half of that time is devoted to the study of *The Odyssey*. Different classes have different personalities and different interests, and some
years it's possible to go into more depth. But every year, there comes a
time when students (and teacher) grow tired of the subject. The trick is to
recognize that point before it actually arrives and finish the unit with a
flourish. For many years now, the final activity has been one of the most
enjoyable: creating a newspaper spoof of *The Odyssey*.

Until near the end, I ask students to approach the story respectfully,
learning as much as they can about it. I don't like doing this spoof too
early in the study; children need time to listen and read and learn details
before they can create informed satire. In addition, I want any published
work to reflect the best that students can do. But after more than two
months, it's time to pull out the stops. Children have little trouble finding
parallels between our society and that of Homer's time. Sex, violence,
drugs, and sports . . . these can all be moved easily from one locale and
time to the other. There is room in the newspaper as well for letters to the
editor, interviews with celebrities, fashion, music and entertainment,
movies and television listings, obituaries, horoscopes, weather forecasts,
cooking tips, and advice to the lovelorn.

Hannes draws on his own experience in reading current events to
shape this rendition of a hot news flash:

After a long chase, police finally cornered and captured the giant
terrorist group dubbed, "The Laestrygonians," in a subterranean

bunker near Bonifacio, Corsica. This is a few minutes walk from the scene of the crime. About a month ago this group allegedly devoured 600 men out of 11 of Odysseus' ships.

Police have a videotape of the incident in their custody. It began with the alleged devouring of a member of an exploration party. All but the flagship of Odysseus' squadron were destroyed by stones and other missiles. Everyone was eaten!

This videotape will be used as evidence for the prosecution. The trial will take place next Tuesday.

Courtney's food feature, on the other hand, combines the tone of Julia Child with an accent and vocabulary acquired in French class:

Bonjour! Je m'appele le Laestrygonian chef Français. Today we will learn how to prepare a feast of crudités.

Capture 550 large, juicy Grecian sailors and dunk them in seawater. Carefully pull off de heads. Destroy de brains (if any) before stuffing with radishes, beans and all 5,500 toe and finger nails mixed with bloody wine.

Yank away any hair left on de head. Remove de eyeballs and have them squished into a fine mash. Arrange de heads in a neat pile on de center of an très gros platter.

The newspaper format encourages children to attempt different voices and to experiment in their writing. Marie's story, for example, allows her to try out a tone that would be difficult to sustain in more serious assignments:

We are the spears of Achilles—the greatest Greek warrior. We have experienced many adventures, such as having our tips clash with the tips of other spears. Sometimes, we feel ourselves going into man's flesh. Then, we sometimes feel ourselves falling down to the ground, still in the flesh. After that, we know that Achilles has killed someone with our help.

We never have to worry about getting clean, because we get daily showers of blood . . .

We organize the newspaper writing differently each year, although the goal is always the same. If students in English class have already completed a newspaper unit, they are familiar with the different parts of a paper and quickly divide up into departments: news, sports, editorial pages, features, and advertising. Other years, to illustrate the different sections, we ask everyone to produce a set number of pieces: one news story, one feature, one ad, and "something else." Some years, children just start writing and drawing as soon as the project is introduced, churning out dozens of pieces in a few days.

With changing technology, we rely more on computers to make the paper attractive. Students now do much of the typing, bringing in stories they have already printed in columns or carrying disks to school with stories they have written at home on any of half a dozen word-processing programs. Other items, such as classified ads, are easier for the teacher to type. We look at our local newspaper's classified section and discuss the different categories. Rather than ask children to create their own ads at home and then keep track of dozens of tiny ads in different styles, I find it easier to take one class period and challenge the class to a race.

> Here's a pile of scrap paper, cut into small squares. We're going to use this paper to write classifieds. While you're writing, I'm going to sit at the Mac and type as fast as I can. As soon as you have an ad finished, have a friend look it over with you and make any corrections and changes, then bring it to me. I'm going to try to type fast enough to keep up with twenty of you. Okay? Go!

Children rise to the challenge, my desk is swamped with scraps of paper, I type furiously, and by the end of the period we have a computer file filled with classifieds, all ready for the school's good printer. (See Figure 6-3 for a sample.)

For the final layout, there are desktop publishing programs that can produce attractive end results, but we usually rely on that tried and true technique from the preelectronic era, cut and paste. Students work in small groups to design and paste up their layouts. They have their own ideas about good layout, and because I tend to be fussy about what I like, based on my own journalism background, I often take on the chores of page layout. That way, the look of the final newspaper is something that pleases me as well as the students.

REFLECTIONS ON THE WRITING PROCESS

Twenty-five years ago, a quiet but major change began in American schools. Teachers and Writers Collaborative in New York sent real writers into classrooms, adults who approached writing from a new perspective and whose pedagogy marked a distinct change in writing instruction. Tackling different genres, attempting different techniques, encouraging individual voices, empowering young people, Teachers and Writers seemed to get children excited about writing.

At about the same time, researchers from the University of New Hampshire were visiting New England classrooms; the two Donalds—Graves and Murray—were bringing the writing process approach to schools around the state. In the late 1970s, when I team-taught third and fourth grade in New Hampshire, they visited our classroom several times. They watched and they listened, they spoke with children, and they kept careful notes. Their comments at teacher workshops had a solid ring. Theirs was not some vague academic prescription to improve writing. On the contrary, these people clearly knew children, they knew writing, and they knew classrooms. There is a better way to teach writing, they said, and we can help you.

What they said made sense and corresponded with our own observations. My teaching colleague and I eagerly jumped on board the bandwagon. The packaged story starters disappeared and were replaced by large hand-written charts listing guidelines for writing conferences. Students learned to act as each other's editors, to ask thoughtful questions, and to offer helpful comments. Tidy deadlines vanished; continual revisions became the new order of the day. Teacher assignments faded away, supplanted by writing folders with lists of individual topics. Children brought special objects into class, which served as starting points for engaging personal narratives. It was a scene repeated countless times in

FIGURE 6-3
Classified ads

PERSONALS
Laestrygonian King looking for wife between 20-30. Should be interested in midnight strolls and fine dining. Send photo if interested.
Olympian Dating Club: Now a separate club for mortals. For the divorced, single and widowed. Meet interested people just like you! Call 1-800-DATING-CLUB.
Calypso's Compatibles: This is how Clytemnestra met Aegisthus! We'll find the right person for you. Don't be shy! Dial 1-800-COMPATIBLES.
Wanted: A man for Aeolus's ex-wife. A person with blonde hair who isn't a wind bag. Call 649-1078.
Come to the **Sirens Singles Bar.** You'll get great music, and live entertainment, and great food. Call at: 1-800-DEATH.
Companion wanted for Laestrygonian Queen. Former King arrested. She is lovely and loves visitors. Contact the Queen at her home in the Mediterranean Sea.

REAL ESTATE
Luxurious cave by the ocean, view of a giant whirlpool, slightly bloodstained. Call 145-8425.
Great city, burned slightly, comes complete with giant horse. Call 623-TROY.
Beautiful seaside cave, great rocks. Call 731-CAVE.

SERVICES
If you're sick and tired of having to pick up after your kids we have the perfect thing for you to get, it's a pet called Scylla. If you would like to have one call 1-800-SCYLLA.

**ODYSSEUS'S
PLOWING SERVICES**
Low rates. Mon-Fri from 9-5. We plant grain, salt and babies. Call 649-1078.

LOST AND FOUND
Missing pigs: 20 Pigs, last seen on black-hulled ship. Call Circe at 649-1048.
LOST: Large gold cattle, without insides, last seen on Thrinakia. REWARD.
Found: Tame lions and tigers found on Circe's island. 555-1010 after 6:00 p.m.
Found: Poly's contact lens in one of his sheep's eyes. Contact the lost and found at Ithaca, 291 Palace Street.
Lost: Ciconian treasure, last seen during raid at Ismarus, Thrace. If found, call 649-1078.
Found: Ghost-like dog, answers to Argos. Call 165-4256.

ENTERTAINMENT
Chair-throwing contest in Antinoös' honor at Odysseus' palace. Tickets cost $7. Almost sold out. Call the box office at 649-1048.
Want a real fun party? Call on the Lotus plant. It makes you real high. Send to Lotus Island, 6784-ZU ZA.

FOR SALE
Used head, body not included; half-eaten man, slightly messy; cave, only a few blood stains. Contact Polyphemus, 1-900-877-6434.
Tons of Sandals is having a big Polyphemus size sale. Route 10, Troy.
Achilles' fighting armor, owned by Achilles himself. To buy, call toll free 1-800-ARMOR.

Book of The Odyssey. Manuscript edition written by Odysseus. Slightly torn but in great condition. Blood signed by the author. Contact Odysseus at his summer residence in Ithaca.
Stuffed Dog. Owned by Odysseus. Faint manure smell. Excite your children! Contact Penelope at palace in Ithaka.
Trojan Horse. Low mileage. Used once. Great for surprise parties. Asking $39.95. Call after 4 p.m. Ask for Fritz or Jake at 802-649-1048.
FOR SALE: Polyphemus's ram, a little big but great for hiding under. Contact Polyphemus at 1-646-POLY-RAM.
Bottled Blood for sale. Lovely taste. Ask for Antiphates at 531-2715.
Zeus's throne, owned by Zeus himself, a little dirty but in great condition. Contact Zeus on Mt. Olympus.

EMPLOYMENT
Wanted: Eye doctor for Polyphemus, someone who is skillful, prepared for danger, and patient. Polyphemus needs serious help. Call 333-3333.
Help wanted: To take care of animals for Circe. They seem to have a mind of their own. Call 1-800-649-1048.
FIGHTERS WANTED! There is a war going on in Turkey. Uncle Agamemnon needs you to help fight the Trojans. Go to Recruiting Office in Aulis.

WANTED!
Charybdis, for sucking a whirlpool every time a ship goes by, and for sucking down the ships too. If seen, please contact the Troy police at 1-800- CHARYBDIS. **Reward** is $2,000,000.

classrooms across the country as The Writing Process laid siege to traditional writing programs in one of the most successful educational reform movements in the last quarter century.

Teachers enamored of this method, in the manner of the newly converted, sometimes lost their balance and their perspective. Reacting to decades of schooling in which all topics were decided and assigned by the teacher, many of us in our first flush of enthusiasm urged children to choose their own subjects. Reacting to fast-paced stories that were little more than rewrites of shallow cartoon shows, some of us insisted that fiction had no place in the classroom, that all writing should be based on the children's experiences, since that is what they know best. Personal narratives assumed new importance in the language arts curriculum.

After years of editing true stories, however, I realized that something was missing. That "something" was fiction writing. What about the precious gift of imagination? Of creativity? Children's writing also thrives when they tap these sources as they are encouraged to write fiction. Some of the best children's writing I've seen teaches us what a vivid part of a child's experiences is the life of the imagination.

Most of my approach follows general writing process procedures. The all-important "prewriting" fills the early months of our *Odyssey* study. By the time they reach fifth grade, most students in our school understand that a polished piece of writing emerges only after a series of messy drafts. Children therefore scribble and scratch out, turn to friends for suggestions, and mark up their early work with personal hieroglyphics. They also help each other through conferences, although rarely as effectively as I would like.

Children publish their work in different ways. At its simplest, they read their stories aloud to their classmates and to others. The final stories are displayed, often next to the rough work, on classroom bulletin boards and in elaborate hallway displays. The school prints dozens of attractive booklets filled with student writing. From time to time, I share my own writing struggles with them, whether it is the step-by-step account of writing a synopsis of a scholarly paper or a short update on the process of writing this book. I want my students to know that writing is a necessary part of adult life as well.

7 | GASTROHIPPOTELECHRON: MOVING BEYOND HOMER

For the ancient Greeks, *The Iliad* and *The Odyssey* were the foundations of culture, two great works that combined literature, history, and religion. Of all the epics—and we know that Homer's stories were two among many—only they survived the centuries intact, in part, perhaps, because there were more copies around to survive. Public recitations of Homer reached Athens by the sixth century B.C. and scribes were kept busy making additional copies of these acclaimed works. In classical times, fifth century B.C., Homer's verses—alone among those of all the poets—were recited regularly at the Panathenaic Festivals. By the Hellenistic era, two centuries later, standardized Homeric texts were created at the Alexandria library. Part McGuffey reader, part history text, part poetry anthology, and part code of behavior, Homer's tales formed the basis of a future citizen's formal education.

For Norwich fifth graders today, the works of Homer form a gateway to ancient Greek culture. The works are worth studying on their own merits as well as for the introduction they provide to later Greek civilization. It would be hard, indeed, to understand much of classical Greece without knowing these books, which were so important to that later society. With only one exception, each year Norwich fifth graders have studied Homer *before* they go on to study the later Greeks and glimpse other ancient civilizations.

Why study the Greeks? Entire volumes have been written on that subject. Political thought, philosophy, mathematics and science, art and architecture, mythology, even our language—we cannot understand Western culture today without appreciating the Greek foundation on which it rests. In order to sample different aspects of classical Greek culture, the fifth-grade exploration lasts another two to three months after our study of *The Odyssey*. A full description of those activities is beyond the scope of this book, but in this chapter I will look at several examples of activities that go beyond strictly Homeric studies, that help children learn about the ancient world and through that process, about themselves.

ROOTS: A JOURNEY INTO THE HISTORY OF WORDS

In an early entry in my *Odyssey* journal, I considered different directions our work might take:

> *Several ideas for the year, which came at odd moments. Actually, two of them came yesterday morning while shaving, and one came this morning while driving on the Interstate toward school:*
>
> *1. Make sure kids get the Roman names this year for the gods and goddesses. We want to concentrate on the Greek ones, obviously, for our story, but there are many references throughout English literature they'll catch if they know the Roman names as well. So one project is to do a family tree of the major gods in both languages.*
>
> *2. Coming out of the Odyssey work as well as #1, have kids make (either on their own or as a class project) a scrapbook of modern use of ancient myths. Hermes and his winged feet speeding FTD florists, Ajax cleanser, etc. Someone from the Odyssey Institute did a project like this, and kids found dozens of references.*
>
> *3. Work on Greek roots and their relatives in English. Each child could have a notebook. We'd put the Greek alphabet in front, along with the sounds of each letter. I'd write each day—each week?—a word in Greek on the board, and we'd figure out how to pronounce it. I'd give them the Greek meaning, and they'd go off for homework trying to find words that derived from the root. In class, we'd make master lists kids could copy into their notebooks and illustrate, and those words in turn would send us to new roots. "Graphos" would be a likely starting point, since that would certainly lead to "telegraph" and we could do "tele" words. It seems an easy enough way to work a whole different dimension into the class, and might lead to an elective in Greek.*

The best-laid plans . . . We never did the family tree of the gods, either Greek or Roman, as a class project that year or any other, although students enjoyed looking at posters showing the Olympian family tree and several created their own versions of Greek genealogies as ambitious independent projects. The Roman names? I still think it would be good for children to know them, but we rarely seem to have the time. I post a chart with the equivalent names, and the mythology enthusiasts teach their classmates informally. Our French teacher has also designed successful assignments that simultaneously reinforce Greek content and French vocabulary. Students review the relationships of mythological characters with exercises like these:

> *Qui est Zeus?*
> *C'est <u>le roi</u> des dieux.*

C'est le mari de Héra.
C'est le père d'Apollon et d'Ártemis et de nombreux autres enfants.
Qui est-ce?
  Le roi d'Ithaque?
  La plus intelligentes des déesses?
  Le dieu de la mer?
Pénélope est la _____ *d'Ulysse et la* _____ *de Télémaque.*

I tried the second idea from my journal, the mythology scrapbook, several times with mixed results. Each year, there were children who really liked looking, who were able to keep an *Odyssey* focus as they walked through their everyday world. (One boy was on vacation in Los Angeles and brought back photographs of the *Odyssey*-related signs he saw there.) Over the years, we have slowly filled several sheets of poster paper but this project never caught on quite the way I had hoped it might.

Thanks to the inspired work of our school librarian, however, the third idea has now become an integral part of our Greek study. For more than a month, as part of their weekly library class, students learn the Greek alphabet and learn to recognize the presence of ancient Greek roots in contemporary English words. Several of these assignments are among the favorites in the entire unit.

Before becoming the school librarian, Susan Voake was a fourth-grade teacher with a passion for literature. She routinely led a study of Greek mythology, which strengthened the *Odyssey* work the following year. When she became the librarian—or "media generalist," as the job is now called—Susan continued her mythology work with all fourth graders. By the time children reach fifth grade now, they already know, if not from first grade then from Susan's study, the names of the major Olympian gods and various associated myths.

An ardent champion of interdisciplinary studies, Susan was eager to find ways to bring the *Odyssey* study into her library classes for fifth graders. We discussed several possibilities, and she agreed to introduce Greek roots. I passed on to her a series of booklets on etymology, most of them purchased through the American Classical League, and over the years we have developed a series of activities and worksheets that combine structure and creative expression.

Susan begins by introducing the Greek alphabet and asking children to write a phonetic rendering of their names using Greek letters. In a conspicuous place in the classroom, I post a chart of the Greek alphabet and its sounds, usually near a large series of strips of paper containing the opening lines of *The Odyssey* written in Greek. I rarely say anything about them, but there are inevitably children who spend class time (and recess time) laboriously trying to figure out how to read them.

Once students are familiar with the alphabet, they move into etymology activities, starting with a worksheet to introduce Greek roots of number words (see Figure 7-1).

Subsequent worksheets move beyond numbers to teach children about the meanings of other common Greek roots: *arch-, bio-, chron-, chlor-,* and so on. Another assignment asks children to take words that derive from several Greek roots, find the roots and their meaning, and write a definition. Students investigate such words as *orthodox, bibliophile, symphony,* and *pseudonym.*

These assignments introduce children to the idea that words come from someplace; they have a history and a reason. They also require children to use dictionaries for research and to differentiate among different kinds of dictionaries. Students quickly discover that their common elementary dictionaries do not show the etymologies of words, so they start using more advanced dictionaries, delighting in finding books that make a point of showing word origins. They discover that just because two words have the same letters in a row, they are not necessarily related; for example, *pan* in *pan-American* or *Panathenaic* is not the same as *pan* in *pants.* The careful word researcher must think about the meanings of the roots as well.

Now it's time to consider the connections between words. Children are invited to create "word webs," which present graphically the relationships among families of words, as shown in Figure 7-2.

Starting from other base words, students create their own word webs, first in rough form and then in finished state. If the earlier etymology worksheets make children aware of differences among dictionaries, the Word Webs assignment transforms some students into avid dictionary readers. Once children get the idea that words are connected through their roots, they start poring through dictionaries in search of related words. The words that we select for the start of the webs (such as *astrology, telepathy, architect,* or *calligraphy*) are chosen because each has many easy-to-find relatives. Children learn that roots take different forms, depending

FIGURE 7-1
Greek root worksheet

---

1. Below are ten Greek number roots. Next to each one is a related Greek form. By using a dictionary (or your own knowledge), write the meaning of each Greek root beside the word.

mono- (μονοσ) _____   **poly-** (πολη–) _____
tri- (τρια) _____   **di-** (δι–) _____
pent- (πεντε) _____   **deca-** (δεκα) _____
hex- (εξ) _____   **oct-** (οκτω) _____
pan- (παν) _____   **kilo-** (χιλιοι) _____

2. Stretch your brain. Choose FOUR of the roots above and list as many words as you can think of (or find) for each root. Be sure the words you list come from these ROOTS!!

on whether they're at the beginning or the end of an English word; hence, *biology* and *logical* both derive from the Greek root *logos*. Some roots, such as *tele,* appear only at the beginning of their English derivative, unless we count such newly minted techno-names as Intel, the manufacturer of computer chips. Figure 7-3 illustrates a detail of one sample.

How can we explain the power of Word Webs? Maybe it is because children are already familiar with that method of connecting words, a residue of seeing and using idea webs and brainstorming maps in previous years. Perhaps it is because Word Webs are the visual representation of a deep-seated human desire to make connections or because the assignment is so clear, so methodical, and so satisfying when completed. Whatever the reason, many students who had invested little in earlier assignments suddenly caught fire. They spent hours completing intricate rough drafts and more hours preparing their final copy, linking words neatly with colored letters or colored underlining.

In junior high school, one of our sons had an exceptionally creative English teacher. As part of a study of the history of language, she asked her class to invent a series of words based on Greek roots. I was able to see, from a parent's perspective, how absorbed Ben was in the process and how much he enjoyed playing with language in that way. We created our own version of that assignment (see Figures 7-4 and 7-5) and eagerly awaited the results.

As with the Word Webs, the response from students was excellent. Dictionaries of invented words poured in, many with those loving

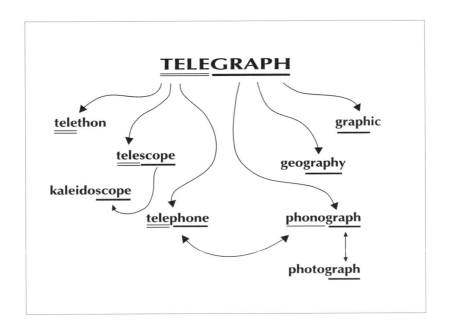

FIGURE 7-2
Sample word web

details—intricate drawings and emotional dedications—that indicate that an assignment has been a success. This project also drew more than the usual comments from parents. One mother stopped me after school to say that her son was staying up late each night filling page after page with new words and occasionally emerging from his room to call out his newest creation for the amusement of the rest of his family. Another described the care her son took in creating a watercolor painting for the book's cover and a hand-sewn binding.

In her introduction to one such dictionary, fifth grader Rebecca explained the process she used to create new words:

> All the words in this dictionary are make-believe but made of real Greek roots. Every Greek root has a meaning. If you put two or more Greek roots together you can have a really neat word! For example: Take the two roots *Ge* and *Scopio*. *Ge* means earth and *scopio* means to look at. If you put the two roots together you can get the word *geoscope* which would mean an instrument used for examining the earth. You can add an O in between the roots or remove a letter or two from a root as I did. I removed io from scopio. I also added the e.

Figure 7-6 shows some examples from individual books and Figure 7-7 is a collection of words from many children's work, a sheet of word puzzles that delighted students and teachers alike.

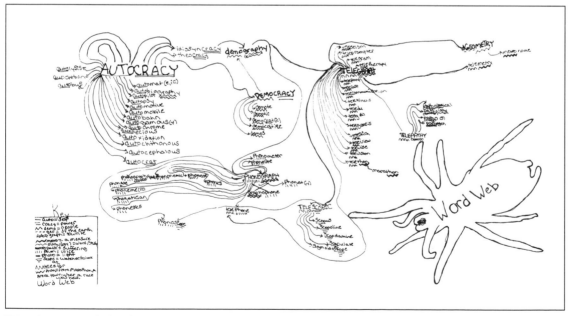

FIGURE 7-3   *Detail of student's word web (Ariel Rothstein)*

A Dictionary of Invented Words

You are well on your way to becoming a **lexicographer**! (From the Greek roots *lego,* to gather and *graph,* to write or draw.) In other words, you are a *gatherer of words* or a dictionary creator.

Having seen how words are created, you now have the opportunity to *invent* some words of your own.

FIGURE 7-4
"Dictionary of Invented Words" assignment sheet

1. Look again at the roots and words you have analyzed in earlier activities. Also refer to the *Beginning List of Greek Roots* on the back side of this sheet.

2. Combine roots in different ways to invent new words.

   The *Beginning List of Greek Roots* can serve as a base for your new words, but you may need to add or subtract a letter to make the words combine neatly. Use a vowel if you need it to combine two roots. For example, imagine that you want to make up a new word to describe the way a sailor looks after going through a horrible storm, "a green sailor." You could combine *chloros-* green with *naut-* sailor. One possible spelling for your new word would be *chlorosnaut,* but an easier word to pronounce would be *chloronaut.*

3. Make a dictionary of at least *five* new words. For each word, be sure to include:

   a. the word

   b. its roots and root meanings

   c. a clear, complete word definition

   d. one sentence using the word correctly

   e. a drawing

   If you want your finished dictionary to come out well, you will have to make several *rough drafts.* Try combining the roots in slightly different ways. Experiment until you have a new word that sounds just right; no one will want to use an ugly word! Test different definitions until you find the best way of explaining the word. Try out different sentences, and vary your sentences so that they don't all sound the same. Finally, experiment with different drawings. You will find it easier to draw pictures of *things* rather than actions, so most of your new words will probably be nouns.

4. To complete your dictionary, be sure that you have:

   a. a front and back cover (heavy paper)

   b. title page

   c. five or more words, arranged in alphabetical order

   Your finished dictionary should not be too large or too small. At its largest, use standard 8 1/2 x 11 inch white paper. You may type or write by hand; ink will look better than pencil. Illustrations may be colored if you wish. Neatness counts!

5. Optional added attractions in your dictionary might include:

   a. introduction and dedication

   b. pronunciation key for each word

   c. part of speech for each word

   d. your own creative touches

Beginning List of Greek Roots

AGOG – to lead

ANGEL– message, messenger

ANTHRO – human being

ARCH – ancient, first, rule

AST(ER) – star

AUT – self

BIBLI – book

BIO – life

CAC – bad

CAL (KAL) – beauty

CANON – a rule

CARDI – heart

CAU – to burn

CENT(R) – center

CHIR – hand

CHLOROS – green

CRACY – rule by

CHROMO – color

CHRON – time

COSM – universe, order, beauty

CRYPT – hidden, secret

CYCL – circle, wheel

DEMON – evil spirit

DI – two

DECA – ten

DEM – people

DERM – skin

DOX, DOG – opinion, teaching

DYN – force, power

GAM – marriage

GASTR – stomach

GE – earth

GLOSS, GLOT – language, tongue

GLYPH – to carve

GNO – to know

GRAPH – writing, thing written

HELI – sun

HEM – blood

HETERO – other, different

HEX – six

HIER – sacred

HIPP – horse

HYDR – water

ICON – image

KILO – thousand

LITH – stone

LOG, LOGY, LOGUE – speech,
     word, study, reasoning

MANIA – passion for

MIM – to imitate

MIS – hatred

MON – one

MORPH – form, shape

NAUT – sailor

NE – new

NECR – the dead

NEUR – nerve

OCT – eight

OD – song, poem

ODON(T) – tooth

ONYM – name

OP, OPT – to see, eye

ORTH – straight, correct

PAN – all

PATH – to suffer, to feel

PED, PEDIA – child, educa-
     tion

PENT – five

PETR – rock

PHA(N) – to show, to appear

PHIL – to love

PHOBIA – fear of

PHON – sound

POL, POLIS – city, state

POLY – many

PSEUD – false

PSYCH – the mind

PYR – fire

SCOPIO – to look at atten-
     tively

TACT, TAX – to arrange, to
     put in order

TELE – distant

TETR – four

THE – god

THERM – heat

TOM – to cut

TOP – a place

TOX – poison

TRI – three

TROPH – to grow, to nourish,
     to raise

TYP – stamp, model

XEN – stranger, foreigner

ZO – animal

FIGURE 7-5 *Beginning list of Greek roots*

from *A Dictionary of Invented Greek Root Words*
by Rebecca

Gastrohippotelechron (Găs· trŏ· hĭp· ō· tĕlĕ· krŏn), noun. A horse that when you touch its stomach it will take you to a distant time. I mounted my gastrohippotelechron and flew back to the seventeenth century. <Gk. Γαστρ (Gastr) = stomach + ιπ (hipp) = horse + Τελε (tele) = far + Κρον (chron) = time>

Biblimorophorochrom (Bĭb· lĕ· mŏr· ō· fŏr· ō· krŏm), noun. A book that changes or forms into different colors. We took our biblimorophorochrom and timed it to see how many times it would change color in one minute. <Gk. Βιβλι (Bibli) = book + Μορφ (Morph) = form + Κρωμω (Chromo) = color>

Pseudopolydonoscope (Sūd· ō· pŏl· ĕ· dŏn· ō· skŏp), noun. A machine used to look closely at many false teeth. The dentist checked her false teeth with his pseudopolydonoscope. <Gk. Συδ (Pseud) = false + Πολη (Poly) = many + Ωδον (Odon) = teeth + Σκωπηω (scopio) = to look at>

Mimekilozomonophon (Mĭm· ĕ· kĕ· lŏ· zŏ· mŏn· ō· phŏn), noun. A machine that will imitate one thousand animals sounds at one time. We used our mimekilozomonophon to find out what sound the peacock made. <Gk. Μιμ (Mim) − to imitate + Κιλω (Kilo) = one thousand + Ζω (Zo) = ani­mal + Μον (Mon) = one + Φον (Phon) = sound>

from *The Rare Flamingo Dictionary*
by Tyler

Chlorozo (klo· ro· zo) A small green animal the size of a rat and looks like a frog. (He thought he saw a clorozo.) { Gk. root = Chloro = green and zo = animal}

Demonotoxin (De· mon· o· toks· in): A sweet liquid that is instant death for anyone evil. (He sipped the demonotoxin.) { Gk. root = demon = evil spirit and tox = poison}

Pyrophono (Pi· ro· fo· no) The crackling sound made by a fire. (He heard the pyrophono as he sat by the fire.) { Gk. root = pyro = fire and phono(s) = sound}

from *Dictionary of the Newest Words*
by Basti

cryptocosm (kriptokosm) Unknown space, like space behind a black hole. The scientists sent out a satellite to investigate the cryptocosm. <Gk. crypt - secret - cosmic - space>

zoxen (tsozen) a foreigner or a barbarian. The Chinese people thought that anyone who didn't live in China was a zoxen. <Gk. zo - animal - xen - foreign>

FIGURE 7-6
Selections from students' invented word dictionaries

FIGURE 7-7
Norwich Students Discover New Words!

Extra! Extra! Read All About It!

Norwich Students Discover New Words!

Directions: Match the definitions in the first column with the words in the second column. One example has been identified, and is shown with the word used properly in a sentence.

A. the power of an evil spirit

B. water that has magical properties so that when women bathe in it they become beautiful

C. skin that turns green

D. a false tooth

E. an instrument to look at two things at one time

F. fear of others

G. one-eyed horse

H. another word for Einstein's theory about space-time

I. time wheel

J. fear of false love

K. a creature that can take on eight forms, from Babylonian mythology

L. a book of language

M. fear of green hearts

N. dead sailor: In Greece a long time ago, when sailors looked at Medusa they turned into <u>necranauts</u>.

O. love of horses

P. animal song

Q. fear of sound

R. poisonous heat that gets stronger as it gets hotter

S. a rock that heats up at the touch

T. a machine that makes doubles of people

U. an image in water

V. fear of evil spirit

W. the way of measuring time in space

X. An instrument used by scientists to look at the center of a fire

Y. fear of new places

Z. another name for a cat, which has nine lives

_____ bibliglot

_____ polybio

_____ demonophobia

_____ toxitherm

_____ hydricon

_____ calahydra

_____ petrotherm

_____ monoptohipp

_____ pyracentascope

_____ neatopaphobia

_____ anthropicon

__N__ necranaut

_____ zoaode

_____ dioscopio

_____ cosmichron

_____ pseudophilaphobia

_____ octomorph

_____ hippomania

_____ cyclochron

_____ pseudodont

_____ cardichlorophobia

_____ heterophobia

_____ chlorosaderm

_____ demodyn

_____ phonophobia

_____ chronocosmic

Civilization®is an extraordinary board game that has become an integral part of our study of the ancient world. On the first day of a new school year, there are usually some fifth graders who walk into the room and ask, "Do we get to play Civilization this year?"

"Maybe," I reply. "We'll see." And then, vaguely, savoring the moment, "It all depends."

"Depends on what?" asks the first child eagerly.

"Please . . ." adds his friend, accompanying the request with Bambi eyes.

By this time, many other children, including those who have never heard of Civilization, have joined in the clamor.

"What is it?"

"Is it fun?"

"When do we get to play?"

"Oh, Civilization! My sister has that game—it's awesome."

I turn the conversation elsewhere, but the question keeps coming back throughout the next few months: "Do we get to play Civilization?" With an introduction like that, the game is assured a receptive audience.

Civilization is a complex game, neither easy to learn nor easy to play. It is aimed at an older audience. But with a careful introduction—we take a week just learning enough rules to get started—it is a game that fifth graders can play successfully. For the overwhelming majority of each year's class, it is a challenging experience. For three weeks, the social studies classroom is filled at recess time, as children from all the fifth-grade sections stop by to see what changes have taken place on the board since they last played and to plot strategy with teammates from other homerooms.

My wife, Sheila, ordered Civilization as a present for me many years ago after reading a review in the annual "100 Best Games" feature in *Games* magazine. I was intrigued as soon as I saw the board, a colorful map of the lands surrounding the eastern Mediterranean Sea. I glanced through the materials and the instruction booklet. No dice! No spinners! No Trivial Pursuit questions! Better and better. The game arrived in time for the two of us to spend many late-night hours over December vacation working our way through the simplified, introductory games. I was hooked and eager to share it with others. We played it with our two boys, and when I went to the Odyssey Institute that next year, I took the game with me. Late one night in Georgetown, I tried teaching it to a group of interested colleagues. They liked the game but weren't sure it was appropriate for fifth graders, citing the twenty-page rule book: "It may be too complicated." That doubt, and my contrariness, probably impelled me to introduce the game to my fifth graders.

The game of Civilization starts off simply enough. Each player places a single token on the board in a space designated for one's own civilization. In each round, the population increases and the player moves the tokens on the board to prevent areas from growing overcrowded. With enough tokens on the board, a player can build cities, although he or she must maintain enough agricultural land to feed the urban population. With the advent of cities, trade begins, which leads to increased wealth and, in turn, the purchase of civilization cards, such as Pottery, Agriculture, Astronomy, Music, and Law. Trade has its drawbacks, though, since it brings an increase in such calamities as epidemic, civil war, and piracy. Conflicts and wars rarely accomplish much besides getting many people killed. A strong civilization develops slowly, but it can be quickly reduced to a shadow of its former glory if it does not balance science with the arts, and crafts with civic institutions. Some years we have played three periods a day—more than two hours—for nearly a month without a winner.

The game is designed for seven players. With three classes of twenty children or more, how do we keep everyone involved? Each child is on a team but during any particular class period, only one person from that team is actually sitting at the board. (The rest of the class is working on other assignments during this time, tasks that can be set easily aside when it becomes one's turn at the Civilization table. Independent research projects on Greek civilization are one particularly suitable activity.) Nonplaying teammates may examine the board at the beginning of class and offer hints, but only one player is in charge of his team's civilization during his time at the board, and he may take it in whatever direction he chooses.

We rarely study civilizations other than the Greeks in any detail, but playing this game whets students' appetites for independent learning. Playing Assyria, Egypt, Thrace, and Babylon gives each child a vested interest in the ancient world. Whenever we play, the walls near the playing table are filled with maps of the region, and as children build a city in a designated city site on the game board, they frequently look at the historical maps to find out where they are: "Oh, this is Carthage . . . Rhodes . . . Thebes . . . Syracuse . . . Jericho." The location of the civilization and the sound of those ancient names is enough to spur some children to seek more information from books in the classroom and in the library.

Although I make everything about the game sound positive here, I worried periodically about whether there was more to it than just the fun of playing. "Yes, I know," went my internal dialogue in the early years, "there are all kinds of good reasons to play. But are the kids actually *learning* anything?" The best way to quiet such doubts was to ask the students directly. Out of my uncertainty came the first Civilization exam, which I've repeated other years:

Final Exam for Civilization

You have been playing the game "Civilization" for three weeks. Imagine that someone comes into school and watches you playing for a while. The visitor complains to the principal that fifth graders are spending their time playing games instead of studying in schoolbooks. Mr. Frye comes to you to learn more about the situation. He is looking for answers to these two basic questions:

1. What skills do you practice when playing this game? What kind of thinking is involved? What do people learn when they play? What kind of learning is involved when you play in teams like these?

2. This is a social studies class and you're supposed to be learning about ancient civilization. Does playing this game teach you anything about ancient civilizations? What do you learn about how civilizations develop and change? Give some examples of what people can learn about the ancient world from playing "Civilization."

I was pleased with the students' responses to the exam. They calmed my worries that first year, and now I keep such answers in a folder to read through and remind me in future years if I have second thoughts. This is a game well worth the time we devote to it. Here are some excerpts from students' answers:

You are not learning facts, you are being that civilization. In the earlier ages civilizations were farther apart but later on, civilizations started fighting for land as they migrated. Also you made friends and enemies.

In the beginning everybody is pretty equal then as the game goes along everybody gets bigger and more powerful. Some civilizations are more powerful than others. It's kind of like today. Other countries are bigger and more powerful than others. Also different inventions help you do more things, these inventions are like the civilization cards. The more you have the more powerful, kind of.

You can learn about trading to get things you needed, the game shows you how the world changed in those specific areas.   (Erin)

In Civilization, you have to make many decisions, and making bad decisions will make you probably lose the game. There are also a lot of pieces in the game, and you have to be very organized. I probably will have to be very organized when I grow older or my family might fall apart. Playing Civilization helps teach me to be organized.

I also learned about all the hardships people went through in the ancient times, like famine, heresy, civil disorder, civil war, piracy, epidemic, flood, volcanic eruption or earthquake.

I also learned how to cooperate in teams, get along, play together, not fight, and make good decisions.

I also had fun. School shouldn't be boring.   (Ben)

I think that playing "Civilization" teaches you about the names of the civilizations, what space they had to function in, what the different cities looked like, and mainly how to survive and move forward to new ages, which is still what we're trying to do.

(Jacob)

"LET NO ONE IGNORANT OF GEOMETRY ENTER"

Legend has it that "Let no one ignorant of geometry enter" was carved above the entrance to Plato's Academy, testimony to the importance the Greeks placed on this branch of mathematics. In the investigations of Pythagoras and his disciples, geometry combined magic and science, a harmonious blend of cosmic mystery and rational investigation. Studying geometry in elementary school offers rigorous discipline and gives students a glimpse of the beauty of mathematics that is often obscured by our heavy-handed emphasis on arithmetic. Geometry is also a branch of mathematics that allows visual thinkers to shine, where logic and proportion are more important than fast recall of facts, and where children who have never considered themselves good mathematicians may discover hidden talents.

Of Greek mathematicians, there is no shortage. Thales (640–545 B.C.), the teacher of Pythagoras, is credited with the founding of deductive reasoning. Thales studied similar triangles, and his theories allow us to calculate the height of a pyramid or a flagpole by measuring the length of its shadow. Pythagoras (c. 550 B.C.) who first used the word *mathematics,* investigated harmonic progression and created the musical scale. He also studied square numbers and triangle numbers, investigated the proportions of the so-called Golden Rectangle, discovered the icosahedron and the dodecahedron, concluded that Earth is a sphere, and is best known for the Pythagorean Theorem, which stipulates the special properties of right triangles. Plato (c. 400 B.C.) and Euclid (c. 300 B.C.) were deeply involved in studying geometric constructions and that class of regular polyhedra known today as Platonic solids. Plato also gave us, in the *Meno,* the famous dialogue on doubling the size of a square, and Euclid's codification of geometric theorems still forms the basis of high school geometry courses. Archimedes (287–212 B.C.) has been called the greatest mathematician of antiquity. In addition to his considerable contributions to science (displacement of water, levers, and the Archimedean screw for raising water), he also investigated exponents, derived an accurate approximation for π, computed the volume of solid figures such as the sphere and the cylinder, and studied the class of polyhedra known to us as Archimedean solids. His contemporary and friend, Eratosthenes, studied prime numbers and composites and devised a method for finding prime numbers, known as the Sieve of Eratosthenes. He also knew that the Earth was a sphere and made a surprisingly accurate calculation (c. 240 B.C.) of the size of the Earth, some 1,750 years before Columbus set off on his voyage with inaccurate information. Appolonius (c. 200 B.C.) wrote about basic geometric shapes (parabola, ellipse, hyperbola) in his treatise, *Conic Sections.* Heron (c. 75 A.D.) devised formulas to determine the area of rectangles, triangles, and circles. Indeed, many of the topics that fit naturally into the upper elementary and middle school math curriculum were the very things that the Greeks thought about.[1]

Different math teachers working with the fifth graders have enjoyed investigating different topics. My favorite topic to introduce in math class, which dates from my own interests and from independent high school investigations with my father, is geometric constructions in the Greek manner, regular figures made with only a compass and a straight edge. We start with the easiest and most familiar shape, a hexagon inscribed in a circle, and move steadily to more complicated constructions—perpendicular lines, a square, bisecting angles, bisected line segments, octagons, and dodecagons. When children have mastered these operations, they learn the same construction that was passed on to a Greek deemed worthy to enter the secret Pythagorean society, the construction with compass and straight edge of a regular pentagon. It is a fitting end to a rigorous mini-unit.

LITERATURE AND DRAMA

Like other elementary school teachers, I read aloud to my class every day, and I like finding books that fit in with our studies. For the Greek unit, I read excerpts from *The Iliad* and *The Odyssey,* of course, but I've found it hard to locate many other appropriate books. The study of the Trojan War does, however, lead naturally to the study of archaeology. Indeed, the single most common question children ask when faced with the complex interrelationships of Greek mythology, is "Was there really a Trojan War?" It's a question that fascinates adults as well; witness Michael Wood's well-received PBS television series and accompanying book, *In Search of the*

---

[1]For detailed discussions of the reasoning employed by many of these great thinkers, see William Dunham, *Journey Through Genius: The Great Theorems of Mathematics.* For more general historical information about Greek mathematics, see Alfred Hooper, *Makers of Mathematics.* For nontraditional mathematical investigations aimed at high school or college students but adaptable for younger grades, see *Mathematics: A Human Endeavor,* a lively textbook written by Harold Jacobs.

Trojan War. The site we now call Troy was excavated in the late 1800s by an amateur, Heinrich Schliemann, who uncovered a buried city at a time when most scholars believed Homer's tales to be a work of literary imagination. Schliemann rose from rags to immense riches, and children enjoy learning more about his life and his Trojan passion. I've found Marjorie Braymer's *The Walls of Windy Troy* a fine introduction to this man's life and work.

The best piece of fiction I know for giving children a taste of classical Greece is *The Avenger,* by Margaret Hodges, which manages to combine details of daily life with important rituals—including the Olympics—and a crucial event in Greek history, the invasion of the Persians that culminated in the decisive battle of Marathon. All this and believable characters, too! One recent addition to my read-aloud list is *Through the Hidden Door,* by Rosemary Wells, a gripping adventure that captures the mysteries and the thrill of archaeological excavation.

In the same way that theater was an important aspect of classical Athenian civilization—prisoners were allowed out of jail to see plays—so, too, has drama been an important part of our study of classical Greece. We have staged musical versions of Pandora and scaled-down adaptations of classic Greek drama, classic comedies such as *The Birds* and tragedies such as *Antigone* and *Iphigenia at Aulis.* Children always respond well to this performing art, which originated in ancient Greece. (See Millstone [1988] for further discussion of children and Greek drama.)

The Norwich Greek program generally runs some six months, and even then, many children are hungry for still more. One year, children in sixth grade asked if they could continue their Greek studies. We established an afterschool Greek club and met all year for two hours late on Friday afternoons. What did we do in that time? Children reviewed the Greek alphabet and learned words and dialogues in modern Greek. We drew a huge map of Greece, acted out skits based on Greek mythology, built models of the Parthenon, and cooked Greek food. We also planned a vacation trip to Greece, which was finally canceled when the Gulf War erupted. More than twenty children, about half of that year's class, participated in the club.

No doubt part of the impetus for the Greek Club came from a strong bond between students and teacher. This was a group of students I had known since third grade, and with whom I had formed an especially strong attachment. They liked being with me, and I liked being with them. The Greek Club provided us with an opportunity to spend time together linked by our common interest in the ancient world. Again, that eternal triangle—student, teacher, subject. Unexpected possibilities, like the Greek Club, are among the joys of teaching.

8 | ODYSSEUS IN FIRST GRADE

The Norwich Odyssey Project has changed over the years but one aspect has always remained constant—the collaboration of first and fifth graders. Why did first-grade teachers get involved in bringing *The Odyssey* to their students? It was not because the teachers were attracted by the content of the epics, a lesson worth noting by those busy writing curriculum standards. Rather, the story provided a rich environment in which teachers could work with their colleagues. As one first-grade teacher explained simply, "It seemed like it would be fun to work with you and Brigid. Forget the curriculum. Let's get on with the people!" In contrast to the close-your-door isolation of so many classrooms, collaboration is a satisfying alternative for teachers and students alike. Teachers enjoy the opportunity to share their professional lives with other adults, and children enjoy teaching and learning from other children. First graders do more than serve as an audience for fifth-grade storytellers. Moreover, first-grade teachers would not settle for the satisfaction of adult collaboration if the project did not also benefit their students academically. This chapter focuses on the study of Homer and ancient Greece in the different first-grade classes in our school.

A note of clarification: in a departmentalized fifth grade, all students share one social studies teacher, so the activities described in earlier chapters have been reasonably consistent for most fifth graders; but first graders have different teachers and, consequently, different *Odyssey* experiences. Likewise, *The Odyssey* is a central part of the social studies curriculum in fifth grade; in first grade, it is one option among several available for teachers to pursue if they are interested. In the early years of the project, only one first-grade teacher studied Homer with her students; in later years, four others have been involved. Since my teaching is concentrated in the upper-elementary grades, in this chapter I rely extensively on examples, ideas, and anecdotes from these five colleagues.

In the fifth grade, students study *The Odyssey* in its own right and as an entry point into the world of ancient Greece. In first grade, teachers incorporate stories from *The Odyssey* into other areas of grade-appropriate study. One of these is strengthening the students' listening skills. As a result of growing up surrounded by television and videotape, notes Terri Ashley, a first-grade teacher at our school, children today have a harder time learning to be an audience for a live performance. "They're used to the pause button," she says. "They're accustomed to being able to get a drink whenever they want, to get up and go to the bathroom." She establishes three rules for listening in her classroom:

- You may not squirm.
- You may not speak when someone else is talking.
- You may not raise your hand until the speaker is finished.

At the beginning of their *Odyssey* work, first graders hear the stories of the Apple of Discord and the Judgment of Paris, sometimes told by outside storytellers, sometimes by their teachers. They then follow many of the same techniques that the fifth graders use to learn their stories—drawing pictures, telling stories with partners using their pictures as a guide, remembering parts of the story as a class activity and then placing those parts in proper sequence. Cindy Pierce, a beginning first-grade teacher, notes, "The most wonderful part was listening to students who struggle academically retell their version with confidence and genuine interest." In first grade, as in fifth, storytelling gives different children an opportunity to succeed.

By listening to their students' retellings of these tales, first-grade teachers discover that the story can take unexpected twists in a first grader's imagination. Retelling the scene in which Odysseus pretends to be crazy by plowing the sand on the beach in Ithaca, one first-grade girl had Odysseus walking back and forth with a power lawnmower, in front of which the baby Telemachus was placed as a test of his father's sanity. Another described the three goddesses Paris had to decide among as wearing go-go boots!

When the fifth graders come to present a new episode each day, how do first graders keep track of the unfolding story? Before each day's telling, teachers and students review the stories previously told so children will know what to expect. Several teachers also ask their first graders to keep their own simple comic strip of the day's adventures, perhaps on a strip of paper that has been accordion-folded into smaller panels. Another teacher finds it effective to make two children responsible for creating a picture from each day's telling. That picture is done collaboratively and entered in the class's ongoing big book of *The Odyssey*.

The story is complicated enough for fifth graders; we usually make it easier for them to follow by presenting episodes in chronological order, rather than in the flashback sequence of Homer's original. For the younger listeners it is even more important to maintain that chronological flow. One year, the fifth-grade girl who was scheduled to tell the story of the Trojan War was absent for several days. The first graders knew the story up through the outbreak of hostilities and they were expecting to hear the next installment. Although they were told that they were skipping ahead when another student came to describe the fall of Troy, without having heard first about the war they were noticeably confused.

Some first graders, like some fifth graders, have exceptionally short attention spans, and, predictably, a harder time sitting still. One first-grade teacher matter-of-factly describes her way of helping them: "They're always pretty itchy. They'd get a hunk of clay to fiddle with or they would sit in my lap. The usual calming stuff." Another comments, "I think the fifth graders thought the first graders were uninterested because they were wiggling, writhing, staring off into space and/or preoccupied." Later on, though, when the listeners ask questions of the tellers, the older children realize that their audience has indeed heard their stories.

First graders listen to dozens of fifth-grade storytellers, every day for a month. In some cases, the fifth graders tell their episode to the entire class. In others, especially when the episode is a long one, the class may be divided, and different storytellers address smaller groups. Storytelling occurs at different times, usually in place of a read-aloud book or, with the rise of whole language techniques, the regular times for poetry, songs, and chants. After hearing a tale, the first graders respond with compliments and questions.

"It's good for the first graders to hear different versions," one teacher says. "They pick up different details from each teller and learn to give comments specific to that particular tale. It's a way of building critical listening skills."

Other first-grade teachers report similar experiences. Brigid Farrell, my original *Odyssey* colleague, mentions the difficulty her first graders experience in listening to each other's writing: "We always try to get first graders to make constructive comments of some sort. I could say, 'I really like the way you used dialogue, or changed your tone of voice,' or I could say, 'Did you ever think of adding some sound effects?' We could model ways to let the fifth graders know whether their story was good or bad without saying, 'I hated it' or 'I loved the whole thing.' " Providing such examples makes it easier for the first graders to give specific feedback to their peers later on.

There is a predictable pattern to most first graders' comments. They often tell their fifth-grade storytellers, "I liked your story." Pressed for more details by the teacher—"Why?"—they frequently respond, "Because it was good." Pushed further—"What was good about it? What part did you think was good?"—they respond instantly, "All of it." As one teacher noted, "This original comment got passed around and sometimes repeated for the same storyteller. The fifth graders are sophisticated enough to accept the comment graciously and get a private chuckle."

In some cases, teachers realize that the first graders are simply being polite. Brigid Farrell notes that "I loved the whole thing" was a common response while the fifth grader was in the room. After the storyteller left, however, children were able to speak more openly about parts of the story that they really liked and parts that they disliked. "They didn't want to hurt the fifth grader's feelings," Brigid says.

Through this process the fifth graders learn to appreciate good storytelling, and the first graders learn to discriminate among the tellers. They appreciate fifth graders who use sound effects or who present new details, and struggle to learn more about these techniques. One fifth grader, who told his story in the first person, was asked, "Why did you say 'I' all the time?"

"Well, I was telling it like I was that character."

This is clearly a new idea to many first graders, who will sit quietly, pondering.

Critical listening carries over into the first graders' reading. First graders ask, "Is that true?," a question that opens many doors. Brigid Farrell turns the question back to her students: "How do you figure out whether any of these stories about Odysseus were true?" Her question sparks a discussion about history and archaeology and an invitation to look through the many books which she provides. Children modify their mental image of Odysseus as a medieval knight and learn to place him in a more ancient context.

"One of the things that would really annoy them," Brigid explains, "was when they'd find out The Truth. You know, they'd find a picture they were sure was Odysseus, somebody realistic, and then they'd find a children's *Odyssey* where the pictures were Roman centurions and definitely *wrong!*" Her students were upset: "Kids would ask, 'Didn't the person who published the book realize that these pictures didn't go with this story?' That kind of critical use of any text is something I'm always trying to get them to do."

MAKING CURRICULUM CONNECTIONS

The Odyssey is a complex story that allows teachers to make connections to other parts of the first-grade curriculum. Different teachers take the story in different directions, and depending on the particular class, the same teacher might use the story in different ways from one year to the next.

Most first-grade teachers agree that the study of *The Odyssey* works best in the context of mythology in general, and they read extensively from *d'Aulaires' Book of Greek Myths*. Children learn that myths are ways of explaining the world, and they spend most of their time hearing different myths and working with that material in various ways. In one frequent activity, first graders choose a favorite character from Greek mythology, assume a typical pose for that character, then have a partner trace around their body onto a large sheet of paper. The partners cut out the picture, paint and decorate it appropriately, and write (or dictate) a short description of the character. The colored silhouettes are displayed in the hall, but some end up in Dartmouth College mythology classes, where they are used to illustrate essential attributes of various gods. First-grade artists, without fail, depict Zeus with a lightning bolt in his hand, Hermes wearing winged sandals, and Athena with an owl on her shoulder. This activity is one of the earliest encounters our students have with Greek gods, and it engenders an awareness that will be refreshed several times in the elementary grades.

First graders enjoy illustrating and writing about imaginary encounters with immortals (see Figures 8-1 and 8-2). In a typical episode, the two characters enjoy each other's company and then go home. Here is an example by first grader Ceileigh; readers may also enjoy looking back at an excerpt of Ceileigh's fifth-grade writing (see Chapter 4, page 68).

> Yesterday I met Persephone, and we went down to Hades. We both didn't like it. Then we came up. Hades was mad. We laughed in his face, and we went to my house. She spent the night. When we woke up we had a good breakfast, then she had to go back to Hades. I missed her. I have never forgotten her. She gave me the clothes she had worn.

FIGURE 8-1
*"Steve and Artemis"
(Steve Winslow, first
grade)*

First graders frequently transform these *Odyssey* stories into their play. In the block corner, blocks become Ithaca, blocks become Troy. Puppets take on new life. A hand puppet of Grover, from Sesame Street, starts knocking on a wooden surface, crying, "Let me out of the horse! I can't breathe! I want to fight!" One year saw a rash of impromptu plays whenever there was a choice period. The teacher came into her classroom at one point and saw creatures making doglike sounds: "I said to whoever was playing Circe, 'Could you please get your dogs—' "

"They're not dogs. They're pigs."

"Could you please take your pigs out and change them into men again?"

"I'm not ready to do that now!"

Sometimes the urge to be dramatic carries an entire class, and students produce plays based on stories from mythology. When first graders produce a play, they start not by putting together a script, but by acting out the story perhaps a dozen times or more. In time, a script emerges. One year's production featured a long cardboard ship that moved slowly across the room from one adventure to the next, while different students narrated and took turns being the monsters that plagued Odysseus on his voyage.

One spring, the playground flooded, producing a giant lake with tufts of snow. A teacher recalled, "For the kids, these were not tufts of snow, they were tufts of lotus, and they went from island to island. They schlopped through and would try to entice other kids: 'Come on! We're having a wonderful time over at this one!' It would get crowded, it might sink, and they would move on, so that again became part of their playground culture."

In some years, teachers have incorporated the collection of fantastic creatures from *The Odyssey* into a larger unit on *monsters* and *giants* around the world, in which Polyphemus is one of many such creatures. First graders hear Roald Dahl's *The BFG* read aloud each year, look at other giants from English and Irish folklore, and consider stories about *dragons*.

FIGURE 8-2
"Hermes and Me"
(Graham Steele, first grade)

Whales, also large creatures, are the subject of a popular first-grade unit that sometimes alternates with dinosaurs. Since Odysseus was always at sea, it made sense to some teachers to integrate *The Odyssey* into a study of *the sea* and different islands and cultures. Studying the sea often means looking at different boats, and that in turn has led to the familiar ESS science unit, *sink and float*. First graders have studied *constellations*, especially those associated with Greek myths, and have explored questions of *archaeology* trying to learn how we know about the past.

Many first graders, of course, have only a hazy notion of the past, so Laurie Ferris uses the Homeric stories as an opportunity to construct a mammoth *timeline of the earth* with her students. The completed timeline, profusely illustrated with children's pictures of what was happening on earth during each era, stretches the entire length of a long hall. As Laurie explains it, "The dinosaur unit always messed up their sense of when *The Odyssey* happened. They figured it might have been just about simultaneous. So it made sense to make that lo-o-o-o-ong timeline and to take a lo-o-o-o-ong time making it so that they would get an inkling of how long ago it happened."

DEVELOPING PRIMARY SKILLS

The Odyssey offers more than links to other topics. Because the story holds children's imagination, teachers are able to use the story to build skills from the first-grade curriculum such as language development. *Sequencing*, the notion of what comes first and what comes next, is an important skill for young children. Children made lists of different episodes and discussed their order. Does it matter? Sometimes it does. Children may remember that Odysseus loses men in different episodes, or that the Laestrygonians destroy eleven of his twelve ships, but if those episodes are put in incorrect order, it changes the story.

Sequencing also emerges in the concept of *alphabetical order*. One year, Brigid Farrell worked on alphabetical order with her first graders for several weeks with no success. Children resisted lining up by name, doing worksheets, all the usual teacher tricks. She finally suggested that they make a list of characters from Homer and put that list in alphabetical order. Instant excitement—they quickly came up with twenty-five names and were hard at work. Helios or Hermes? Which one comes first? One girl—"I thought she barely knew her ABC's"—said Helios. Brigid asked her how she knew. "Well, I thought R was somewhere back there near S, near the back of the alphabet, and I guessed that L was in front of it."

First graders also use sequencing skills when they *design* board games. These are simpler than the fifth-grade games but follow similar principles of design. Games might be similar to the commercial games the six-year-olds know, like Candy Land (players move by colors, but if a player lands on a space, he might lose his life or have to stay for three days). Other games demand that a player landing on a space naming any episode must summarize that story in order to leave. First-grade teachers copy the same quizzes that fifth graders are taking and share them with first graders, letting them test their memories and feel proud of how much they know.

Odyssey stories also provide first-grade teachers a way of developing the skills of *emerging writers*. If the constraints of retelling an existing episode lead older children to produce excellent written stories, they can also push first graders to extend their writing. They learn to develop characters, to provide a setting, and to build a story before moving into the conclusion. By using a story that everyone already knows as an example, a good teacher can teach the basic elements of story structure. Armed with these elements, first-grade writers have enjoyed creating further adventures for Odysseus and his crew, usually involving an encounter with other monsters.

In the early years of the Odyssey Project, whole language was a new teaching philosophy, even though the school had long ago abandoned basal readers. First-grade teachers found that they could take *Odyssey* characters and place them in new situations as a way of helping children develop oral language and *reading skills*. Brigid remembers helping children learn to use predictable language patterns. "You know, 'Brown bear, brown bear, what do you see? I see a red bird looking at me.' You don't even have to turn the pages or look at the word to be able to read it. Some classes went through a whole slew of 'Odysseus, Odysseus, who do you see?' 'I see a Laestrygonian looking at me.' And then, 'Big woman, big woman, what do you see?' 'I see Odysseus looking at me.' We did a lot of patterned things, playing with the story in that way. We made up big books, and chants. It's certainly not controlled vocabulary, but by now, we're in spring of first grade so we can have some big words."

First graders enjoy playing many of the same games as their fifth-grade counterparts. "Twenty Questions," for example, develops the same language and thinking skills in young children as it does in fifth graders. The younger children learn to move away from "Twenty Guesses" by asking useful preliminary questions instead of randomly coming up with a character's name. "Are you a person or something else?" might eliminate half the possibilities, and "Are you male or female" narrows the choices further.

They discuss the language of the epics, playing with the *imagery* of a "wine-dark" sea. What color is wine? Red? How can the sea look red? Or "fat-bellied" sails? Does that say more than "the sails were filled with wind"? Did you ever see someone with a fat belly? Can you draw a ship with fat-bellied sails?

Some first graders are fascinated by *maps*, and teachers have used the travels of Odysseus to extend that fascination. One teacher helps her class create a large map of the Aegean and Mediterranean Seas, onto which students place their own drawings of Odysseus' various adventures. Another teacher takes the bulletin board that covers the entire end of her classroom and lets children pin up pictures of different episodes and drawings of boats, which they move from episode to episode. Other teachers reproduce maps, such as the one on endpapers of the Robin Lister edition of *The Odyssey,* and encourage children to draw stick figures at the appropriate places. When fifth graders finish their storytelling, they are sometimes asked, "You said the wind blew. Do you know if it blew up or down?" (meaning north or south). With luck, the fifth graders sometimes remember from their own classmates' maps the general direction in which the ships had been sailing in that episode and can pass the information along to their listeners. On several occasions, we have been able to develop a burgeoning interest in cartography just by pairing an avid map lover from first grade with an older student who shares that passion.

The Odyssey also makes appearances in first-grade *arithmetic* lessons, providing a subject for numerous word problems:

> "Scylla had six heads and two were fed. How many were still hungry?"
> "Odysseus went in with twelve boats and came out minus three. How many were left?"

One year, a science product to create instant whirlpools appeared on the market. Students could fasten the small plastic piece between two liter soda bottles, twist them, turn them upside down, and poof!, a whirlpool appeared. If students watched carefully to the very end, the whirlpool would make a small burp, and they could see how the infamous Charybdis might spit out the wreckage of Odysseus' raft, providing him with a great beam to cling to for safety. Once, months after the *Odyssey* unit had come and gone, children studying moths noticed that one large specimen was called a Polyphemus moth. A first grader wondered, "Does the name have anything to do with the big eye he has at the bottom of his wing?"

Children make many unexpected connections with their *Odyssey* studies. One first grader came to school one day having heard part of a news story on "All Things Considered," the news show on National Public Radio. The story made reference to a bed that couldn't be moved. The boy hadn't heard the whole story, but he got into a conversation with his parent, who had been listening.

"Oh, that was like Odysseus' bed," explained the boy. "It was built into a tree that was planted, and they used that as a trick to see if Odysseus was really Odysseus." Suddenly, his mother understood the point of the news story, which she had missed before because she didn't know about Odysseus' bed.

Similarly, it was first graders who proposed—an idea seconded by their parents—that students compile a *dictionary* of Homer's characters, which parents could use to help them keep up with the story. The rationale? "It's hard always having to explain things to them."

First graders *do* try to teach the story to their families and to others. One year, young Brooke went home every night after hearing stories told by fifth graders and repeated the tales to her younger brother, who was five at the time. Another year, Brigid Farrell had a group of girls "who were really into teaching. They made a big book of *The Odyssey* with a two-sentence story on each page and lots of illustrations because they wanted to tell the story to the kindergarteners. So they took the book to kindergarten and read the story. As they would read the two sentences they would also say, 'Well, that's only the beginning, this is what really happened' and tell the story more and get into it." I am reminded of the fifth grader's comment, quoted in Chapter 4: "Once you've learned it, you just want to go around and tell the story to everybody you know." Clearly, the desire to share what you have learned is common to first graders and older students alike.

Odyssey extensions even make their way into first-grade physical education classes. The gym teacher made up several games, one drawn on a large piece of scrap carpet, in which children would hop from one adventure to the next. Another game involved shooting marbles into Odyssean traps. The teacher also recycled a popular game from the fall, a run-and-chase game called "Old Mother Witch." This is one of the children's favorite games, and they frequently rename Old Mother Witch. Sometimes, students pick the names of *Odyssey* characters and change the rules to fit. For example, if the active person is Scylla, he or she can catch no more than six people because Scylla has only six heads. Our gym teacher has no particular background in the classics, but the children teach her how to modify the game appropriately according to their new knowledge.

WHAT DOES IT MEAN?

Adult critics argue over the meaning of "honor" in Homer. Fifth graders learn an exciting adventure story and reflect on what it means to be a hero. What, however, does *The Odyssey* mean to a six-year-old?

I would argue that we cannot know the ultimate impact these stories have on young children. After ten years I am starting to hear stories from former fifth graders who are now young adults in college. Spurred by a vague memory of something enjoyable associated with Greek pottery, they sign up for an art history class and later change their major to Classics. I have little doubt that much of the enthusiasm brought by each year's group of fifth graders comes from a good first-grade experience nourished by additional tastes of Greek mythology in third or fourth grade.

Laurie Ferris, an experienced first-grade teacher, says that *Odyssey* stories work so well with first graders "because kids that age are fascinated with power and its use. Good guys and bad guys. The characters could fall in behind lines that were black and white." (In contrast, the complexity of the characters is part of the appeal for fifth graders; Odysseus is not a Saturday morning two-dimensional cartoon figure.) Other first-grade teachers agree with Laurie. First graders sort through the large cast list and pick out the heroes and the heroines. The boys, not surprisingly, find plenty of models in the fighters, but the girls also delight in playing out the various goddesses—they have power that is obvious. Others love Penelope, whose deceitfulness with the suitors, weaving by day and unweaving at night, is a tactic they can appreciate. And Odysseus? "There's not a bad thing about Odysseus," agreed Brigid Farrell. "For first graders, he's good. There's nothing bad. 'Yeah, we get to get booty, that's good, that's for me.' There's just nothing bad. They don't see him being deceitful or tricky. He's good."

Working with complex stories is an important part of growing up, and *The Odyssey* gives children rich material to work with. They re-create *The Odyssey* in their play, and, as Maria Montessori noted, play is the work of children. Homer's tales and the larger body of Greek mythology give first graders (as they do fifth graders and adults alike) a shared collection of characters and stories through which they can explore what it means to be human.

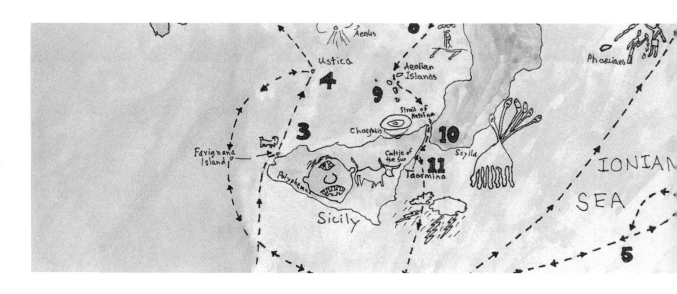

WHY DOES
IT WORK?

9 | ORGANIZATION AND EVALUATION

Creative ideas alone do not guarantee classroom success. Creativity in the classroom needs a foundation of coherent organization and clear presentation so that students know what is expected of them. My journal entries indicate that my teaching is often energized by instinct, although I then strive to bring order to unformed ideas. Even assignments I have presented many times sometimes fall flat and force me to rethink my plans. Those problems are true of any creative work, and good teaching is both art and craft.

The *Odyssey* study is a rich mixture of many different simultaneous activities. Each year, the specific tasks change slightly, but even those activities that occur every year take place in a slightly different order, pushed about by the calendar and by the continual desire to adjust and adapt. Some teachers, including many whom I admire a great deal, follow the same plans year after year. They are able to find fresh life in the same routine by focusing on the new group of children in their classroom. I generally enjoy the personal stimulation of tackling different subjects, different grades, even different ways of presenting the same material. Teaching Homer has been the exception.

Certain principles guide the organization of the *Odyssey* unit. Many of those principles should be clear already from the organization of this book, although taking a complex (and sometimes messy) whole and breaking it into discrete chapters is a difficult process. Rather than discuss organization in the abstract, let's examine an actual *Odyssey* schedule from start to finish.

After ten years, I know in broad outline how our study will progress. Children first listen to the story and then spend several weeks reviewing that information and completing the activities described in Chapter 2. They learn storytelling techniques. They complete independent projects and, sometimes, classwide art projects. They write, both serious pieces and the newspaper spoof. I know that each year will follow this general pattern, but I rarely plan in more detail. Therefore, it is easier to look at the daily *Odyssey* schedule after the fact (see Appendix B).

The schedule was compiled by Ingrid Stallsmith, a teaching intern in the 1991–92 school year. Every day, Ingrid spent a few minutes at the computer recording what we actually did that day in the *Odyssey* unit. I have changed her format slightly and shortened several entries. I have also marked with italics the major starting and stopping points along the way. After the initial storytelling, which brings all homerooms together at one time, this schedule captures the nitty-gritty of the Social Studies classroom and our forty-five-minute periods each day. The work on puppets and playwriting in Weeks 4 through 10 takes place in English class.

Looking back through the daily account of the classroom, I see a flow to the events, an underlying order that makes sense. Certain activities precede others. New projects are introduced, practiced, and completed, and other projects appear at strategic moments to provide a fresh focus. What kind of planning leads to such a schedule? And how do we evaluate the work that children produce?

PLANNING AND PREPARATION

A teacher's enthusiasm goes a long way. In our early years in the classroom, we rely far more on enthusiasm than on experience, simply because experience is what we are lacking. Enthusiasm takes many forms, from in-your-face, rapid-fire delivery and eager gesticulation to a more controlled but no less fierce determination marked by a formal stance. Students know, of course, whether the teacher is interested. As we think back on our own schooling from elementary school right through college, we can remember those teachers who went through the motions and those few electric teachers who palpably cared about their subject and their students. Enthusiasm alone, however, is rarely enough to sustain a classroom over time. If this is the teacher's major method of motivation, overload and burnout are in the wings.

There is no substitute for knowing the subject we are teaching. A large part of the success of the Norwich Odyssey Project lies in my own continuing interest in the subject and in my growing expertise. After that initial month-long summer immersion, I was excited *and* I knew a great deal about the topic. Since then, I've continued my education, and I'm able to bring more and more knowledge with me into the classroom. Good graduate courses and workshops are stimulating; summer seminars and institutes, locally funded or backed by such organizations as the National Endowment for the Humanities, are a delightful way for the adult learner to experience fresh intellectual challenges.[1]

On the other hand, there is a danger in too much emphasis on academic preparation. Knowledge of the subject matter can obscure the need for good teaching techniques. Teachers can hide behind academic content; students in such classrooms and lecture halls are merely adjuncts to scholarly presentations.

Ultimately, the skilled teacher needs all three—enthusiasm, knowledge, and effective techniques—to build bridges between student and subject. Inevitably, we will teach many things that we don't fully understand; that's where our enthusiasm helps carry the day, while we patiently go about learning more.

I find it helpful to start my preparations for a new unit of study by brainstorming ideas, working with others if possible. Sometimes I just make a long list of possibilities, no matter how farfetched. At other times, I like organizing ideas in a web—a useful alternative to the formal outline—with major topics branching off into details, and arrows showing possible connections between different clusters.

During planning, we often think in terms of content: What do we want children to learn? What material should be covered? Equally important, and sometimes lost, are the process questions: What will children actually be doing in class? How will they support each other's learning? What assumptions am I making about what they already know and what they can do? How can they apply what they learn to new challenges?

A crucial part of successful preparation is anticipating outcomes. How will students publish their work? In what ways will they share what they learn? Knowing ahead of time what such outlets will be helps shape the work itself. Publication—in all forms—is of such importance that it needs to be built in, not left to chance.

One final preparation step is to let parents and colleagues know your intentions. Parents will offer new and unexpected ideas, and act as our advance guard. Parental enthusiasm for a classroom activity can play an important part in getting children interested; the more parents know what is coming, the more they can involve their child.

Informing parents means more than sending home a note every week or so. Any teacher (or parent) can tell you how rarely notes arrive at their destination on time. In our school, we use a variety of methods to let parents know what we have planned. On the first day of school, we send home a letter from each teacher as part of the opening day's huge mail.

---

[1] For information on summer seminars and institutes, contact the National Endowment for the Humanities, 1100 Pennsylvania Avenue, N.W., Washington, DC 20506. Teachers, librarians, and principals may also be interested in a program of rigorous independent study in the humanities. Such opportunities are supported by the Council for Basic Education, P.O. Box 135, Ashton, MD 20861.

Parents know that they should expect large quantities of letters, calendars, and forms on the first day, and that is when students' notebooks and backpacks are neat and orderly. That letter briefly explains the curriculum for the year and describes in more detail those activities that will occupy our first month of school. Two weeks later, we hold our first parents' night, during which we describe the curriculum and our expectations for students. We also provide written descriptions of the curriculum and of the upcoming activities and invite parents to ask questions. About 90 percent or more of the families attend this meeting. Most of their questions are answered in turn by other parents, those whose older children have passed through the school. A month later, in mid-October, we schedule our first Open House for parents and students; again, the vast majority of families turn out. By this time, relatively early in the year, we've already explained our plans on several occasions. Now we can show what it is that students have already accomplished. Teachers hold additional Open Houses throughout the year to share ongoing work with parents or to celebrate a study just completed.

Most of our teachers schedule parent conferences shortly after the October Open House. These meetings are an opportunity to compare first impressions, to learn how the child is adjusting to the demands of increased homework, to get to know parents better, and to garner information they think is important for us to know. We follow up with the first report card in November, which often includes a cover letter describing the term's activities.

Such meetings and letters, combined with the comments of other parents, go a long way toward informing parents about curriculum and expectations. In addition, I find it helpful to send home letters describing specific long-term activities that I expect to be done as homework. (See Chapter 5 for a discussion of one such letter, which accompanies independent *Odyssey* projects.) Faced with the all-too-common exchange— "What did you do in school today?" "Nothing"—parents with the best intentions often do not know how to help. Many have said that such letters and phone calls are among the most useful things a teacher can do to help them help their child with schoolwork.

Collaboration with other adults establishes an environment in which the whole is greater than the sum of the parts; collaboration offers a powerful model for working together. Students who see teachers locked inside closed classrooms may have a difficult time imagining themselves working closely with others; conversely, students who see adults laughing and learning from each other gain valuable insights into the benefits of cooperation. It is important to coordinate in advance with other professionals in the building. Other classroom teachers at the same grade level, specialists in such areas as music and art, and teachers in other grades all have valuable ideas that will shape your plans.

Coordination helps ensure variety. Creative tasks need to be supplemented with the routine, drawing with writing. Even the freshest approach will sour if it is overused. If students are building puppets in English class, for example, that may not a good time for them to be constructing dioramas in social studies. Asking children to start several new things at once may be overwhelming. The 1992 daily log (see Appendix B) shows clearly that major new tasks are introduced gradually as children near completion on other assignments. Children can work on several tasks simultaneously, but their work goes more smoothly when their assignments are coordinated. Thus, in Week 6, students in our homeroom were in the final stages of their scriptwriting. With one project drawing to a close, it was a good moment to introduce a new one, creating an *Odyssey* board game. Similarly, the newspaper spoof started in Week 10, as the board games, filmstrip, and mobile were all finishing.

I find it especially helpful to speak in advance with the learning specialists who give additional assistance to children with special needs. In some cases, they can take extra time to help a child with an assignment. With certain projects, they can help the child get an early start, so that the child is able to complete a task on time with his peers. In all cases, their experience in teaching children with learning difficulties is a valuable asset. By discussing assignments in advance and by anticipating how a particular assignment might be implemented for a nonreader, I am able to do a better job of creating tasks for all the children in the class.

WHAT ROLE DOES EVALUATION PLAY?

Preparation is the advance work that enhances student performance, but as teachers everywhere know, the job is not over when students finish their work. Children need support as they take new risks, and they want honest reactions to their work. In my kind of teaching, with no textbook to follow and no organized series of content lectures as the foundation for learning, I must devise methods of evaluation that differ significantly from end-of-chapter quizzes.

Paradoxically, one of the most important things we can do as teachers is to learn when *not* to evaluate. Too many children look to others to decide the worth of what they do. Schools help train children to accept the word of authorities as the measure of them and of their work, preparing them to fit neatly into a hierarchical structure in the American work force. Children are already under intense pressure to meet the standards, real or imaginary, set by their peers; indeed, learning to find one's own place within a social group is a necessary part of growing up. But by insisting that the locus of control lies with others, schools contribute to the individual's sense of powerlessness. The drug and alcohol education programs so prevalent—and so necessary—in our schools today, start from the premise that the individual must learn to take increased responsibility for his or her actions. In the same way, we help our students when we enable them to take increased responsibility for the quality of their academic work. Here are some guidelines I keep in mind.

The work speaks for itself.

Much of the time, our evaluation is superfluous, unnecessary, redundant. Adults and children alike respond to quality. (Perhaps it is appropriate now to reread Robert Pirsig's *Zen and the Art of Motorcycle Maintenance,* a philosophical journey in search of that elusive trait, Quality.) Yes, it takes time to learn the value of something, but a grade often short-circuits the process of learning to see. "What did I get?" asks the child. That's usually the end of the process. The grade erases other, more valuable questions: How could this be better? What can I take from this to use next time? Does this represent the best I can do?

Teachers familiar with the writing process catechism know the importance of "publishing" students' work. Publishing reminds students that there is a wider audience than the teacher, and they need to think of that wider audience when they write. Publishing validates the young writer's work. It provides children with the thrill of seeing their name in print. Publishing allows that wider audience to learn from each child's work, turning a piece of writing into a resource for continued learning. Publishing also allows parents and community members to appreciate the achievements of the writers. A comment in passing, a note from a family friend, an acknowledgment from neighbor to parent to child—each makes the child feel more confident and eager to tackle the next task.

Computers and word-processing technology have made publishing student work much easier than it was even ten years ago. In our community, where home computers are common, many upper-elementary students bring written work to school on disk or already printed out to a specified page size, which makes the final paste-up into booklet or newspaper much faster. The photocopier, too, has simplified the task. Years ago, I remember spending long hours typing student work onto ditto masters, which made me think twice before undertaking a publishing project.

Make high standards visible.

Even the simple act of displaying work on a bulletin board, in the classroom, or in the hall, shares a child's work with a wider audience. That sharing allows for additional learning. There are really only two philosophies for displaying papers: display some or all. Each conveys a useful message.

Picking a few good examples for display gives those children a reason for particular pride, a brief time in the spotlight. (I assume that teachers keep track of whose work is displayed and make a serious effort to spotlight quality work from different students throughout the year.) These examples are models for other students, showing them how an assignment might successfully be completed. More than the teacher's words, the outstanding work of peers can lift the quality of other children's efforts. I think here of the independent *Odyssey* projects, which build so success-fully on the work of preceding years' students. Such a display, with attrac-tive labels and accompanying text, also educates parents and community members about the teacher's standards.

Make the range of products visible.   Displaying everyone's work, if space allows, is even more effective for parent education. Many parents are concerned about their child's skills in relation to those of others in the grade, and the displays at Open Houses and throughout the year provide eloquent testimony. Displaying everyone's work also provides an opportu-nity to create a worksheet based on the display. At its simplest, this forces students to look carefully at each other's work. The display identifies a re-source for continued learning.

A class display should not hold individuals up to ridicule. Students with handwriting problems should have the opportunity to type their written work, or in special cases, to have adult assistance. Children who cannot write need the assistance of a scribe, either peer or adult. Learn-ing-disabled students need additional assistance from tutors; this is where planning with other professionals pays off.

If good work teaches by example, so does poor work. One of the more useful techniques in a teacher's repertoire is to present for discus-sion a sample of a problematic piece of work. Armed with a list of criteria to use in examining the work, children can learn from identifying the weaknesses. Going through such an exercise before they begin work on their own similar project heightens children's awareness of the expecta-tions.

Announce the criteria in advance.   Before children start work on an assignment, let them know what you expect in as much detail as possi-ble and in writing if possible. This may seem harder than simply taking fi-nal papers home and grading them, but it actually simplifies the entire process. It does force teachers to decide ahead of time on the objectives of a particular assignment. Unlike grading on the curve, where some will al-ways do better than others and some must, by definition, fail, specific cri-teria and standards make it possible for all children to succeed. If they know in advance what they are being asked to do, everyone can learn the names of the major characters in *The Odyssey*. Everyone can complete a simplified comic strip of a particular episode. This notion of mastery for all is at the heart of the continuing debate over quality *versus* equity in ed-ucation. I do not know if mastery of everything is indeed possible for each child, but it's a goal worth attempting.

Use red ink on rough drafts only.   Although children sometimes see rough drafts as simply one more task designed by sadistic teachers, their purpose is to help students work through their ideas and to create a stronger final product. Many of us remember getting papers back with a sea of red ink in the margins; no matter how valid the comments, it's easy to feel disheartened. As a teacher now, I have lots to say—and red ink does stand out—but I'd rather make my marks on children's rough work, when they still have an opportunity to change it. I find children are far more receptive to such comments, critical though they may be, because they can take advantage of my reactions. The point of teacher comments is neither to demonstrate the adult's understanding nor to stamp the paper with an indelible grade, it is to help students improve their work.

If specific comments and suggestions for improvement are made on the rough drafts, comments on the final product might fit neatly into a few categories, such as this short form, which I have used several times to react to independent *Odyssey* projects:

> **Evaluation Sheet**
> Project title:
> Did you meet the deadline?
> Overall attractiveness:
> Information presented:
> Details:
> Suggestions for further improvement:

Such a brief form allows me to note the improvements I notice since earlier drafts, to celebrate the student's success, and to point out—in the final section—major flaws that still need fixing.

Documentation is "authentic assessment."

In Vermont, there is widespread interest in portfolio assessment, which is based in part on the notion that children and teachers alike need clear, objective criteria when looking at samples of actual work. It has taken several years to develop such benchmarks, and it will take many more before teachers are trained to interpret them in a reasonably uniform manner. Vermont is one of eighteen states in the New Standards Project, "arguably the most complex and ambitious school-reform effort in this century," which uses portfolios and other assessments to investigate "what is worth teaching and how to tell when students have mastered it" (Viadero 1994).

If grades recede as a written evaluation of student work, how will parents know what progress their child is making? How will future teachers know how well the child did? Unlike our common evaluation methods, portfolios allow others to look at student work directly or to know what has been accomplished. As our school systems become more accustomed to working with portfolios, all of us—students, parents, and teachers— may find it easier to think in terms of *documentation,* a careful record of students' improving work.

Keeping a file of completed work seems easy enough. Classroom teachers often use a series of manila folders and a milk crate as a storage system for most student work. Such a file can also include photographs, cassette tapes, videocassettes, and computer disks. These alternative media enable us to record much valuable information that goes beyond print materials. Nearly twenty years ago, when I team-taught third and fourth grade, we gave the children an individual cassette tape to be used once a month to record themselves reading a passage aloud. At parent conferences that tape was one way of documenting a child's progress in oral reading. Likewise, keeping a recording of children telling *Odyssey* stories is a useful way of looking back at a transitory moment.

Although establishing such a documentation system is challenging enough, it is even harder knowing how to use such information effectively. For nearly twenty years, the Prospect School, in Bennington, Vermont, maintained archives of student work, written stories and artwork alike, comprising all work that the student did not take home. Unfortunately, this meant that much of the best work disappeared. In time, though, as the community began to grow more aware of the existence of these archives, students would bring back their work and ask that it be placed in their files. Parents started bringing in scribbles from children as preschoolers. Graduates would send copies of their work back from college. For some children, the archives grew to include work from many stages of their life.

The Prospect School developed a stylized, formal technique for reflection in which the teachers study together a single piece of work by a child. One at a time, the participants take turns simply describing what they see, avoiding interpretation, analysis, psychological guesswork, and judgment. One person takes notes and summarizes what has been said. Unlike our usual system of evaluation, which emphasizes the weaknesses in a finished piece, the Prospect exercise forces one to look ever more closely at the child's work, to note all that is there rather than to find that which is not. The stress is on the positive, not the negative.

Beware of numbers.

Our society has a passion for the quantifiable. When report cards are due, I inevitably dream about averaging columns of numbers and having a single grade emerge. The time-consuming reality is that I prefer to write a descriptive paragraph—even a short one—about each child. Fortunately, I work in a small school where teachers develop their own report cards; we have none of the top-down requirements to conform to a single, districtwide reporting form. In the upper elementary grades, we check "outstanding," "satisfactory," or "having difficulty" for a handful of categories, but the bulk of my report is anecdotal. Written reports give us the opportunity to describe, to tell a story, which may be more informative than a numerical grade.

Some work *is* easily quantifiable. With no qualms, I can indicate that a child correctly identified forty-six of the fifty U.S. states on a map, or 92 percent; correctly matching twenty-two of twenty-five named individuals on a quiz of *Odyssey* characters, is 88 percent. But these are two very specific and relatively low-level tasks. Instead of asking children to match characters with descriptions, what if the quiz simply presented the names of twenty characters and asked the student to write a short identification? Set aside for the moment the reality that some individuals have significantly more difficulty writing an answer that reflects what they know. Just how much detail does an identification need to earn full credit?

Grading a quiz is easy compared to the myriad classroom tasks of greater complexity. How does one determine that a three-page written report deserves an 82? Why not a 79? Why not an 85? Why an 82 and not an 83? How is a numerical grade assigned to a piece of sculpture, a painting, a short story? Rather than cloak opinions in the guise of numbers, which have such a powerful aura, I prefer to state my opinions in words.

The teacher is not detached and objective.   Is this too obvious? Children and parents often look to the teacher as The One Who Knows. Especially at report card time when they must produce a summary of student progress, teachers are pushed into playing the role of judge. Like all human beings, however, teachers can be opinionated and myopic. At times our attention is turned in the wrong direction, we misunderstand student questions, and we make incorrect assumptions. Despite good intentions, teachers bring their personal lives to school with them. We procrastinate, we cut corners, we don't get enough exercise or enough sleep. We may be withdrawn or remote, harsh or grouchy. One excerpt from my journal illustrates the point:

> I'm in a definite mood of low energy, staying up late and cranky with kids at school, low tolerance for the bickering of the boys at home, not finding time to do much schoolwork (or as much as I think is needed). And lurking overhead are report cards, due in two weeks. I don't want to go into detail, evaluating kids on their knowledge of The Odyssey and putting that as their content grade on the report card. Almost everyone has been working hard, or about as hard as can be expected, and some have been really caught up in it . . .
>
> Kids worked diligently on their Odyssey stories, which came in last week. About half the kids had their stories finished on time, and most of the remainder came in the following day with little prompting. It's hard to summon up the same kind of enthusiasm that I felt several years ago when first I saw them write on these topics. In truth, I just haven't made the time to sit down and read their pieces through—I'm sure that there will be excellent pieces of writing, and that will in turn get me excited. The problem isn't so much with them as it is with me.

Different teachers also have different reactions to the same work. One of the hardest challenges facing our writing portfolio assessment is training different teachers to reach common ground; at the moment, two individuals evaluating the same piece of writing may arrive at different scores.

Closer to home, I know that when I ask my students to design a map of an imaginary world, I have an idealized picture of what constitutes quality work; other teachers have different ideas. Each of us has a rationale for what we like, but a child being graded by me could receive a very different grade from my colleague.

Can such subjectivity be eliminated from the classroom? What messages would children receive in a supposedly objective environment? Perhaps what teachers should do instead is admit our biases and encourage others to share their perceptions. And there is one more crucial voice to be heard—that of the child.

KNOW THYSELF

When the writing process wave reached my classroom in the late 1970s, I was struck by the power it granted to young writers. The author, not the teacher, must decide what changes from the rough draft should be made in subsequent drafts. The teacher's role, and that of peers, was to offer support and suggestions. Writing is a fragile act, we heard, and a young author needs encouragement. For many of us, this was a refreshing if unsettling change in our roles. Formerly, the teacher set the task, received the work, and took it home to grade. Now, responsibility for improving writing became a shared task, and the writing conference moved to center stage.

For a successful writing conference, the author needs to set the agenda by offering certain areas up for examination: "I'm not sure about the lead. Is it strong enough? Should I be more specific? Do the conversations sound realistic? What do you think about the descriptions—can you picture the setting of my story? Should I include more details? Is the story too long?" The readers, classmates and teachers alike, ignore other areas and focus on that designated topic. The writer listens carefully to suggestions but retains the authority of the author, making only those changes that she or he agrees with.

We saw earlier examples of student evaluation. In Chapter 4, we looked at student evaluation of adult storytellers; in Chapter 7, we discussed children's evaluations of the game of Civilization. Children can bring that same analytical eye to bear on their own educational progress, whether at the conclusion of a specific task or in a broader summary such as that demanded by a quarterly report card. In the same way that specific criteria make it easier to understand a task, specific guidelines offer a framework for children attempting to assess the quality of their own work. After the independent *Odyssey* projects are completed, the questions shown on one simple self-evaluation form (see Figure 9-1) help children consider both process and product.

Teachers can expand on such opportunities for self-reflection. Since report cards loom large in a child's universe in even the most supportive

environment, I like to give my students an opportunity to tell the rest of
the story. After I've finished writing reports, but before the cards go home,
I assemble my students at our meeting area and introduce the task.

> I just spent the last week writing your report cards. When I write re-
> ports, I try to state as honestly as I can what you've done in this
> class. If I think you're working hard, I will say so; if I think you're
> coasting, I'll say that, too. I will describe your successes and those
> areas that have been difficult. But you have to keep in mind that
> this report is the opinion of one person, myself.
>
> You're all old enough to know that there is more than one side to
> most stories. I'd like you to write your own report card. Yes, I will

FIGURE 9–1
*Project Self-
Evaluation Sheet*

Project: _____   Name: _____

Project Self-Evaluation Sheet

Topic selection

Did you discuss your project choice with a parent?

Why did you pick this project?

Now that you're finished, do you think it was a good choice for you? Explain.

Preparation

Research: What research, if any, did you need to do?
How did you find the necessary information?
Was there information you wanted but couldn't find? Please explain.

Rough work:
Did you need to write a rough draft, or make sketches, or do other
preliminary work? Please explain.

Did you have any surprises along the way? Did things go easier or
harder than you expected, or was it about what you had anticipated?

Did you learn any new skills in the process of completing your project?

Planning your time

How did you budget your time? Did you do a lot of work at one time?
Did you spread it out over several weeks? Explain.

If you had it to do over again, would you make any changes in planning
your time?

About how many hours did you spend on your project, from start to
finish?

Final Project

Is your finished project attractive?
How does your project fit with our study of *The Iliad* or *The Odyssey*?
What parts of it do you especially like?
If you had it to do over again, are there changes you'd make? Explain.
Overall, what do you think about your final project?

---

send home your report, just like I'm sending home my report. I will also photocopy your self-evaluation and place it in your permanent school file. This is a chance for you to describe, as honestly and as accurately as you can, the work you are doing.

One thing to keep in mind, though. Don't be too hard on yourself; emphasize the good points. After reading student-written reports for many years now, I've realized that it's hard for most people to write good things about themselves. In our society, if you say something good about yourself, you worry that people will think you're bragging. That's not going to happen with this assignment. Your classmates are not going to be reading your report. Your parents will read it and I'll read it, but what you say isn't going to change my report on you; I've already written that. So be as honest as you can. If you think you're working hard and doing good work, please say so.

This is a difficult assignment for most children; it is often greeted by muted groans. The words that seem to convince students of my seriousness are "your permanent school file." Writing for me? Yawn. Writing for parents? Maybe. Writing for your school file? That's significant! Perhaps in the same way that publishing gives importance to a piece of writing, this task exudes the aura of writing for posterity, adding their words to a terribly weighty document.

Year after year, I learn a great deal about my students from what they write. Parents also say that they find it refreshing to read their child's self-reflections. Although I have no evidence to back this opinion, I believe that this exercise is one of the more worthwhile assignments of the year. Writers need to write a lot to improve their ability to produce a polished piece; musicians need to practice before they can play harmoniously with others. In much the same way, young children need to look inward and learn to say good things about themselves in order to develop higher standards for themselves.

WHO EVALUATES THE EVALUATOR?

One piece remains in the evaluation package. How do teachers grow? How do we learn what is effective? What assistance do we receive in improving our skills? Three helpful sources of such aid are colleagues, parents, and students.

One advantage of working in a school where teachers collaborate is the opportunity to receive help from peers. Teachers involved in the *Odyssey* unit meet to coordinate activities, and inherent in such coordination is an assessment of what worked in prior years. Before following the same schedule, my colleagues review which projects clicked with students in the past. We look at this year's students and their particular needs—some groups need more structure, while others can support each other in a looser environment. We think back to great ideas we had that flopped—I remember abandoning one ill-conceived project after two weeks and apologizing to the class for having wasted their time. We work together as we create a plan for the new year.

Collaboration also brings teachers together during the day. In a profession noted for its solitary character, where teachers spend most of their working hours behind closed doors and removed from contact with other adults, collaboration opens the doors. When first graders are dictating the Apple of Discord to my fifth graders, I have time during the school day to visit a first-grade classroom and listen to one of my colleagues giving directions or answering questions. I get to look at a different room arrangement, to read the bulletin boards, to skim the class's recently written big books, to comment on what I notice. Similarly, when the younger children come upstairs to paint pictures with their fifth-grade partner, a first-grade teacher might follow along and look at my teaching. Such opportunities to share each other's professional lives are as valuable as they are rare.

Parents are a second source of worthwhile feedback, but they need to be encouraged to speak up. Many adults had less-than-successful experiences in school and have grown up with the idea that they are in no position to criticize schools and teachers. (Some adults, of course, feel perfectly comfortable criticizing schools and teachers alike, with only the vaguest understanding of the school's mission, appropriate state and federal laws, child development, confidentiality, educational research, and changes in the social structure of American life in the past forty years. That's another story.) Consequently, I make a special point of encouraging parents to let me know what is on their minds. There is one fixed line in the speech I give at the first parent meeting of the year, a thought I first heard expressed by David Whitin, with whom I team-taught for three years: "You don't have to wait until there's a problem to contact me. Please let me know when you're pleased." Parents respond to that invitation. At parent conferences and open houses, through short notes and telephone calls, and in countless conversations in the aisle of the local general store, I see my classroom reflected through parents' eyes. Parents talk to the principal as well, and he passes their comments along to me. I learn about homework that was difficult and homework that was exceptionally satisfying; often, the same assignment produces vastly different reactions in children. "We like all this mythology," comments one mother of a rural family. "My husband and I never studied those things, and it's fun to have this as a topic at the dinner table." I learn what skills are important to different adults in the community; I learn that different families have different goals for their children; I learn which parts of my messages home are unclear. Over time, I improve what I do.

Finally, and fundamentally, I learn from my students. Our relationship and their performance on particular tasks let me know how well I am doing as a teacher. If no one wants to talk with me, I need to work harder at making myself accessible. If many students are confused, I discover that I have to make my directions clearer. If projects are disappointing, I find a better way of communicating high expectations. If day after day brings listless responses, I know that it is time to rethink my lesson plans.

Schools mix informal and formal evaluations of students, ranging from a teacher's file of daily anecdotes (mental or written) through standardized tests. Those tests, fortunately, are only a small part of our picture of each child, but they do provide one more piece of information. Each year, I ask children to provide two other formal assessments to improve my teaching in general and the *Odyssey* unit in particular. The first is a continuation of that meeting my principal held with students in 1985, the very first year of the project. It was the day after the Open House and I was suffering the collapse of an adrenalin high that had sustained me throughout many weeks. The principal gathered students in a circle and asked them what they remembered from the unit. "What specific activities do you recall?" he asked, and then, after dozens of children fondly recalled scores of moments, "What do you think you learned?"

We start the process today in much same way. I stand at the chalkboard or at an easel, and for half an hour or more I function as the group's scribe. Children call out their memories and I write furiously. There is something immensely satisfying in being reminded of all that took place during the preceding months. Children delight in remembering those wonderful, funny moments, and they take special pleasure in recalling the tiniest details in the interest of developing a complete record of our accomplishments. Each recollection prompts another, and I marvel at how much information is stored in our collective memory. Each specific incident also elicits reactions from the rest of the class, ranging from "Huh? What?" to wild grins and cries of "I remember that!" Both reactions, and the gradations in between, tell me a lot about the value of each task. Specific tasks from months ago, challenging at the time, are viewed with a different perspective, as children discover in retrospect how one assignment laid the foundation for later learning. The fondness with which certain moments are recalled also speaks eloquently.

After the list is finished, I ask students to write a formal evaluation:

> Think back on all that we've done, and write a report card for the *Odyssey* unit. What parts of it worked? What parts were the most valuable? What assignments were hard? Maybe at the time you didn't enjoy them much, but now you realize that you learned a lot from them. What did we do that was fun but you have to admit that you didn't get much from doing it? What do you wish we did more of? If we could only keep a few activities for next year's class, which ones should they be?

Children's responses to these questions do influence the shape of the project in future years; they provide invaluable information about how students react to my plans. Like writing a self-evaluation, this is a difficult assignment, perhaps because it is so unfamiliar. Consequently, I rarely ask children to undertake this kind of evaluation more than once or twice in a year. They take such requests seriously, perhaps because I make them infrequently and therefore they seem especially serious. I worry that making frequent demands for evaluation will tarnish the glow of their achievements.

Teaching is more than a series of assignments made and work completed. Yet much emphasis in teacher training and in curriculum design goes into these two relationships, between teacher and curriculum, and student and curriculum. The teacher develops the curriculum and the curriculum in turn shapes the teacher. Students respond to the curriculum, and the subject itself has a way of testing students. One formal evaluation remains.

At the end of the year, often as an assignment due on the last day of school, I ask my students to write a report card of me as a teacher. We talk about the sorts of things that might enter into a report card, about the qualities one seeks in a good teacher. Unlike so many other assignments, however, I provide no criteria and few guidelines. Some children create elaborate grids and fill in grades. Some write detached—almost clinical—reports. Some write warm and personal letters, describing in rich detail what the year has been like for them. All responses, from the sketchiest to the most elaborate, provide one more evaluation of the elusive component that is difficult to document but which lies at the heart of good education, and that is the human link between teacher and student.

10 | A TEACHING PHILOSOPHY

We work in the dark.
We do what we can.
We give what we have.
—Henry James

Norwich, Vermont, population 3,100, lies on the eastern edge of a state whose total population of African Americans only recently passed the one thousand mark. The Franco-American population of Vermont lives primarily to the north, and that of neighboring New Hampshire is either in former mill towns or in remote logging regions. The home community of the indigenous Abenaki nation lies far away in the extreme northwest corner of the state. There is no significant Latino population, the number of Jewish families is small, and the town has largely missed the new immigrants from Southeast Asia. Norwich is a town of Yankee families learning to accommodate an influx of professionals coming to work at the nearby college and medical center. In short, the community where I teach is marked by a notable lack of ethnic diversity and is removed from the strident debate about multiculturalism and the canon.

In recent years, as classical humanities have been championed by such conservative critics as Allan Bloom and William Bennett, I sometimes find the Norwich Odyssey Project cited as an example of quality education by individuals with whom I have major political differences. Indeed, the summer institute where I fell in love with Homer's text was sponsored by the National Endowment for the Humanities during Bennett's chairmanship, and I have been told that he took a personal interest in having such an institute established specifically for elementary school teachers. Bennett went on to become Secretary of Education in the Reagan Cabinet, where he used his bully pulpit to argue against much of what I hold true in education. Such critics heralded Greece and Rome as more worthy of study than other ancient cultures. In the face of mounting cries for a multicultural curriculum, the argument was that these classical civilizations offered exemplars of the good, the true, the eternal. As cornerstones of Western democracy, we heard, classics had much to offer that the study of other cultures lacked.

Year after year, I saw children responding eagerly to our study of Homer and Greek civilization, but despite that continuing success I felt uncomfortable leading a project that would lend credence to these arguments, which left such a bitter, elitist, and sometimes racist aftertaste. If ancient Greece was at the core of the curriculum championed by the cultural conservatives, I questioned the value of what I was doing. If they liked it, there must be something wrong.

Help for my dilemma came in the form of a journal article in which classicist Susan Ford Wiltshire (1988) tackled head-on the "return to the basics" elitism of Bloom and Bennett. As I read her essay, I found myself nodding vigorously in agreement. Wiltshire argues that we each need a "second identity" in order to understand "that our immediate world is not the only one that exists." The classical world is one rich source of such an identity, she continues, but it is not the only source:

> Mastery of a prescribed list of texts or phrases does not constitute an educated person, and neither, alone, does a knowledge of Greece and Rome. Rather, the purpose of education and especially of the humanities is to make us larger than our own immediate experience. It enhances the habits of our minds in ways that expand the habits of our hearts. (24)

Greek mythology is one powerful source of a second identity, but Wiltshire stresses that other cultures have different ways of developing that wider vision. In the United States, Greek and Roman classics have for years been at the heart of a democratic educational system, she argues, education for the many:

> On at least two occasions, however, the classical humanities have been distorted to justify parochialism and homogeneity rather than to foster generosity and diversity of thought. In the 19th century, arguments from Greece and Rome were invoked to defend the institution of slavery in the American South. More recently, certain proponents have urged the classics as a defense against the democratic pluralism of American education. . . .
>
> The elitist ideology dreams of a past that never existed in order to avoid the challenges of a present that does. Certain preselected texts and ideas are identified as "good and true," then promulgated as the unchanging standard to which we all must adhere. We are told to apprehend texts, rather than formulate judgment.
>
> By contrast, the democratic view is that the classical humanities engender a respect for the past at the same time that they equip us for change. They teach us simultaneously to maintain and revise our values. . . .

The elitist ideology promotes narrow parochialism by misappropriating the western humanities in order to reinforce simplistic forms of superiority, whether based on gender, wealth, nation, or race. In this view, education is a bulwark rather than a bridge, a barrier to keep out those who are different rather than a common ground that brings us together.

In the democratic perspective, the classical humanities promote a global view of the world. The goal of education finally is not merely to understand ourselves but to understand our place in history. It is to know the larger story of which our own story is a part. It is to feel our connectedness with the whole of human experience. (27–28)

Wiltshire offers a calm and thoughtful middle ground in what is becoming an increasingly contentious arena. Schools and the school curricula have always been linked to broader social and political concerns, but the debate in recent years is taking a decidedly strident tone, as advocacy groups attack schools for doing too little—we need more drug and alcohol and AIDS education—or for doing too much—schools have no place providing drug and alcohol and AIDS education. The challenge to the elitist view of the classics comes primarily from ethnic groups in the United States who argue that their children need to understand their own unique cultural background and history. Some argue that such a background is the key component of a good education, while others see their own cultural identity as a necessary complement to the classical Western civilization of the dominant society. In particular, African Americans point out that the history and contributions of their ancestors have been systematically removed from the history texts. Despite the extreme positions taken by some, most voices call for—in the words of Shelley Haley (1993), a black classicist—"the restoration of ancient Africa to the history of human civilization."

Moving from the political battlegrounds of school district curriculum adoption committees and into the halls of classical academe, the argument took on a new dimension in 1987 with the publication of Martin Bernal's book, *Black Athena: The AfroAsiatic Roots of Classical Civilization*. Bernal argued that racist attitudes in its founders distorted classics as a discipline. In her analysis of *Black Athena*, Haley explains that this racist tradition lives on:

It distorts and ignores much ancient evidence affirming the influence of African and Semitic cultures. This model has seen the intellectual split of ancient Egypt from the rest of ancient Africa; the miscegenation of ancient Egypt is ignored and the ancient Egyptians are constructed as white; ancient Greece, through spontaneous generation and in cultural isolation gave birth to all that is beautiful and good in the western European tradition.

Over the years, as my own understanding of the period grows, I find myself teaching a more complex story of classical Greece. Yes, Athenian democracy provided an important leap ahead in political theory that children should understand. But there is more to the story than the ideals expressed in Pericles' "Funeral Oration." Such political developments rested on the backs of a large class of slaves, and the touted democracy of Athenian society included a severely constrained role for women. Our children are well served by looking at such social complexities rather than the cleansed versions put forward in many texts.

As an African American, a woman, and a classicist, Haley formulates her own version of the problem that so bothered me: "If the paradigm of classics as we know it is fundamentally racist, are we racist if we teach classics?" She concludes that the fault lies not in the ancient texts but in the interpretation of those texts: "Our job is to produce textbooks where men and women from all over the ancient world are represented."

I am not urging everyone to rush out and teach Greek epics. For me, this body of literature and this time in history offer particularly rich possibilities for inquiry and understanding. However, I respect teachers who find their inspiration in other cultures and other times, and I believe that good teaching transcends the specific details of the subject nominally under study. My goal is to challenge students, to acquaint them with larger ideas and distant places, to broaden their horizons, to help them think more deeply about the world they inherit. Other elementary teachers inspired by other NEH summer institutes have successfully designed major units of study based on Vergil's *Aeneid* or Ovid's *Metamorphoses*. The subject need not be classical. Many disparate topics—the Middle Ages, or ancient Egypt, or the literature of the Indian subcontinent, or the European encounter with the Americas, or even Richard Adams' epic novel about rabbits, *Watership Down*—can provide an appropriate focus for a thoughtful investigation in elementary school. Regardless of the particular topic, however, during a child's dash through the myriad items in a school curriculum it is vitally important at some point to explore one area in depth.

WHY IS THIS APPROACH SO SUCCESSFUL?

Norwich students usually explain their *Odyssey* success in one word: "Fun." The introductory activities are, in fact, fun, an enjoyable change of pace even in a good school such as ours. The opening storytelling requires a major change in the schedule and the follow-up activities are varied enough to interest most students. Teachers in other grades are beginning to incorporate storytelling into their curriculum; as part of a lengthy study of India, for example, our second graders heard a storyteller's version of *The Ramayana*. Humans seem to have a deep need for stories in their lives and I doubt that our students will tire of hearing too many stories, especially ones of such depth.

"Fun" is not in vogue in many schools today. Politicians and business leaders urge us to look at Japan for models of educational reform, and no educational journal links "Japan," "schools," and "fun" in the same article. Granted, not everything in school, as in life, can be made fun, but it is true that we learn best when things are fun. A varied diet of assignments holds children's interests longer, and they report learning almost "without thinking about it."

Several other factors play a role in this process. Children this age have a passion for detail, and take pleasure in knowing something thoroughly. (Witness a young figure skater's total familiarity with the Olympic records of her heroines, or a Little Leaguer's detailed knowledge of the baseball cards in his collection.)

Children are also fascinated by the exotic. *The Odyssey* perches on the edge of reality; parts of it are clearly possible and other parts are—well, who knows? For the younger children, the fantastic elements of the story pose little problem. One year, for example, first-grade teacher Brigid Farrell realized there wasn't time enough in her first-grade curriculum for *The Odyssey;* something had to come out. (State officials are quick to add to the list of what should be taught but are conspicuously silent when asked what should be removed to make room for the new.) Brigid dropped her usual unit on dinosaurs and substituted Homer. Children showed the same fascination with the Laestrygonians and Polyphemus as they had with Triceratops and Tyrannosaurus Rex. In each case, they were learning about creatures larger than life, endowed with enormous power.

Fifth graders are young enough to be believers and old enough to be hard-headed realists. This story takes place in ancient times; that much they know early on, and for a ten-year-old, "ancient" is almost as distant as "once upon a time." As the *Odyssey* unit develops, children gain a more accurate sense of its place in time, but the ancient setting is still a major stumbling block for many. Who knows what might have been possible so long ago?

Unlike their younger partners, the fifth graders frequently try to fit the fantastic into an increasingly logical view of the world. Faced with the unlikely yet graphic description of the monster Scylla, a yipping, six-headed creature with snaky necks who devours six men from each passing ship, one child searched for a rational explanation:

I think Scylla was probably the last of an endangered species. You know how different animals have to adapt to the environment as it changes? Well, we learned that different societies in the Mediterranean traded a lot with each other. Maybe a kingdom was ruined and people couldn't trade with them any more. When the trade routes changed, ships didn't pass by Scylla's cave any more, so she ran out of her special diet and she eventually died without any children so they became extinct.

How do students acquire their knowledge of the men and women in Homer's story? The *Odyssey* experience is a process similar to language acquisition. Infants do not work their way through a series of structured workbook exercises or phonics drills in order to speak their native tongue; rather, they grow up surrounded by spoken language in use in a variety of contexts. Similarly, our fifth graders are surrounded by Homer's stories and through their immersion they learn challenging material with surprising ease.

VARIETY AND BALANCE

What does one consider when selecting a subject for extended study? One set of suggestions comes from Jack McKernan, who for more than twenty-five years has taught ancient Greece as the central subject in his fourth-grade class at the Shady Hill School, an independent school in Cambridge, Massachusetts. Shady Hill was founded more than sixty years ago and continues in the progressive tradition of Frances Parker, although "central subject" no longer dominates the lower grades. Central subject's thematic teaching follows three rules, says McKernan:

- It has to be the study of the people.
- It must be age-appropriate.
- It must be based in literature.

Literature is key to maintaining student interest, he asserts, because literature best reminds us of the humanity of others.

Literature indeed forms a strong base for learning, but we do our students a disservice if we expect them all to learn in one way and to share their learning in one way. Yes, I have exceptionally competent readers in each class, but there are also many for whom print is a challenge. Instead of assuming that every student will be able to learn from the printed page, let's ask, "What are the different strengths of each child?" A typical class includes artists, speakers and listeners, animal lovers, cartoonists, group organizers, social butterflies and introverts, athletes, memorizers. Some love to be creative, to tackle open-ended tasks; others function better when they're told specifically what to do.

A varied academic diet makes the year more interesting. Many adults remember only too well the sinking feeling that came a week or two into a new course when they realized that every day was going to be a repeat of "Open your books to page . . ." When my students ask if we're going to continue an activity the next day, I frequently reply, "Come back tomorrow and find out." It's a joke and an invitation at the same time. I periodically look at the shape of the entire year, weighing the content to be covered as well as the possibilities for developing different skills.

Each activity offers children a fresh start, a new opportunity to succeed. The storytellers are different from the artists, the researchers are different from the actors, the cartographers are different from the chart makers. Over the course of a varied year, each gets a chance to shine. Sometimes the variety comes through a child's choice; at other times, I expect everyone to attempt the same task, but the tasks change throughout the year, increasing the likelihood that children will discover something new and to their liking.

In recent years, I've realized that each exercise also provides students with a new opportunity to be frustrated. When a student complains about a particularly difficult assignment, I might sit down and explain my goal: "During the course of the year, I hope to ask each of you to do something that is hard for you." This usually takes the listener aback. Our students are accustomed to parents and teachers constantly encouraging them; being told that I am deliberately seeking to make things hard requires some thought. However, learning to overcome frustration is a skill worth acquiring at a young age. I love building a classroom environment where the multiplication whiz coaches her friend on the times tables and turns to the same friend for help in drawing the human figure. In such a climate, those children who breeze through academia's common pencil-and-paper tasks can learn humility. In time, all can come to value the varied talents of others in the classroom community.

SET HIGH STANDARDS

Good teaching means paying attention to the process by which children learn and setting high standards for the work they produce. The two are intertwined. In a classroom where inquiry is encouraged and children support each other, they will learn more. Similarly, setting high standards—giving students a vision of what they might achieve—helps motivate students in their work.

Throughout this book, I have demonstrated that *how* students work is fundamental to their success. Children need to be engaged, need to have fun, need variety, need to savor that energizing mixture of competence and challenge. At the same time, no amount of creative activities or structured instruction will bring out the best in children if they are not inspired by something in the subject itself. What I have tried to do with Homeric epics works in large part because the overall story itself is so rich, with something for every taste. If students want love and romance, consider Odysseus and Penelope. If the goal is a story about an adolescent in search of self, look at Telemachus. If the demand is for blood and guts and action, revel in the gore of such episodes as the Cyclops and the Laestrygonians. One student argued simply, "The Odyssey unit is so big that everyone probably had to have one favorite part in it that they really like." Imagine producing powerful murals, emotional retellings or minutely detailed dioramas based on the family life of Dick and Jane and

Spot. If we want our students to feast, we need to offer them more than stale bread.

I believe that there is something inherently uplifting in *The Odyssey,* some intangible quality—inspiration from the Muses?—that stimulates these students to produce such fine work. In many ways, my job is to introduce them to the story and then stand back out of the way so that it can work its own magic.

It's not quite that simple. The other part of our job as teachers is to help children extend their grasp. The independent *Odyssey* projects certainly benefit from the detailed list of proposals that children receive. For that matter, each year's classes have already been inspired by four years of looking at the projects that came before. Each new round of successful work sets a new and higher standard for the next year. Time and again, children and parents and teacher alike end up being surprised and pleased by what the student has done, which is as it should be. If our expectations are not appropriate, let's err on the side of expecting too much.

DOING IT RIGHT TAKES TIME

There are no shortcuts to learning. If our students are to savor the satisfaction that comes only from succeeding at a difficult undertaking, they need lots of time. Hearing *The Odyssey* initially is the work of a week; mastering the names of the characters takes several more. At that point, we can begin our study in earnest.

It is clear by now that I value learning in depth. Given a month in the classroom, I would rather plunge deeper into one area than skim rapidly over a large surface. I'm that way when I travel, too. While some can cover Europe in seventeen days, I prefer to stay in one part of one country and move slowly. Yes, there are vast lands I will never visit, but I have a richer sense of where I have been.

Driven by a textbook or by a centrally adopted social studies curriculum, we often race through time and space when teaching history, the centuries blurring as they rapidly recede from view. At the end of this jolting journey, students often recall only those few odd, disconnected bits that stand out for their novelty.

It is easy to decry the diminished work ethic of the younger generation, raised by television, cursed with a short attention span, constantly needing fresh stimulation. Must we adopt that same fast pace in our teaching? To be effective teachers, must we hone our skills as stand-up comedians? A sense of theater works to our advantage, but that is nothing new. Instead of more rapid-fire entertainment, our students benefit from grounding. In place of the ever-changing dash from one topic to another, I propose that we slow down and help children take time to explore our surroundings.

Taking time benefits everyone. Children who need external structure have the satisfaction of knowing where they are. Longer-term assignments allow them the opportunity to reflect on what they're doing, instead of having to respond immediately to the latest new task. Though the particular set of activities is new, the child knows that this day's work is related to some larger scheme. When different teachers coordinate their work and the child encounters related material in different classes throughout the week, that sense of calm is enhanced. Life rarely presents itself in neat compartments—English, math, history, art. Many are the rewards of tackling a complex subject in its entirety, and that takes time.

This is not a new idea. Several groups proposing changes in the history curriculum of American schools recommend setting aside four years for such study in middle and high school. (See "Who Shapes the Curriculum?" for further discussion of these issues.) In releasing one such recommendation, Kenneth T. Jackson, a history professor at Columbia University and chair of the Bradley Commission on History in the Schools, said:

> History should not be just a mad dash through the centuries with teachers trying desperately to get to the 1980s before school lets out in June. If history is to be properly taught and understood, teachers must have enough time to provide context for facts and training in critical judgment based upon evidence.

Most parents understand the value of this approach. When I invited parents to evaluate the *Odyssey* unit, one mother wrote:

> It was an in-depth experience. Just about every course until the third year of college is an introductory survey that results in superficial knowledge of a broad topic. I always found it difficult to get involved in subjects treated in that manner; and it's more difficult to get through courses like that too because you have to know something about everything. The classics unit gave the kids a chance to have total immersion in a subject at a very young age. (Maybe it will give them a taste for graduate school.) . . . I wish I could say I thought there was something about classics specifically that made the experience so valuable, but secretly I think it's mostly that you all did such a good job of it. There are probably other topics that could have been delved into with the same intensity with the same result.

Taking time has implications for teachers as well as students. At a teachers' workparty once, I met Fred Locke, a teacher of teachers from Philadelphia. Fred argued passionately for taking time in teaching, but on this occasion he spoke from the teacher's perspective. "When you set out to teach a major thematic unit," Fred said, "plan to teach it at least three or four years." When you have chosen a subject of enough importance and interest that you can foresee returning to it time and again, the first year's task is simply to get started; there has to be a first time to teach anything.

You do so knowing that your work will be flawed. That first year provides a baseline, a reference point for the work to come. You make notes as you go or you sit down at the end and think back. Indeed, the best time to revise a unit of study is immediately after teaching it. While it's still fresh in mind, I write notes to myself about what worked well and what failed. I make fresh copies of necessary materials, restock supplies for the next time, and discuss additional books that the library might acquire. This is the time to fill in the calendar indicating how long we actually spent on each activity, and where we ended up squeezed for time. I file away maps, posters, and charts, organized and ready for the next time. (A truth-in-advertising disclaimer: Do I do this all the time? No. This is an imperfect world. Does it work when I do take the time? Definitely.)

The second year is an opportunity to refine plans, to make major adjustments if needed, to try the same materials with a different group of children. We know that we need to allow more time for certain activities. We try a different approach, or even different wording, for activities that did not work as planned the first time through. This second time we're also able to include that visit from the speaker that—too late!—we thought about inviting last year.

By the third year, the teacher has developed a wide repertoire of activities. We have files on the computer, dittos arranged in the file cabinet, plans for enrichment, and that certain calm that comes only with experience. We have planned activities with the art and music teachers, and the math specialist is willing to try a related project. With steady purchases, we've built up a worthwhile collection of materials in both the classroom and the library—large maps for display, colorful posters, a game, some software. We have located a relevant film and have chosen an appropriate read-aloud book. Everything is starting to click.

The next several years offer the opportunity to relax and enjoy the fruits of our labors. The core of the unit is firmly in place, and this is the time to attempt variations on an established theme. (In my case, this was when we staged Greek dramas, a major undertaking that took both teacher and students in different directions.) We can vary the order in which we present activities, since we have a clearer grasp of what we're trying to accomplish. At this point, we're flying. If we continue the study after that, we know what benefits we can reasonably expect for our students and we have clear reasons for adhering to our choice.

WHO SHAPES THE CURRICULUM?

One recent development in the latest school reform movement, dating from the release of *A Nation At Risk* in 1983, is the effort to adopt national standards of what students should know. Such attempts come from individuals such as E. D. Hirsch, Jr. (author of *Cultural Literacy: What Every American Should Know* and subsequent dictionaries and grade-level lists) and from a plethora of blue-ribbon panels with august members. About the only certainty is that such proposals will appear more frequently in the years ahead. National standards are being developed in all core curriculum areas; in the area I know best, there are no fewer than three distinct groups competing to establish the standards that will govern the social studies curricula. (One group's framework is social studies, one is history, and one is citizenship; geography is already well established and is making strong inroads, thanks in part to generous funding and vigorous support by the National Geographic Society.) Not surprisingly, the textbook publishing industry is confused by conflicting messages (Rothman, 1988).

These groups are responding to the changing nature of the American workplace, the challenge of newly emerging economic powers, and the perceived demands of the next century. Their efforts are fueled by reports of low scores on standardized tests, increased violence in public schools, illiterate high school graduates, the rising number of teenage pregnancies, and adults who fail to meet even the most basic job skills expected by employers. SCHOOLS ARE NOT DOING THEIR JOB, reads the common banner raised on high. FOLLOW OUR RECOMMENDATIONS!

For several years, I was on the Advisory Board of the National Center for History in the Schools, an organization founded at UCLA with more than a million dollars in start-up funding provided by the National Endowment for the Humanities and subsequent funding by the NEH and the U.S. Department of Education. The National Center's ultimate goal, which I fully endorsed, was for students graduating from American high schools to understand history better. Seen as fundamental to the Center's work was Project 1: "the identification and justification of the essential understandings and materials in history that should be the substance of history instruction in the schools." Other projects included analyzing current history textbooks, collecting data on the amount of history actually taught in American schools, publishing a series of model teaching units on selected aspects of U.S. and world history, and organizing a series of summer institutes "to work with teachers toward restoring history to its rightful place as the most vital synthetic discipline at the core of the humanities."

Although wary of the centralized push for "essential understandings and materials," I agreed to participate because part of the Center's mission included improving the way that history is taught in American schools. Four years of intense effort on the part of Center Scholars and staff led to the publication of *Lessons from History,* a 314-page volume listing "essential understandings and historical perspectives students should acquire." The Center, agreeing with its predecessor, the Bradley Commission on History in the Schools, advocates major changes in the amount of time devoted to history in the curriculum, beginning in the elementary grades; the recommended time is no less than two years of United States history and two years of world history between grades 7 and 12, although three years are preferred. As one indicator of how much change will be needed to meet the Center's goals, in many school districts today, U.S. history is covered in a single year or less.

Why am I concerned about this national effort for curriculum standards? We certainly need a change from the present system; study after study shows that social studies or history ranks first on the list of least-liked subjects. An evaluation critical of the San Diego social studies program stated, "Too often, social studies instruction is a dry and uninviting race over mounds of facts that leaves students bored and teachers and administrators frustrated" (Gaines, 1988).

The problem, though, lies less in what should be taught than in the ineffective methods of instruction that are widely employed. There is nothing intrinsically boring about history; indeed, when taught well, history and literature excite the imagination as do few other disciplines. Classics as an amalgam of both history and literature offers especially rich possibilities. However, the curriculum reform movements that would establish "world-class" standards are unlikely to bring about meaningful change with their top-down push to change curriculum.

The core of a good education, the moment when learning becomes electric, lies in that magical three-way connection among teacher, student, and subject. The curriculum reform movements concentrate on one element of the triangle—content—and, in many cases, the content recommendations are not new. *Lessons from History* includes the United States Constitution as a topic to be studied: "The Philadelphia Convention deserves careful attention because it was distinguished by one of the greatest debates in American history and produced the Constitution under which Americans have lived for two centuries" (Crabtree et al. 1992, 82). Is this news? Is there a textbook of United States history anywhere that does not devote significant space to this extraordinary gathering? Is the reason students come away with an imperfect understanding of the Constitution because their teachers did not think it was worthy of study? Or is the problem that those teachers themselves lacked the understanding of how to animate the discussion of the document? In how many classrooms do students and teachers alike simply slog through a series of textbook questions on the background of the Revolution and the subsequent framing of the Constitution? In contrast, there are those classrooms described in long-time education reporter Fred Hechinger's (1988) account in which two good teachers actively involve students and push them hard to understand those complex issues:

> There is widespread agreement that Americans are alarmingly ignorant of their own history. History classes are often boring. Dull textbooks, poorly prepared teachers, rote learning and superficial "coverage" virtually assure that what is studied is soon forgotten. . . .
> The point is that teachers with different styles can make history come to life. What they have in common is skill at organiz-

ing classrooms and conveying goals to students. Both, the report says, "are masters of their subject" but they also know that knowledge of content alone does not assure good teaching.

History is not easy but it need not be dull.

Every teacher with ten years of experience has seen recurring waves of educational reform. Faced with new directives, most veteran teachers can look back through their curriculum folders and find the same approach from years, or even decades, before. Policymakers come and go, school boards change, and the pendulum swings steadily, although the swinging is sometimes accompanied by more frenzied shouts. Watching these changes over time, knowing well that today's comprehensive reform will be replaced by something new in another few years, career teachers are good at closing their classroom doors and continuing to do what we have always done. School systems are tradition-bound institutions that are exceptionally resistant to change. They follow a centuries-old agrarian calendar and are based on an industrial model that is rapidly becoming obsolete. Younger teachers sometimes enter the profession with ideas for change, only to grow frustrated by the ponderous reality they encounter.

WHAT WILL HELP TEACHERS?

The most important person in determining the quality of a school is the principal. Similarly, the teacher is the key person in determining the quality of education that students receive. Curriculum reform efforts are too often aimed at Boards of Education, legislators, and superintendents willing to move into the policy-making arena. Such efforts attempt to create a teacher-proof curriculum, a framework specific and rigid enough to withstand inept and lackluster teaching. What such attempts all too often guarantee is a uniform standard of mediocrity. Meaningful changes will only come about when classroom teachers embrace the change. A poor teacher can sabotage an exemplary curriculum, either consciously or through neglect; by contrast, in the worst surroundings, with minimal resources, a good teacher can create a vibrant educational environment for students of all abilities.

Researchers support the idea that professional development is crucial to implementing the changes that are being discussed for American schools. Twenty years ago, that notion was part of federal policy, although President Reagan began cutting teacher development programs that were in place at that time. Now, as part of the Goals 2000 law, states are being pushed to develop plans to improve the quality of instruction. Undersecretary of Education Marshall S. Smith is quoted in support: "If what we're trying to do is to change teaching and learning, isn't the most important thing we can do is try to help teachers get the training they need to be able to work with students in an effective manner?" (Bradley 1994).

How *do* we create better teachers? How can we take advantage of the ability of good teachers to implement meaningful curriculum change? Why is so little attention paid to this crucial element in improving our schools?

A stimulating classroom begins with a deep understanding of the needs, interests, and strengths of the students in that classroom, and a similar understanding of the particular abilities of the teacher. Bright moments in education come from a particular teacher's enthusiasm, a passion for learning that the teacher is able to share with his or her students. Good education also grows out of a teacher's ability to create a path of study that takes full advantage of the particular students in the class. Good teaching does not occur within the confines of a rigid framework imposed from above. I spoke earlier of the slow revolution brought about by the emergence of the writing process approach, but it is worth remembering that these changes—which are still far from influencing all schools—are happening only as a result of more than two decades of classroom-based research, education, and one-on-one support and training.

The changes I envision will require a massive investment in teacher preparation and in continuing education. They will come about through a series of changes implemented on the local level—sabbatical leaves, small class size, educational aides in the classrooms, mentors for beginning teachers, access to new technologies, internship programs toward certification, incentives for advanced study, summer institutes, peer coaching, institutes where teachers teach teachers . . . the list goes on.

The single greatest force for change in the school where I work, aside from the overall quality of the individual teachers on our faculty, is a program of sabbatical leaves. Over the last twelve years, ten teachers have taken a year at full pay to pursue diverse professional interests, investigating such topics as children's literature, hands-on science, computers and writing, portfolio-based mathematics assessment, modern French culture, and Vermont natural history. Without exception, the teachers have returned with increased levels of personal enthusiasm and professional competence. This program has been maintained at the expense of higher individual teacher salaries, but year after year in contract negotiations, teachers have argued that the benefit to the school community at large outweighs the individual drawbacks. To their credit, members of the local school board over the years have supported this research and development program, recognizing its value even in a time of increasing pressure on the school budget.

None of the ideas above is a new idea; everything listed there can be found already in schools around the country. But these ideas cost money, at a time when the American economy has been sliding downhill for twenty years. (We often hear that the problems of the schools will not be solved by throwing money at them; researchers have yet to show that spending less money will solve the problems.) Major new initiatives produce bold headlines for a few leaders. The proposals I mention, in contrast, bring about gradual, meaningful change in small doses. That is the kind of educational change that endures.

TEACH WHAT YOU LOVE

The Norwich Odyssey Project began because two teachers shared an interest in an old story and wanted to work together. Many factors coalesced to make that possible—my good experience in an undergraduate humanities seminar, Brigid's background as a classics major, our shared teacher training in a program that valued the liberal arts, a conservative political climate in which the NEH provided funding for a summer institute on *The Odyssey,* an intelligent and talented faculty assembled in one school under the leadership of Milton Frye—but it is worth remembering ten years later that everything started simply.

We were not trying to implement the latest directive from the Vermont Department of Education. Despite the flood of programs and pronouncements from that office in recent years, compared to that of most states Vermont's educational bureaucracy is small and relatively benign.

We were not creating a new area of study in response to a curriculum review. The tradition of local control is strong in rural New England, and unlike our neighbor, New York, there have been few state requirements to interfere with quality education. At the local level, our school district has seen a steady flow, coming and going, of assistant superintendents, those administrators who specialize in expediting curriculum reviews. When we started, the fifth grade's social studies curriculum of "geography and ancient civilization" provided the only boundaries.

We were not attempting anything grand. I wanted my fifth graders to hear *The Odyssey* from a storyteller, and I hoped that in time they would come to love the story as I did. Brigid wanted her first graders to have some contact with older children in the building; *The Odyssey* could provide a vehicle for such interaction.

No other teachers were involved in our decision to work together. We explained to our principal what we thought we were going to do and enlisted his support to apply for a local grant to pay for part of the first year's storytelling. Other teachers in the upper-elementary grades willingly allowed us to rearrange the all-important schedule for the week of the storyteller's residency. We made no plans to extend our work into art or music classes. We had little enough idea of what we were doing ourselves; how could we ask others to participate?

We had no particular model we were trying to copy. Most of the summer institute, by design, was spent being scholarly, studying Homer and related topics. The methods portion of the program was weaker than the academic, and the sixty of us did little together to create classroom applications for what we were learning. Still, in dinner conversations and at informal gatherings late into the night, we swapped stories and shared our successes from back home. That summer in Georgetown was a multifaceted awakening for me. I was hooked by the fascinating lure of the Greek world, I found fresh intellectual energy in myself, and I discovered that there were excellent teachers around the country, with different styles of teaching that were all effective. My world changed.

Years earlier, before I had ever considered teaching, I had a friend who taught second grade in inner-city Oakland, California. She regaled me with stories of her students and she described teaching yoga in class to help them focus. She had her share of rough days. "It's not the kids who drive you out of the classroom," she explained. "It's everything else. Whatever happens with the kids, you can deal with. It's the other stuff that gets to you—the principal and the superintendent, the parents, the School Committee." I quote her often, warning my interns to develop their skills in coping with that "other stuff." The other part of her message is equally strong. The kids *are* always there, always ready to try something new. Coming back from my summer study, I had fresh energy. More important, I had a clear focus. We had something to work on. The triangle—student, teacher, subject—was complete.

At teacher workshops, I'm sometimes challenged: "Aren't these stories pretty violent? What do you think about the role of women as they are portrayed? Do you really think it appropriate to spend so much time studying Greek society?" I realize that the speaker has missed my usual disclaimer, and I repeat it. If teaching Greece does not appeal to you, don't do it. We have all suffered through classes where teachers were teaching something that someone had decided should be taught, a subject that had no personal meaning. (*Silas Marner,* anyone?) Let it be, so that students might discover it later on their own or in the company of a trusted guide.

We start as teachers and stumble along, developing our skills, sustained initially by hope and by teacher's guides and increasingly by intuition and experience. In time, encouraged by friends and family, supported by our colleagues and the parents, and taught by our students, we discover what matters and we share that as best we can.

To teach well, a teacher must know what matters, not to a committee appointed by the state legislature or to the textbook publishers, but to himself. Every good teacher can say, "This is what I know; this is what I believe. This is who I am. This is why I teach. This is what I do. This is what I have to give."

APPENDIX A
Dictionary of Homer
by Fritz Krembs 5th grade

Achilles   The greatest Greek fighter who was invincible except for a place on his heel which we now call the Achilles tendon. His armor was made by Hephaestus. He got in an argument with Agamemnon and stopped fighting until Hector killed his friend Patroclus. He killed Hector and dragged the body around Troy seven times. Paris killed him by hitting him in the heel with an arrow.

Adriatic Sea   The sea to the north east of the heel of what is now Italy.

Aegean Sea   A large body of water to the east of what is now Greece.

Aeolia   Floating island of Aeolus, king of the winds.

Aeolus   King of the winds. Gave Odysseus a bag with all of the winds that would blow him off course. His greedy men opened the bag, thinking that it contained gold and silver letting out all the winds creating a hurricane.

Agamemnon   War leader of the Greeks. Ruler of Mycenae. Brother of Menelaus. Husband of Clytemnestra. Father of Iphigenia and Orestes. It was his idea to attack Troy. Some call him the king of men.

Aiaia   Island of Circe. Odysseus and his men stayed there for one year until leaving for the land of the dead.

Ajax   One of the Greeks' greatest fighters. Fought Hector until night fell. Helios stopped while driving his sun chariot to watch. He stopped for such a long time that a forest fire started at what is now the Sahara Desert.

Alcinous   King of the Phaeacians. Father of Nausicaa and wife of Queen Arete.

Antinoös   One of the suitors. He was the most cruel to Odysseus. Odysseus in turn buried an arrow to the feathers in his neck.

Aphrodite   Goddess of love and beauty. She is married to Hephaestus and had an affair with Ares.

Apollo   God of music and light. Twin brother of Artemis. Son of Zeus and Leto.

Apple of Discord 1   The wedding to which Eris was not invited.

Apple of Discord 2   The apple that Eris throws between people to start wars for Ares.

Ares   God of war. Brother of Hephaestus. Is very proud and conceited. Drives war chariot into battle. Eris, Pain, Panic, Famine and Oblivion are usually close behind him.

Arete   Queen of the Phaeacians. Mother of Nausicaa and wife of King Alcinous.

Argus   Odysseus' dog. He was the only thing that could recognize him under Athena's disguise.

Artemis   Goddess of the hunt. Twin sister of Apollo. Daughter of Zeus and Leto. Agamemnon had boasted that he could shoot an arrow more accurately than she could. She got very angry and took away all the wind so that they could not sail for Troy until Agamemnon had sacrificed his daughter, Iphigenia.

Athena   Goddess of wisdom. Always with her companion Nike, the spirit of victory. Was born full grown out of Zeus' head. She was very fond of Odysseus and she helped Odysseus on his travels.

Calchas   The priest of Artemis who said that Agamemnon had to sacrifice his daughter, Iphigenia, to get wind to sail for Troy.

Calypso   A sea nymph who loved Odysseus and kept him on her island for seven long years until Zeus sent Hermes down to make her let Odysseus go. She loves to weave.

Cassandra   Apollo loved her and when their friendship was broken Apollo gave her the ability to see the future except no one would believe her.

Cattle of the Sun   An episode in the Odyssey where Odysseus' men kill the cattle of the sun god Helios because they were starving.

Charybdis   A giant whirlpool that sucks in water three times and then spits it back out. She is across from Scylla.

Ciconians   The first place that Odysseus went on his travels. The men plundered a city and spared only the life of a priest of Apollo. In gratitude he gave Odysseus a skin of very strong wine.

Circe   An evil enchantress who turned Eurylochus' men into swine and only he could get away to warn Odysseus. On the way to Circe's palace Odysseus got a visit from Hermes who warned Odysseus to be careful and he gave him a root to eat which would protect him from Circe's magic. After he had made Circe change his men back to men they stayed on her island, Aiaia, for one year.

Clytemnestra   Wife of Agamemnon. Mother of Iphigenia and Orestes. Was married before Agamemnon came along and killed her first husband. She was angry at Agamemnon for killing Iphigenia and her first husband so she killed Agamemnon and later was killed by Orestes.

Cronus   Son of Gaea or Mother Earth. He killed his father, Uranus, the sky. Afraid of one of his children killing him he swallowed them. The sixth one, Zeus was hidden and Cronus was given a rock. Zeus grew to be very strong and he killed Cronus and cut him open and inside were his brothers and sisters, alive and well.

Cyclops   See Polyphemus

Demeter   Goddess of the harvest. Daughter of Cronus. Mother of Persephone.

Discord   See Eris

Elpenor   One of Odysseus' men. He died at Circe's palace because he was drunk and he slept on the roof, he woke up and saw the ship leaving so he forgot where he was and fell to his death. Odysseus met him in Hades.

Eris   The spirit of strife. Follows Ares and his chariot. She is known for her golden apple which if she throws between friends, their friendship would come to a rapid end. If she threw between enemies, war would break out which Ares likes a lot.

Eumaeus   The old swine herd who showed Odysseus his son Telemachus.

Eurykleia   The old nurse who was giving the disguised Odysseus a foot bath when she noticed a scar on his foot and knew it was Odysseus.

Eurylochus   Odysseus' second in command. He warned Odysseus of Circe. It was his idea to kill the cattle of the sun.

Eurymachus   One of the suitors.

Hades   Lord of the dead, dark and gloomy god of few words. Son of Cronus. Brother of Zeus and Poseidon. Husband of Persephone. He took Persephone down to the underworld against her will.

Hector   Son of King Priam and Hecuba. The greatest Trojan fighter. He killed Patroclus which made Achilles mad. Enraged he killed Hector and dragged the body around Troy seven times. King Priam went on to the battle field and asked Achilles for his sons body to give it a proper burial.

Helen   Wife of Menelaus. She was the most beautiful woman in all of Greece. All of the princes wanted to marry her so her father made two rules, no fighting and if she is in trouble all the other princes would help. After Paris gave Aphrodite the golden apple he was awarded with the most beautiful woman in Greece, Helen. Menelaus got angry and started the Trojan War.

Helios   God of the sun. Son of Hyperion. He drives the sun chariot across the sky every day. His sacred cattle graze on the island of Thrinakia. After Odysseus had warned them not to his crew ate the cattle of the sun. Helios was very angry and he made Zeus throw a lightning bolt at the ship. Odysseus was the only survivor.

Hephaestus   God of fire and smiths. Son of Zeus and Hera. Husband of Aphrodite. He is very fond of his mother and tries to cool her temper with gentle words. He is very peaceful. Once when Zeus and Hera where fighting he stepped between them and Zeus flung him down to earth. For a whole day he fell until he hit the small island of Lemnos where the sea goddess Thetis bound his wounds and nursed him back to health. He has been lame ever since. He made Achilles his armor.

Hera   Daughter of Cronus. Wife of Zeus but a very jealous one. Even Zeus is afraid of her fits of temper. She hated all of his other wives. The first time Zeus asked her to be his wife she refused him. He tricked her by creating a thunderstorm and changed himself into a little cuckoo in distress and flew into her arms. She pitied the little wet bird and she hugged it close to keep it warm and soon she realized she was hugging the mighty Zeus.

Hermes   The god of shepherds, travelers, merchants, thieves and others who live by their wits. The messenger of the gods. He is known for his winged sandals and helmet. He is the merriest of the Olympians. He leads the dead down to Hades. When he was a newborn child he stole Apollo's cattle. He was forgiven by Apollo, the god of music, because he played the lyre so beautifully.

Hyperion   Often confused with Helios, sun god. Is the father of Helios.

Ionian Sea   The sea to the west of what is now Greece.

Ino   The sea nymph who saved Odysseus' life by giving him a scarf that kept him afloat.

Iphigenia   Daughter of Agamemnon and Clytemnestra. Sister of Orestes. Agamemnon sacrificed her to Artemis to get wind to sail for Troy.

Ithaca   Kingdom of Odysseus. The island home of Odysseus, Eumaeus, Penelope, Telemachus, Eurykleia, Laertes and Argus.

Laertes   Odysseus' father.

Laestrygonians   The cannibals who destroyed eleven of Odysseus' twelve ships. The only reason Odysseus' ship escaped was because he did not dock it inside the huge cliffs.

Laocoon   A priest who was suspicious of the Greeks and was saying not to bring the wooden horse into the city. The gods (who had had enough of the war) send down a serpent to strangle him and his sons.

Lotus Eaters   The people who only cared about eating the Lotus blossom. After some of Odysseus' men had tried it they forgot about their voyage.

Mediterranean Sea   The sea that separates northern Africa from south western Europe.

Menelaus   King of Sparta. Brother of Agamemnon. Husband of Helen. He fought Paris for Helen. Paris would have been killed except Aphrodite saved him.

Mycenae   Kingdom of Agamemnon. Home to Agamemnon, Clytemnestra, Iphigenia and Orestes. Known for its Lion Gate.

Nausicaa   Princess of the Phaeacians. Daughter of King Alcinous and Queen Arete. She found Odysseus while doing her laundry. She loved Odysseus.

Nike   The spirit of Victory. A constant companion of Athena.

Odysseus   King of Ithaca. Husband of Penelope. Father of Telemachus. Son of Laertes. He was pretending to be mad by plowing with an ox and a mule when Agamemnon came to ask him to fight in the Trojan war. Agamemnon knew he was not mad because he put Odysseus' son in front of the plow. Odysseus carefully turned the plow to the side. He thought of the wooden horse which won the war. The Odyssey is about his travels after Troy's fall. He blinded Polyphemus. The lone survivor on his journey. He killed all the suitors in his house.

Ogygia   Island of Calypso, the sea nymph.

Orestes   Son of Agamemnon and Clytemnestra. Brother of Iphigenia. He killed Clytemnestra and her new husband after she killed Agamemnon and his men. He was driven away for one year until returned to rule Mycenae.

Paris   Son of King Priam. Brother of Hector. King Priam took him away from Troy because seers said that he would destroy the city. He did not want to kill his son so he left him in the country where he became a shepherd. He was made to choose the most beautiful goddess. Hera said she would make him the most powerful man in the world. Athena said she would make him the wisest man in the world. Aphrodite said she would give him the most beautiful woman in the world. He chose Aphrodite. He went to Sparta and stole Helen which started the Trojan war. So he did help in the destruction of Troy.

Patroclus   A close friend of Achilles. He died when wearing Achilles' armor.

Peleus   Husband of Thetis. Father of Achilles. One of the few mortals to marry a god.

Penelope   Wife of Odysseus. Mother of Telemachus. She put off marrying them by saying she was making a funeral shroud for her dead father. Every day she would weave, and every night she would unravel it. She never forgot her husband. She tested Odysseus by having him string his great bow which none of the suitors could do. She also asked him to move her bed which was carved out of a live olive tree. When he said that was impossible she knew it was really him.

Persephone   Queen of the dead. She was taken down to the underworld by Hades. Her mother, Demeter, was so sad that nothing could grow and it was it was cold and barren. Demeter found out from a swineherd that Hades had kidnapped her. Demeter went to Zeus and told him that she would never let anything grow again if she could not get back her Daughter. Persephone had eaten six pomegranate seeds and once someone has eaten the food of the dead they must stay in the underworld. Persephone stays with Hades for a month of the year for every pomegranate seed she ate.

Phaecia   The kingdom of King Alcinous, Queen Arete and Nausicaa.

Polyphemus   Son of Poseidon. A giant one eyed cyclops. Odysseus and his men went into his cave and when he found them he ate by bashing their brains against the rock walls. Odysseus was about to stab him in the liver, except he realized he would never get out because a huge boulder had covered the entrance to keep in his sheep. He gave him some very strong wine and in his sleep they blinded him. In his gloating he told Polyphemus who he was. Poseidon was very mad and he tried to destroy Odysseus' ships.

Poseidon   God of the sea and earthquakes. Father of Polyphemus. He tried to stop Odysseus from reaching Ithaca because Odysseus blinded his son. With his mighty trident he can make water sprout from the earth or make an earthquake. He is sometimes called the earthshaker.

Priam   King of Troy. Husband of Hecuba. Father of Paris and Hector. After Hector had been killed he went to ask Achilles for his son's body to give it a proper burial.

Scylla   The six headed monster who lives in a cave on the opposite side from Charybdis. She ate six of Odysseus' men.

Sirens   Three enchantresses who with their lovely singing, lure ships to their rocky island where they crash and are eaten. Odysseus wanted to hear the song so he was tied to the mast and the men put wax in their ears.

Sisyphus   One of the shades in the underworld. He tricked the gods by chaining Hades to a tree when he came to bring him to the underworld. The fates control all life, even the gods. Their strings of life got all tangled and no one could die. Zeus finally made him release Hades so then people could die, starting with Sisyphus. His punishment in the underworld was to push a huge rock up a hill, and just when it reached the top it would roll back down again.

Sparta   The kingdom of Menelaus. Home of Menelaus and Helen.

Tantalus   One of the shades in Hades. He was one of Zeus' sons and favored by the gods. He was invited to a feast on Mt. Olympus so he invited the gods to his palace in Asia Minor. He was a rich king but he did not think he had anything good enough for the gods. He sacrificed his son and made a stew and put it in front of the gods. The gods hate human sacrifice. So when he died he suffered in the underworld. He stands up to his neck in water, but when he bends to drink the water goes away. There are branches full of fruit, but when he reaches for them, they go out of his reach.

Telemachus   Son of Odysseus and Penelope. He was just an infant when Odysseus left for Troy. He went to look for his father after he heard of the fall of Troy.

Thetis   A sea nymph. Wife of Peleus. Father of Achilles. Seers said that her son would be stronger than the father, so Zeus let her marry a mortal man. Hephaestus fell onto her island after Zeus threw him. She bound his wounds and nursed him back to health.

Teiresias   The blind prophet of Thebes. Odysseus went to the underworld to find him and ask what would happen on the rest of his journey.

Trojan War   The war over Helen which lasted ten years. Menelaus, her husband, wanted Helen back after Paris had taken her and half of his treasure. Fighting on the Greek side were Agamemnon, Menelaus, Odysseus, Achilles, Ajax, and Patroclus. Hector and Paris fought for the Trojans. The war was finally won by the Greeks because of Odysseus' idea . . . **The Wooden Horse!**

Troy   The city where the Trojan war was fought. The biggest city in trade in all of the Mediterranean Sea because of its location just south of the Dardanelles. Is known for its huge walls which are tall as a three story building and as thick as a street.

Zeus   God of lightning. Son of Cronus. Brother of Poseidon and Hades. Husband of Hera, Demeter and Leto. Father of Persephone, Hermes, Hephaestus, Ares, Athena, Apollo, Artemis and Dionysus, god of wine. His father had swallowed his brothers and sisters being afraid of one of them killing him. Zeus killed him and cut him open and there were his brothers and sisters alive and well.

Special thanks to: The storytellers who came to our school, *d'Aulaires' Book of Greek Myths* and my mother.

APPENDIX B
Odyssey Unit ~Winter 1992

Week 1: January 27–31

Monday	Meet with first-grade partners for Apple of Discord story dictation
Tuesday	Review Apple of Discord story with fifth graders
Wednesday	Mary Sinclair, storyteller, tells entire *Odyssey*
Thursday	Story-editing conferences with first-grade partners
Friday	Jim Hunt, storyteller, tells Scylla and Charybdis episode Meet with first-grade partners to begin collage pictures for stories

Week 2: February 3–7

Monday	Storytelling with Becca Ashley: Phaeacians/Nausicaä
Tuesday	Debriefing List episodes in chronological order Storyteller Judy Witters tells the tale of Circe Storyteller Laurence Davies recalls the Homecoming as far as the test of the bow
Wednesday	Debriefing Begin cartoons sequencing the story Listen to Odds Bodkin tape of some *Odyssey* episodes
Thursday	Become familiar with names, places, and episodes by using "Who am I?" cards (names on the back), concentration cards, and picture sequencing cards Listen to more Odds Bodkin tapes
Friday	Continue familiarization with names, places, and episodes by using same techniques as Thursday and also crossword puzzles Listen to Odds Bodkin tapes

Week 3: February 10–14

Monday
Read various episodes in different translations and retellings

Tuesday
Make a preliminary choice of episode to tell
Continue reading and researching episodes
Review cards with names on the back game

Wednesday
Continue reading various versions of episode choices
Optional comic strip of episode choice
Optional crossword of *Odyssey* characters

Thursday
Review storytellers that were seen and/or heard
Generate a list of techniques used that could be incorporated in good storytelling
Begin storytelling exercises—adapt voices and body gestures of various characters

Friday
Make final choice of episode to tell
Guided imagery session

February 17–21   WINTER VACATION WEEK

Week 4: February 24–28

Monday
Introduce puppet project, discuss papier-mâché and play scriptwriting

Tuesday
Begin storytelling workshop with Mary Sinclair

Wednesday
Storytelling workshop continues
Meet in groups for puppet productions—list characters needed, do rough draft sketches of puppet, begin final sketch

Thursday
Storytelling workshop—day 3
Finish final puppet sketches—front and side view

Friday
Final day of storytelling workshop
Begin papier-mâché puppet heads—balloon with three layers

Week 5: March 2–6

Monday
Debrief storytelling workshop; student-written evaluation of workshop
Read storytelling episode in translation
Continue puppets—three more layers of papier-mâché

Tuesday
Read, compare, and contrast Fitzgerald and Lattimore translations of the invocation of the Muse
Continue reading translations of episode to tell
Tell stories in small groups
Puppets—attach neck (oaktag) using tape and then papier-mâché

Wednesday   Read, compare, and contrast translations of Calypso's island

Choice: 1. illustrate one of the Calypso translations
2. tell stories in small groups
3. read translations of episode
4. start memorizing a passage in the *Odyssey*

Continue puppets—reinforce necks with more papier-mâché

Briefly *introduce scriptwriting technique*; divide play episode into scenes for individuals to write script

Thursday   *Introduce individual project assignment*
Hand out translations of Polyphemus' cave
Begin molding facial features on puppets
Continue scriptwriting—introduce ideas of foreshadowing; clarify stage and script directions

Friday   Answer questions about individual projects
Do thirty-second telling of episode
Continue adding papier-mâché features to puppets
Continue scriptwriting

Week 6: March 9–13

Monday   *Individual project choices due*
Reactions to project assignment; suggest materials to use for projects
Continue adding features to puppets
Cover puppets with final layer of paper towels for even texture
Continue scriptwriting

Tuesday   Present research materials for individual projects
Begin research
Finish adding features to puppets
Finish writing individual scripts
Begin board game group project with homeroom

Wednesday   Continue research for individual projects
Begin storytelling to first graders
Begin to paint puppets
Begin to compile individual scenes for group scripts

Thursday   Check in and review information sources for individual projects
Write questions for *Odyssey* computer game
Continue painting puppets
Continue script compilations and proofreading

Friday   Begin gluing hair and costumes on puppets
Finish scripts and proofreading

Week 7: March 16–20

Monday	No School—Teacher Workshop Day
Tuesday	Progress check on individual projects Look at map of Greece and discuss plausible locations of some events in *The Odyssey* Continue board game unit with homeroom—Jerice Bergstrom [parent and game designer] talked about board game theory and shared several games with class Continue work on puppets—glue costumes, hair, etc.
Wednesday	*Introduce group projects for other two classes* 1. large mobile of *Odyssey* characters 2. *Odyssey* filmstrip or video created by black and red-orange "Greek style" drawings of scenes with narration Continue board game project—timetable due Continue gluing puppets and practicing with playscripts
Thursday	Discuss new group projects—how to represent characters with certain identifying symbols and what to include in scene Begin drawing sketches for character, or scene and/or border design Board game groups continue sketching and planning Edit scripts and practice puppet plays
Friday	Continue sketches for mobile or scenes with borders for filmstrip Continue working on board games Practice puppet plays

Week 8: March 23–27

Monday	Emphasize "bigness" for mobile characters and continue drawing More scene and border drawing for video filmstrip Meet with all fifth graders to observe and critique run-through of two puppet plays
Tuesday	Video: Complete enough of scene and border sketch to copy so that on Wednesday students can experiment with black on red-orange and red-orange on black Mobile: Finish drawing character figure and cut out so on Wednesday figure may be traced and cut out of foamcore More game work—board, directions, accessories Practice puppet plays
Wednesday	Trace and cut out mobile characters Experiment with scene/border drawings using black marker, crayon, Cray-Pas, or pen and orange-red water-color wash Games group—work on board, directions, accessories

Thursday	Begin drawing and decorating foamcore figures using paints, markers, fabrics
	Begin final scene and border drawings on 12″x 18″ white paper
	Games—continue work on boards, accessories, directions, packaging
Friday	Write rough draft descriptions and draw miniature character sketch for mobile key—use blank 4″x 6″ index cards
	Sequence sketches and narrate story of *The Odyssey* while tape player records
	Board game work continues
	Present puppet plays for entire fifth grade
	LAST DAY for individual projects to be handed in

Week 9: March 30—April 3

Monday	Work on final sketches for video
	Cut out and decorate mobile figures
	Work toward completion of board games
	Perform puppet plays for other fifth graders
Tuesday	Continue all group projects—mobile, video, and board games
	Practice puppet plays in class groups
Wednesday	All project work continues—decorating figures, drawing final sketches, completing board games
	Practice puppet plays with stage
Thursday	MORE group project work: finish and test play games
	Video: finish black sketching, apply watercolor wash
	Mobile: continue decorating figures and work on description cards
Friday	Mobile: discuss and decide how to categorize characters in order to hang them
	Video: more drawing and painting; listen to and comment on first take of sound track
	Stage puppet plays for one class of second graders

Week 10: April 6–10

Monday	Video: finish drawing and painting *all* scenes; make preparations for filming—credits, title "frame"
	Mobile: work on characters and description cards—two per character, begin stringing and hanging characters
	Complete board games
	Introduce Odyssey *newspaper*
Tuesday	*Videotape* Odyssey *filmstrip*
	Complete mobile characters and description cards, hang figures
	Rehearse puppet plays

Wednesday	*All mobile work completed*
	Play *Odyssey* games from other class
	View video, debrief
	Share individual projects
	More puppet play rehearsal
Thursday	View video
	Share individual projects
	Play games
	Rehearse puppet plays
	Write articles and design ads for newspaper
	Perform puppet plays in Rep [school assembly]
	8th Annual Odyssey *Open House*
Friday	Debrief Open House
	Play *Odyssey* board games
	Work on *Odyssey* newspaper

Week 11: April 13–17

Monday	View slide show of individual projects from previous years
Tuesday	*Writing assignment introduced*—write own version of an *Odyssey* episode
	Continue newspaper work—write classified ads
Wednesday	Work on episode writing assignment
	Finish up all newspaper writing and ad designs
Thursday	Continue writing assignment
	Layout newspaper and choose banner for front page
Friday	*Complete episode writing—due end of class*
	Newspaper collated, read by students
	Play *Odyssey* board games

April 20–24   SPRING VACATION WEEK

Week 12: April 27

Monday	*Evaluate entire* Odyssey *unit*
	In small groups: brainstorm and list activities included as part of the extensive unit
	Homework assignment: complete written evaluation using list for ideas to write about

REFERENCES

ATTEBERRY, MARY WADE. 1988. "Commission Gives History Curriculum Failing Grade." *Indianapolis Star,* Sept. 29:A-16.

BARBER, ELIZABETH. 1992. "The *Peplos* of Athena and the Transmission of Bronze Age Information by Women." Paper presented at a symposium, Athens and Beyond, at Dartmouth College, October 24.

BERGER, JOSEPH. 1990. "Now the Regents Must Decide If History Will Be Recast." *New York Times,* Feb. 11.

BERNAL, MARTIN. 1987. *Black Athena, Vol. I: The Afroasiatic Roots of Classical Civilization: The Fabrication of Ancient Greece, 1785–1985.* New Brunswick, NJ: Rutgers University Press.

BRADLEY, ANN. 1994. "Teacher Training a Key Focus for Administration." *Education Week,* July 13:1.

BRITTON, JAMES. 1970. *Language and Learning.* Coral Gables: University of Miami Press.

CAVAFY, CONSTANTINE. 1976. *The Complete Poems of Cavafy.* Trans. Rae Dalven. New York: Harcourt Brace Jovanovich.

CHATWIN, BRUCE. 1987. *The Songlines.* New York: Viking.

COLES, ROBERT. 1987. "Gatsby at the B School." *New York Times Book Review* 92 (October 25): 1.

―――. 1989. *The Call of Stories.* Boston: Houghton Mifflin.

COOPER, PATSY. 1993. *When Stories Come to School: Telling, Writing, and Performing Stories in the Early Childhood Classroom.* New York: Teachers & Writers Collaborative.

CRABTREE, CHARLOTTE, AND DIANE RAVITCH. 1987. *History–Social Science Framework for California Public Schools.* Sacramento: California State Department of Education.

CRABTREE, CHARLOTTE, GARY B. NASH, PAUL GAGNON, AND SCOTT WAUGH. 1992. *Lessons from History.* Los Angeles: National Center for History in the Schools.

DUNHAM, WILLIAM. 1990. *Journey Through Genius: The Great Theorems of Mathematics in Historical Context.* New York: Penguin Books.

EGAN, KIERAN. 1987. "Literacy and the Oral Foundations of Education." *Harvard Educational Review* 57:445–72.

———. 1989. *Teaching as Story-telling.* London, Ont.: Althouse Press, and London: Methuen.

FADIMAN, CLIFTON, ED. 1958. *Fantasia Mathematica.* New York: Simon and Schuster.

FISKE, EDWARD B. 1992. *Smart Schools, Smart Kids: Why Do Some Schools Work?* New York: Simon & Schuster/Touchstone.

GAGNON, PAUL, ED., AND THE BRADLEY COMMISSION ON HISTORY IN SCHOOLS. 1989. *Historical Literacy: The Case for History in American Education.* New York: Macmillan.

GAINES, JOHN. 1988. "Classes Don't Make the Grade." *San Diego Union,* Sept. 19.

HALEY, SHELLEY P. 1993. "Classics Pedagogy Begs Race Question." *American Classical League Newsletter,* Fall. Text of a speech presented under the title "*Black Athena* in the Context of America" at the American Classical League Institute and Workshops, Boulder, Colorado, June 23.

HAVELOCK, ERIC. 1986. *The Muse Learns to Write.* New Haven: Yale University Press.

HECHINGER, FRED. 1988. "Good Teachers Find New Ways to Make History Leap Off Dusty Pages." *New York Times,* Oct. 12: B9.

HIRSCH, E. D., JR. 1987. *Cultural Literacy: What Every American Should Know.* Boston: Houghton Mifflin.

HOOPER, ALFRED. 1948. *Makers of Mathematics.* New York: Random House.

INNERTS, CAROL. 1990. "Black Educators Seek to Rewrite Curriculum to Counter 'Genocide.'" *Washington Times,* Feb. 26: 1.

JACOBS, HAROLD R. 1970. *Mathematics: A Human Endeavor.* San Francisco: W. H. Freeman.

KAKUTANI, M. 1989. "Goodbye Minimalists; Hello Tellers of Tales." *New York Times,* May 31: C15.

LORD, ALBERT. 1960. *The Singer of Tales.* Cambridge: Harvard University Press.

MARSHALL, SYBIL. 1963. *An Experiment in Education.* Cambridge: Cambridge University Press.

NATIONAL STANDARDS FOR HISTORY FOR GRADES K–4: EXPANDING CHILDREN'S WORLD IN TIME AND SPACE. 1994. Los Angeles: National Center for History in the Schools. Also, *National Standards for United States History: Exploring the American Experience* (1994) and *National Standards for World History: Exploring Paths to the Present* (1994).

ONG, WALTER. 1982. *Orality and Literacy.* New York: Methuen.

"PANEL FAULTS 'INADEQUATE' HISTORY CURRICULUMS." 1988. *New York Times,* Sept. 30: A36.

PIRSIG, ROBERT M. 1974. *Zen and the Art of Motorcycle Maintenance.* New York: William Morrow.

RAVITCH, DIANE. 1990. "A Phony Case of Classroom Bias." *Daily News,* Jan. 28: 41.

ROTHMAN, ROBERT. 1988. "Discord Over Social Studies Vexes Publishers." *Education Week,* April 6: 6.

SOBEL, DAVID. 1993. *Children's Special Places.* Tucson: Zephyr Press.

STARNA, WILLIAM A. 1990. "Whose History Will Be Taught, and What Is History Anyway?" Letter to *New York Times* dated Feb. 12.

THOMAS, C. G. 1977. *Homer's History: Mycenaean or Dark Age?* Huntington, NY: Robert E. Krieger.

VIADERO, DEBRA. 1994. "Teaching to the Test." *Education Week,* July 13: 21–25.

WELLS, GORDON. 1986. *The Meaning Makers: Children Learning Language and Using Language to Learn.* Portsmouth, NH: Heinemann.

WILTSHIRE, SUSAN FORD. 1988. "A Second Identity: Two Views of the Classics." *Prima* 1 (Fall): 24–28.

WINERIP, MICHAEL. 1993. "As Superintendents Go Out the Revolving Door, Reform Efforts May Go with Them: A Case in Point." *New York Times,* Dec. 8: B7.

WOLKSTEIN, DIANE. 1978. *The Magic Tree and Other Haitian Folktales.* New York: Alfred A. Knopf.

RESOURCES ON
HOMERIC GREECE
Materials of Particular Use
in the Elementary
School Classroom

Author's note: Compiling a bibliography is a sorry task. Most of the materials listed here have been useful in our study of Greek mythology, *The Odyssey,* and the ancient world; most were purchased within the past ten years. However, changes in tax laws have increased the taxes that publishers pay on their inventory, making it less profitable to keep books in print, meaning stored in warehouses. The publishing industry today works on a short cycle: books emerge, sell for a short time, and are quietly remaindered, often before they have had a chance to find their market. Even high-quality volumes disappear sooner than one might expect. As a result, this bibliography contains numerous O.P. (out of print) designations to aid library users and those readers who frequent used book sales or are willing to use the book-find services. Between the time of writing and publication, other titles will surely join the O.P. list. Rather than assume that good volumes will remain in print, readers who find an appropriate book are advised to purchase it quickly. Readers might also contact publishers in an attempt to convince them to reissue worthy titles. Recent years have seen an outpouring of attractive and informative children's books on aspects of life in classical Greece. For the most part, this bibliography concentrates on mythology and topics related to our study of Homer.

———

ALIKI. 1994. *The Gods and Goddesses of Olympus.* New York: Harper-Collins. This book summarizes the Greek creation myths, the struggles among the early gods, and the coming of the Olympians. Each deity receives a double-page spread with several paragraphs of simple stories. Young readers interested in a different view of the gods may enjoy comparing these brilliantly colorful pictures with the somber ones in Leonard Everett Fisher's *The Olympians.*

BAKER, CHARLES F. 1991. "Odysseus's Homecoming." *Calliope* 1:3. This retelling of the final section of the *Odyssey* is part of an issue devoted to epic heroes. Other stories describe Gilgamesh, Beowulf, and the *Mahabharata.* Maps, activities, puzzles, timelines, and articles about relevant archaeology, all useful for the classroom. *Calliope* is published by the same company that produces *Cobblestone* and *Faces* magazines for children.

BAKER, ROSALIE F. 1994. "At the Walls of Troy." *Calliope* 4:3. Free translations of two well-known scenes from *The Iliad,* Hector's farewell to his wife and young son, and the fight between Hector and Achilles. This "Epic Heroes II" issue also discusses Aeneas, El Cid, Sundiata of Mali, the African griot, epics from Finland and from Chile, as well as activities and sources for additional information.

BASS, GEORGE. 1987. "Oldest Known Shipwreck." *National Geographic,* Dec. The author, founder of the Institute for Naval Archaeology, directed the team investigating the wreck of a Bronze Age cargo ship, located off the south coast of Turkey. This article summarizes the first four years' work, with diagrams of the site and stunning photographs of objects recovered. An excellent look at Bronze Age crafts and trade, as well as a fascinating glimpse of underwater archaeology.

BOLTON, JAMES. 1968. *Ancient Crete and Mycenae.* New York: Longman. A good book on the subject, aimed at middle school but also providing young readers far more information than they will find in more general books of ancient history. The 100 pages treat the two subjects equally, with illustrations from ancient art and artifacts. The text treats each civilization in parallel fashion, moving from excavations through detailed descriptions of architecture, daily life, and language. Fifteen other titles in the "Then and There" series also examine the ancient world, including China, Egypt, Babylon and Jerusalem, Athens, Alexander the Great, and Rome. Illustrated with black and white photos, maps, diagrams. O.P.

BOWRA, C. M. 1965. *Classical Greece.* New York: Time-Life Books. Although the text is too difficult for children, this Time-Life volume contains many maps and photographs, both color and black and white. (The opening relief map powerfully conveys the mountainous terrain of the lands bordering the Aegean.) One unusual photo essay depicts scenes from a rarely photographed, ancient 600-foot-long sandstone frieze of the Homeric epics. O.P., but widely available in used book stores.

BRADFORD, ERNLE. 1964. *Ulysses Found.* London: Century Hutchinson. Too difficult for most elementary children, although useful for adults working with children. A detailed account of Bradford's theories, based on years of sailing around the Mediterranean. Bradford is also featured in a film of the same name, which some find sappy (long shots of him gazing thoughtfully off across the sea) but which does show glimpses of Mediterranean lands. O.P.

BRADFORD, ERNLE. 1968. "Voyage in Search of Fabled Lands," *Greece and Rome: Builders of our World.* Washington, DC: National Geographic Society. A shorter, illustrated version of the previous book. Comparing Bradford with Severin is an excellent introduction to the question of where Odysseus sailed. O.P.

BRAYMER, MARJORIE. 1960. *The Walls of Windy Troy.* New York: Harcourt, Brace & World. A detailed biography of Heinrich Schliemann, the successful businessman who made a fortune and then turned his passionate attention to locating and excavating ancient Troy. A fine read-aloud to introduce students to archaeology. O.P.

BRITT, HELEN. 1987. *Ye Gods.* New York: Longman. This introduction to classical mythology is aimed at a high school audience, but younger readers with a strong interest in mythology may well enjoy reading these retellings. Complete with study questions which could also serve as review questions for younger students.

BROOKS, ROBERT A. 1991. *Gods and Heroes of Ancient Greece.* Chapel Hill, NC: University of North Carolina Press. A huge (48˝x 35˝) illustrated wallchart "showing the legends, descent and relationships . . ." A striking compilation, revealing at one glance the complex interrelationships of the names in Greek mythology. Totally fascinating for some children and a useful classroom reference for all.

BURRELL, ROY. 1990. *The Greeks.* Oxford: Oxford University Press. The informative text and Peter Connolly's vivid paintings combine to yield an excellent volume for the classroom library. This has been one of the books most frequently used by student researchers. Topics include the Minoans (including a simple discussion of the process of decoding Linear B writing), the Mycenaeans, the rise of cities, the Golden Age of Athens, the Persian and Peloponnesian wars, and Alexander. Burrell has a companion volume, *The Romans.*

CAIRNS, TREVOR. 1974. *People Become Civilized.* Minneapolis: Lerner/Cambridge University Press. One part of the *Cambridge Introduction to the History of Mankind,* this book traces the transition from hunters and gatherers to the earliest civilizations, with emphasis on Egypt and Mesopotamia. The next section covers classical Greece, including city-states, the Persian Wars, the rise and fall of Athens and Sparta, and Alexander. An excellent textbook introduction to the ancient world, 100 pages written and illustrated clearly with maps, diagrams, photographs, and drawings. Suitable for upper elementary and higher grades. O.P.

CASELLI, GIOVANNI. 1983. *The First Civilizations.* New York: Peter Bedrick Books. Part of a series (*History of Everyday Things*) that also includes a volume on the Roman Empire and the Dark Ages. This book, aimed at middle school readers, attempts to show common objects in context. A typical double-page presentation of the Greeks at home includes thirty pictures of clothing, footwear, and jewelry; a grouping of furniture; a cutaway view of a house; and a street map of ancient Olynthus. Other topics include the first cities, the Neolithic agricultural revolution, Egyptian craftsmen, Minoan Crete, northern Europe, ancient China, and the Etruscans. See also the author's *A Greek Potter,* in the "Everyday Life" series.

CHURCH, ALFRED J. 1964. *The Iliad and The Odyssey of Homer.* New York: Macmillan. A well-written version, detailed and complete, with a lofty feel to the language, an excellent edition for reading aloud. O.P. Available through used-book stores and worth the search. The 275-page text includes both Homeric epics, recounting in full the travels of Odysseus and the other plots, such as the travels of Telemachus. The twenty illustrations are attractive black and white line drawings by Eugene Karlin. A companion volume tells Vergil's *Aeneid.*

CIVILIZATION. Avalon Hill Game Company, 4517 Harford Road, Baltimore, MD 21214. The game can also be purchased through game stores and bookstores. See Chapter 7 for a brief description of the game.

COBBLESTONE. 1983. Archaeology: Digging Up History, June. *Cobblestone* is a history magazine for children that devotes each issue to a different theme; archaeology is the theme of this entire issue. Among the topics: what archaeology does, digging into local history, dating discoveries, biographies of two archaeologists of the American Southwest, a map (with descriptions and phone numbers of major sites in the United States) and an article on the Paleo-Indians who reached America across the present Bering Strait.

COLUM, PADRAIC. 1918. *The Children's Homer.* New York: Collier/Macmillan. This version is seventy years old, recently reissued in inexpensive paperback and widely available. It is a literary retelling with the feel of an epic, 250 pages long, including both tales from Homer. Some readers might be put off by the use of archaic speech: "But wilt thou not be brotherly to us? Tell us by what name they call thee in thine own land."

CONNOLLY, PETER. 1977. *The Greek Armies.* Morristown, NJ: Silver Burdett. The top of each page includes information taken from Greek history based on Homer, Herodotus, Thucydides, and Xenophon—tales from Troy, battles of Marathon and Salamis, the struggle at Thermopylae, the siege of Syracuse, and Alexander's campaigns against the Persians. The bottom of each page includes detailed information based on literary and archaeological sources. Topics include body armor and helmets, chariots, swords and shields, organization of the phalanx, warships, siege tactics, and cavalry formations. Some boys spend hours looking at this book. O.P.

CONNOLLY, PETER. 1986. *The Legend of Odysseus.* Oxford: Oxford University Press. A beautifully illustrated retelling of the story of Odysseus interspersed with a detailed look at the archaeological evidence, including maps, Mycenaean grave relics, details of ships, costumes and hairstyles, the Pylos palace, excavations at Troy, and information on religion and burial rites. (Some of this information appears in other forms in Connolly's earlier book, above.) This book is an excellent way of moving from the literary story to the possible historical reality underlying the tale.

COOK, ALBERT. 1974. *The Odyssey: Critical Edition.* New York: W.W. Norton. Cook's translation aims "to render the poem not only literally, but line by line," and to remain "wholly faithful to the formulaic character of the poem." Also includes 150 pages of collected scholarly commentary, useful for adults to read in one place a selection of Homeric criticism.

COOLIDGE, OLIVIA. 1952. *The Trojan War.* Boston: Houghton Mifflin. An older retelling of the epics for young readers, this version concentrates on the action at Troy, although it also describes the events leading up to the war and the return of the Greeks. See also the author's *Greek Myths.*

COOTES, R. J., AND L. E. SNELLGROVE. 1970. *The Ancient World.* New York: Longman. An introductory British textbook aimed at eleven- or twelve-year-olds. Some 200 pages of well-written text supplemented by photographs, maps, diagrams, and timelines; a workbook is available. After a section on the beginnings of civilization, we move through ten-page chapters on Mesopotamia, Egypt, India, the Chinese, the Persians, and the Hebrews. Thirty-five pages are devoted to the Greek world, from Minoan Crete through fifth-century Athens. The last half of the book covers the Roman Empire and Roman Britain.

CORK, BARBARA, AND STRUAN REID. 1984. *Young Scientist Book of Archaeology.* Tulsa: Usborne/Hayes. A breezy overview of archaeology, with text set off in short paragraphs and profusely illustrated. Sites range from Egypt to Pompeii, from England to China. Among the topics are site excavation, pottery, burials, animal and plant remains, dating, fakes, experimental archaeology, and underwater exploration. The informal style and lively graphics will appeal to many children, though other sources will be needed to provide a deeper look at any one subject.

CULLUM, ALBERT. 1970. *Greek Tears and Roman Laughter.* New York: Citation Press/Scholastic. Useful collection of adaptations of classic plays aimed at middle school children; includes ten Greek tragedies and five Roman comedies. Cullum shortens and simplifies the original texts, yet maintains the compelling complexities. Includes suggestions for introducing the plays, vocabulary for each script, suggestions for staging. Teachers seeking a fuller version might add additional lines for the Chorus. The book has recently been reprinted in a larger format as *Greek and Roman Plays for the Intermediate Grades* (Carthage, IL: Fearon Teacher Aids).

D'AULAIRE, INGRID AND EDGAR. 1962. *D'Aulaires' Book of Greek Myths.* New York: Doubleday. It's hard to imagine teaching young children without this book—literate and lavishly illustrated with colorful lithographs. Indeed, some elementary school teachers have organized months-long mythology studies with little more than this volume in their classroom. The d'Aulaires begin their book with the creation myths, followed by stories of the Olympian gods, the minor deities, and mortals. The text presents the stories simply, without talking down to the reader. Essential reading.

DEETZ, JAMES. 1967. *Invitation to Archaeology.* New York: Natural History Press. A thoroughly satisfying little volume exploring the principles, methods, and problems of modern archaeology. Topics include techniques of excavation, record-keeping, methods of dating, structure and function of artifacts, and the importance of context. An excellent introduction for teachers interested in pursuing archaeology in their classrooms, although the book itself is too difficult for younger readers. O.P. Try looking in a university library, or contacting a nearby archaeologist to borrow a copy.

EVSLIN, BERNARD. 1969. *The Adventures of Ulysses.* New York: Scholastic. A full-length retelling of the *Iliad* and the *Odyssey* by an author well known for his adaptations of classical mythology. This version is certainly dramatic, but the author has taken considerable liberty with Homer's text. Worth reading to compare with other versions, but not faithful enough to the original to use as a basis of study.

EVSLIN, BERNARD. 1987. *The Cyclopes.* New York: Chelsea House. Illustrated with forty excellent selections from masterpieces of western art. Part of an attractive twenty-five-volume series, *Monsters of Mythology.* (Librarians report attacks on the series by fundamentalist groups angered by frontal nudity and alleged Satanism in the masterworks.) Most books deal with monsters from Greek tales, including the Sirens, and Scylla and Charybdis. Each book compiles fragments from different myths and attempts to piece them together. Some children like Evslin's vigorous writing; I am bothered by the hip tone of the dialogue and the number of episodes that have been changed or invented. In Evslin's tale, for example, Ulysses proposes doing eye surgery and Polyphemus agrees. Later on, after the blinding, Artemis—not Poseidon—swears revenge. These changes are masked by the author's air of authority: "We have the exact words that Ulysses spoke to his crew."

FINLEY, M. I. 1978. *The World of Odysseus.* New York: Pelican. Who was Homer? Was there a Trojan War, and if so, when did it occur? What sort of society did Odysseus inhabit? This introduction to Homeric scholarship was called "one of the treasures of my library" by Mary Renault; it is a fascinating glimpse into Bronze Age Greece. An excellent starting point for adult readers interested in moving beyond Homer's poetry to the history that might underlie the verse. Originally published in 1954, and later revised.

FISHER, LEONARD EVERETT. 1984. *The Olympians: Great Gods and Goddesses of Ancient Greece*. New York: Holiday House. An excellent introduction to these key characters of Greek mythology. Fisher's bold color pictures provide a vivid portrait of each deity; a paragraph of text is followed by the god's Roman name and information on parents and symbols. Young readers will also enjoy Fisher's *Cyclops* (1991), where dramatic lighting in each picture magnifies the scale of the cannibal in relation to the Greek sailors. Fisher has written and/or illustrated more than 200 books; other titles from Greek mythology include *Theseus and the Minotaur* (1988) and *Jason and the Golden Fleece* (1990).

FITZGERALD, ROBERT, TRANS. 1961. *The Odyssey*. New York: Doubleday. Hailed as "a masterpiece" and "a great achievement," Fitzgerald's work is one of two frequently cited modern, poetic translations of *The Odyssey*, along with Lattimore's (each has been called "the best"). Fitzgerald gives the reader in English a feel for what it's like to read Homer in Greek. Critics who favor this version cite the freshness and delight of his words, the sense of heroic dignity, the poetic imagery. Excellent for reading aloud, letting the rich sounds and images wash over a listener.

FRENKEL, EMILY. 1986. *Aeneas*. Bedminster, Eng.: Bristol Classical Press. Much of the story of the fall of Troy, including the details of the Trojan Horse, comes not from Homer but from Vergil's epic, *The Aeneid*. This fresh retelling will interest children interested in the adventures of the hero, who fled the ruins of burning Troy to embark on his own epic journey; 175 pages, with black and white illustrations by Simon Weller.

GATES, DORIS. 1976. *A Fair Wind for Troy*. New York: Puffin Books. A simple and literate retelling of the background of the Trojan War, aimed at children ages 8–12. The war itself is described in only a few pages at the end. This book concentrates instead on the oath that bound the Greeks together to rescue Helen, her flight with Paris, the gathering of the chieftains and—rare in children's literature—a lengthy version of the sacrifice of Iphigenia. An excellent addition to the classroom library; five other books by the same author relate the myths of Apollo, Zeus, Heracles, Aphrodite and Demeter, and Athena.

GIBSON, MICHAEL. 1977. *Gods, Men and Monsters from the Greek Myths*. New York: Peter Bedrick. Gibson tells his stories in detail, and students might learn much from his versions of the myths, although he sometimes makes puzzling changes. For example, Polyphemus simply enters his cave and falls asleep, ignoring Odysseus and his companions instead of eating them two by two. The text is well served by the illustrations. Giovanni Caselli provides bold black and white drawings in classical Greek style at the start of each chapter, as well as an attractive title page illustration of the major gods. Scattered throughout the book are brilliantly colorful pictures in double-page spreads. Some are rich fantasy illustrations, while others (such as the picture of Athena) provide informative images to supplement the text. Caselli's picture of the fighting at Troy is a powerful image of the horrors of war.

GONEN, RIVKA. 1973. *Pottery in Ancient Times.* Minneapolis: Lerner. A useful book for upper elementary children wanting more than the brief introduction to pottery found in survey books about archaeology. Topics include how pottery is made; designs, decorations, and finishes; pottery in the ancient world, and how an archaeologist uses pottery. Other titles in the Lerner Archaeology Series are *Jewelry of the Ancient World, Search for the Past,* and *City Planning in Ancient Times,* each 80+ pages and illustrated with photographs. O.P., but see the author's more recent *Fired Up! How Ancient Pottery Was Made,* same publisher.

GOTTLIEB, GERALD. 1959. *The Adventures of Ulysses.* New York: Random House. This book shares the traits of its companions in the venerable "Landmark" history series. It is a straightforward tale not marked by elaborate literary style but accessible to upper elementary readers. Like most retellings, this takes the story of Odysseus chronologically. It begins with the boyhood boar hunt that gave him the scar on his leg, which Eurykleia would recognize so many years later at his homecoming.

GRAVES, ROBERT. 1962. *The Siege and Fall of Troy.* New York: Dell. A detailed account for children, based on Homer and on other Greek and Latin authors. Graves combines scholarship with vigorous writing. This may be too detailed for young readers for their first encounter with the tale; it serves well as a reference or second source. O.P. Readers may be able to assemble a similar version by consulting Graves' many other works on mythology.

GREEN, ROGER LANCELYN. 1958. *Tales of the Greek Heroes.* New York: Puffin. "Once found, the magic web of old Greek myth and legend is ours by right," declares the author in his postscript. In 200 pages he covers the bulk of Greek mythology, setting aside entire chapters for the adventures of Perseus, Theseus, Heracles, and the Argonauts. A literary achievement, filled with information for the diligent reader.

GREEN, ROGER LANCELYN. 1958. *The Tale of Troy.* New York: Puffin. A companion volume to *Tales of the Greek Heroes* aimed at grades 5–7, this book tells the complete story of the Trojan War: the marriage of Peleus and Thetis, the Judgment of Paris, Helen of Sparta, the gathering of heroes and the siege of Troy, the fall of Troy, and the subsequent adventures of Agamemnon, Menelaus, and Odysseus. Highly readable, direct, lofty in spirit and language without being hard to follow.

GREIG, CLARENCE. 1974. *Greece/Crete.* Loughborough, Eng.: Ladybird. Two small books, 50 pages each with text and facing illustration. The size and simple language, coupled with the organization of the books, appeal to younger readers. *Greece* centers on classical Athens and discusses festivals and plays, athletics, Pericles, Socrates, Hippocrates, Athenian women, and the fall of Athens. *Crete* begins with several myths, then moves to Arthur Evans, the palace at Knossos, private houses, farming, crafts and trade, bull-jumping, and religion. O.P.

HAMILTON, EDITH. 1940. *Mythology.* New York: New American Library. One of the best-known mythology books, 300 pages of detailed stories with a thorough index. After a brief introduction on the nature of myths, Hamilton introduces the Greek and Roman gods, followed by tales of love and adventure. Each story is preceded by a description of the source, although critics sometimes fault her for taking liberties with the tales. Difficult reading for elementary students, who might find Rouse's informal style more accessible.

HARTZELL, D. J. 1978. *Odysseus. The Complete Adventures.* New York: Longman. This reads more like a small textbook than a story, but it successfully presents for a middle or high school audience the complete story of Odysseus, drawing on Homer and non-Homeric sources. The seventy-five pages are illustrated with black and white photographs of Greek sculpture and pottery.

HODGES, MARGARET. 1982. *The Avenger.* New York: Charles Scribner's Sons. This historical novel, set in classical Greece, works as both a story and a way to learn about daily life in ancient times. With an exciting plot and realistic characters, it has been a popular read-aloud book in my classroom for several years. For the most part, though, we are still awaiting a Mary Renault for younger readers, an author versed in classical scholarship to create stories which will hold readers' attention. O.P.

HUTTON, WARWICK. 1992. *The Trojan Horse.* New York: Macmillan. A picture-book account of the fall of Troy, clearly written, with attractive pen and watercolor paintings. If Peter Connolly's books depict every piece of metal armor, this book is less accurate but suggests moods and feelings. Hutton's watercolors sparkle; see Leonard Fisher's darker style for a different atmosphere. Hutton has also created picture books of Theseus, Perseus, and biblical tales.

LANG, ANDREW. 1907. *Tales of Troy and Greece.* London: Faber & Faber. One of the classic retellings of Greek mythology for young audiences. Lang devotes two-thirds of this 300-page volume to the Trojan War and the wanderings of Odysseus; the remainder describes the Golden Fleece, Theseus, and Perseus. Like Colum, Lang can sound old-fashioned at times: "If indeed thou art a goddess of them that keep the wide heaven, to Artemis, then, the daughter of great Zeus, I mainly liken thee for beauty and stature and shapeliness." Nonetheless, he is a fine storyteller. O.P.

LATTIMORE, RICHMOND, TRANS. 1956. *The Odyssey of Homer.* New York: Harper & Row. Acclaimed as a "dazzling and well-nigh flawless performance," one of the two most common modern translations, along with Fitzgerald's. Lattimore's is a much more literal translation, often cited for accurately conveying the poem's imagery. If Fitzgerald presents the feel of Homer, Lattimore gives us his words. Lacking the opportunity to read the original Greek, teachers and children interested in Homer's language should read different translations to gain their own understanding of the story. Also, see Mandelbaum.

LEVI, PETER. 1984. *Atlas of the Greek World.* New York: Facts on File. A large-format volume, less useful as an atlas than as a source of wide-ranging information, from the geography of ancient Greece through various historical eras. The text is aimed at an adult audience. Topics include history, architecture, arts and sciences, economics, and religion. Especially attractive are twenty-six inserts describing specific sites. Detailed index, glossary, and lavish reproductions of Greek art.

LITTLE, EMILY. 1988. *The Trojan Horse.* New York: Random House. Aimed at readers in grades 2–4, a fine book to have in a primary grade classroom or for weaker readers in the upper grades. In addition to the simplified story, the author includes a modern explanation for the war, that the Trojans controlled access to the Black Sea and demanded tolls for passage. A final chapter discusses Homer writing the epics and the discoveries by Heinrich Schliemann.

LISTER, ROBIN. 1987. *The Odyssey.* New York: Doubleday. Well written, literate, and lavishly illustrated; a colorful volume seamlessly melding text and pictures. The story starts with Odysseus in the land of the Phaeacians, where he recounts his adventures. Any retelling must shorten the story; eliminated here are the details of Telemachus' search for information about his father, the discussions of the gods on Olympus, and the meeting with Penelope. The text is placed carefully around Alan Baker's illustrations; every double-page spread contains at least one picture. All in all, an excellent adaptation for a young child's introduction to Homer. Because it is so new, it should be widely available in libraries.

LLOYD-JONES, HUGH. 1991. "Welcome Homer!" *New York Review of Books,* Feb. 14: 28–33. This review of three recent translations of *The Iliad* and *The Odyssey* also provides an introduction to the issues involved in translating Homer, a subject much discussed in the last century. For adults interested in the differences among translations, Lloyd-Jones provides a useful and opinionated starting point.

LOW, ALICE. 1985. *Greek Gods and Heroes.* New York: Macmillan. Illustrated by Arvis Stewart. For twenty years, the d'Aulaires' *Book of Greek Myths* was unchallenged as a mythology book for children. This volume is attractively illustrated with bright watercolors and is a worth-while companion. The text is simple and direct; children will enjoy comparing two different versions of the same story.

MACAULAY, DAVID. 1979. *Motel of the Mysteries.* Boston: Houghton Mifflin. In the year 4022, an amateur archaeologist is exploring a site in the ancient buried country of Usa. A witty takeoff on great moments in the history of archaeology, by the well-known author and illustrator of *City, Pyramid, Castle,* and *Cathedral.* This book fits nicely into an activity in which students try to reconstruct a civilization from arti-facts made by their peers.

MANDELBAUM, ALLEN. 1990. *The Odyssey of Homer.* Berkeley: University of California Press. If, indeed, each generation needs its own transla-tions of Homer, here is the most recent contender, an attractive and fresh translation. Mandelbaum's verse is direct and accessible to mod-ern readers.

MASON, ANTONY. 1994. *The Children's Atlas of Civilizations.* Brookfield, CT: Millbrook Press. A useful reference book to help students broaden their historical horizons, this illustrated atlas ranges from the Sumeri-ans and Akkadians through Minoans and Mycenaeans, early African kingdoms, the Hittites, empires of southeast Asia, and the Americas. Each double-page spread (forty in all) presents a capsule history, pho-tographs of artifacts, and a map of the region. The text is too dense for most elementary students, but the colorful illustrations and maps will attract the attention of browsers.

MASON, HERBERT. 1970. *Gilgamesh.* New York: New American Library. This retelling of the ancient tale reads smoothly, unlike the more literal translations.

MASON, JAMES. 1991. *Greek Heroes and Monsters.* New York: Longman. An attractive little volume combining retellings of two myths—Theseus and the Minotaur, and the tale of Odysseus—with historical and ar-chaeological information. Complex ideas are presented simply and clearly. Attractively illustrated, both with colored drawings and pho-tographs of sites and artifacts.

MCEVEDY, COLIN. 1967. *The Penguin Atlas of Ancient History.* New York: Penguin. A collection of forty clear maps (black, white, and blue), with facing text, illustrating topics up to the fourth century A.D. The same base map is used throughout, depicting Europe, the Near East, and northern Africa. Helpful for adults interested in, say, the spread of bronze working, trade routes in Mycenaean times, the extent of the Persian empire, or the aftermath of Alexander.

MCLEISH, KENNETH AND VALERIE, EDS. 1972. *Aspects of Greek Life.* New York: Longman. An outstanding series for the elementary classroom. Each 64-page book is illustrated with black and white photographs, maps, and drawings. Excellent text, detailed and factual, with occasional ex-cerpts from Greek sources. Each volume is written by a different author, but the overall quality of the series is uniformly high. Books include questions, suggested projects, and an annotated bibliography. These books stand as models of a good text: inviting, informative, satisfying. Titles are *Mycenae, The Greek Theatre, Greek Exploration and Seafaring, Greek Art and Architecture, Greek Athletics, Minoan Crete,* and *Greek Everyday Life.* Not all may still be in print. A companion series presents aspects of Roman life.

MILLARD, ANNE, AND PATRICIA VANAGS. 1977. *First Civilisations to the Fall of Rome.* Tulsa, OK: Usborne/Hayes. This simplified history of the ancient world offers short text blocks organized around extensive pictures; written for grade 4⁺. Devotes two to four pages to such groups as the Babylonians, Chinese, Minoans, Celts, and Persians, with more coverage of Sumerians, Egyptians, Greeks, and Romans. Attempts to describe how people lived, their inventions, conflicts with other civilizations, and contributions to our culture. As the publishers admit, "a vast amount of detail has, of course, had to be omitted." This volume also appeared as three separate titles, *First Civilisations, Warriors and Seafarers,* and *Empires and Barbarians.* O.P.

MILLSTONE, DAVID. 1988. "Greek Drama: Child's Play." *Prima* 1 (Fall): 19–23. A classroom teacher's account of producing several classic Greek plays with upper elementary students, arguing that the formal structure and sophistication of Greek tragedies make them an ideal vehicle to help children explore complex emotional and personal questions.

MILLSTONE, DAVID. 1989. "Immersion in Confusion: Reflections on Learning Language." *Teaching & Learning* 3:3: 28–36. Compares the experience of learning modern Greek as a second language with that of children learning their first language; cites the importance for both processes of having rich oral language experiences.

OLIVER, PETER. 1992. *The Odyssey.* Newmarket, Eng.: Brimax. A large-format volume with vivid illustrations on all pages. The text provides a detailed retelling of the tale. Roger Payne's illustrations gleam with golden light, but his Bronze Age figures wear clothing from the Classical Period hundreds of years later. Some children find the pictures appealing; some adults may be reminded of 1950s Hollywood epics.

PEARSON, ANNE. 1992. *See Through History: Ancient Greece.* New York: Alfred A. Knopf. This book features crisp photographs of beautiful objects displayed on luminous white backgrounds. The photographs include historic sites as well as sculptures, paintings, and vases; the artwork will inspire many young artists. Several pages discuss the Mycenaean world and Troy, while most of the book presents aspects of life in classical Greece.

RAPHAEL, ELAINE, AND DON BOLOGNESE. 1989. *Drawing History: Ancient Greece.* New York: Franklin Watts. A dozen two-page spreads, each describing one topic from ancient Greece and giving three-step instructions on how to draw an appropriate picture for that topic. Subjects include Greek temples, vases, masks for drama, an Athenian orator, a Spartan hoplite, and a trireme.

RICHARDSON, I. M. 1984. *Odysseus and the Cyclops.* Mahwah, NJ: Troll Associates. One in a series of seven, aimed at younger readers. Most pages have only five lines of text, with simple color illustrations filling the page. The retelling is straightforward, conveying the basic details of the story but lacking much literary style. Worth including in a classroom library, where its simple language and easy format will appeal to certain children; teachers may also enjoy having seven booklets rather than one text. Other titles include *Odysseus and the Giants, Odysseus and the Great Challenge, Odysseus and the Magic of Circe, The Return of Odysseus, The Voyage of Odysseus,* and *The Wooden Horse.* See also other mythology books in similar format by same publisher.

RIEU, E. V., TRANS. 1950. *The Odyssey.* New York: Penguin. A prose translation, easier to follow for many students than verse. The publishers list this as grades 9 and up. See Rouse (1971) for an alternative many find easier to read.

ROCKWELL, ANNE. 1994. *The Robber Baby: Stories from the Greek Myths.* New York: Greenwillow Books. This collection presents fifteen well-known tales from Greek mythology, and includes a Greek pronunciation guide. *Odyssey* enthusiasts browsing here will learn more about Aeolus, king of the winds. The bright and sprightly illustrations, like those of Warwick Hutton, create a different mood than the somber palette of Leonard Everett Fisher. Students in primary and upper elementary grades alike may enjoy comparing different treatments of the same material.

ROUSE, W. H. D. 1957. *Gods, Heroes and Men of Ancient Greece.* New York: New American Library. An informal introduction to Greek mythology written as though these are stories being told aloud to a listening audience. As a result, the stories are lively and entertaining, rather than scholarly, and they will appeal to many readers; the reading level is grade 5. Good index makes the text available for easy reference.

ROUSE, WILLIAM H. 1971. *The Odyssey.* New York: New American Library. I find Rouse's informal style appealing, and to me, this prose version reads more easily than, say, Rieu's translation. Again, readers must find the version of Homer that speaks most clearly to them.

RUSSELL, WILLIAM F. 1989. *Classic Myths to Read Aloud.* New York: Crown. Russell's book follows in the wake of his earlier *Classics to Read Aloud to Your Children.* He attempts to choose old-fashioned language, and he sprinkles pronunciation guides throughout the text, along with estimates of how long each chapter will take to read. Most children will prefer illustrated versions or retellings without the didactic overtones of his work, but some adults might find this a useful starting point in approaching Greek myths.

SCHODER, RAYMOND V. 1974. *Ancient Greece from the Air.* London: Thames and Hudson. An inspiring collection of aerial photographs of 80 ancient Greek sites. Each photograph is accompanied by a clear map labeling the features shown. The accompanying text describes the site and in one short page explains its importance. O.P.

SCHODER, RAYMOND V., AND V. C. HORRIGAN. 1986. *A Reading Course in Homeric Greek* (Loyola University Press). Appendix D to Volume II presents a concise description of the travels of Odysseus, helpful because it mentions the specific references (book and line numbers) from Homer's text to aid those who want to interpret Homer's geography for themselves. O.P.

SEVERIN, TIM. 1986. "The Quest for Ulysses." *National Geographic,* August. This is only the most recent attempt to fix the route of Odysseus in the actual Mediterranean. Illustrated with dramatic photographs and maps for which *National Geographic* is justly famous, this is the story of adventurer Severin's attempt to re-create the voyage of Odysseus. (An earlier voyage with the same 54-foot model of a late Bronze Age ship saw Severin sailing from Greece to the Black Sea following Jason's quest for the Golden Fleece.) This time, using Homer as his source, Severin starts out at Troy and ends up with a route that differs considerably from that proposed by Ernle Bradford. Students may enjoy comparing the two routes and the reasoning behind each.

SEVERIN, TIM. 1987. *The Ulysses Voyage: Sea Search for the Odyssey.* New York: E. P. Dutton. The book amplifies the *National Geographic* article listed above—more details, more photos, a book worth putting on display in the school library. O.P.

SPIGEL, TRUDI. 1986. "The Lure of the Dig." *Washington University Magazine* 56:4 (Autumn): 8–16. A journalistic account of an ongoing dig on Odysseus' island of Ithaca, directed by Prof. Sarantis Symeonoglou. Color photographs give students a feel for the land of Greece. Starting from his own reading of Homer, Symeonoglou has been testing sites on Ithaca since 1983, searching for the home of Odysseus. Those interested in keeping up with each season's progress reports can receive copies of his newsletter, "The Siren," The Odyssey Project, Campus Box 1189, Washington University, St. Louis, MO 63130.

SUTCLIFF, ROSEMARY. 1993. *Black Ships Before Troy.* New York: Delacorte Press. At last, a worthy illustrated retelling of *The Iliad.* Sutcliff is well known for her other historical novels for children, including those set in Roman England. This attractive book tells of the judgment of Paris, the gathering of the troops, the quarrel between Agamemnon and Achilles, the endless fights in front of Troy and the eventual fall of the city. There is also a helpful pronunciation guide. The sombre greys and browns that dominate Alan Lee's palette seem appropriate to this tale of men at war; on occasion, he introduces vivid colors to good effect, as in the illustration of Achilles crossing the bloody river.

TAYLOR, B. C. 1984. *The Greeks Had a Word for It.* Toronto: Guidance Centre. A useful little handbook of nearly 100 Greek words and concise explanations of how those forms appear in English derivatives. Exercises and activities can easily be adopted by a teacher interested in presenting etymology exercises in class. Includes words written in Greek, as well as pronunciation guides.

VENTURA, PIERO. 1985. *In Search of Troy*. Morristown, NJ: Silver Burdett. An inviting introduction to Homeric studies aimed at a young audience. Includes information about Heinrich Schliemann, his dig at Troy, and the story of the Trojan War. Attractive illustrations by Gian Paolo Cesarani, though not as detailed as those in Peter Connolly's books. A classroom might well include this book, Connolly's, and Wood's adult volume; each examines the same subject in increasing detail. O.P.

THE VISUAL DICTIONARY OF ANCIENT CIVILIZATIONS. 1994. New York: Dorling Kindersley. This volume in the *Eyewitness Visual Dictionary* series depicts objects from sixteen civilizations around the world. Illustrated in the distinctive Dorling Kindersley style (see Anne Pearson, *Ancient Greece*), this book features photographs of 200 artifacts with thousands of details pointed out and named. The large format allows the reader to notice details which might be obscured in smaller photographs.

WATSON, JANE WERNER. 1956. *The Iliad and the Odyssey*. New York: Golden Press. An outstanding edition, published as a Giant Golden Book and unfortunately O.P.; worth a major search. A rich text is set off by stirring illustrations by Alice and Martin Provensen, with dramatic and varied page layouts. Pictures are stylized and colorful, and include superb depictions of the gods on Olympus watching the mortals below. The text also weaves the gods into the story, unlike many retellings, which present just the exploits of the mortals. An excellent version for reading aloud to younger children. The Provensens also illustrated *The Golden Treasury of Myths and Legends* by Anne Terry White (1959).

WEBB, VIVIAN, AND HEATHER AMERY. 1981. *The Amazing Adventures of Ulysses*. Tulsa, OK: Usborne/Hayes. Illustrated in lighthearted cartoon style, told in simple language for very young readers. Older readers, though, will enjoy this book as a change of pace from full translations and lengthy retellings. The text is arranged in small blocks of three or four lines, each block of text with its own picture. O.P.

WEILER, SUSAN K. 1986. *Mini Myths and Maxi Words*. New York: Longman. Aimed at middle school or high school students, this collection of twenty-six lessons contains simple retellings of major myths as well as explanations of a dozen or more English words that derive from the myth. Elementary school teachers might simplify some lessons for classroom use; young readers with a love of words would enjoy browsing in it.

WELLS, ROSEMARY. 1987. *Through the Hidden Door*. New York: Dial Books. Seeking to escape the social pressures of their prep school, two boys stumble on the remains of an unusual civilization. A good book to give students a feel for the excitement and the uncertainties of an archaeological find.

WOOD, MICHAEL. 1985. *In Search of the Trojan War.* New York: New American Library. Based on a six-part public television series, this weighty book is aimed at an intelligent adult audience. Was there ever an actual siege of Troy? How do we know? This book is a detailed look at the complex archaeological, literary, and historical records that help answer these questions. Wood explains oral and written epics, the history of Greek excavations, the decipherment of Linear B, the Hittites and the Mycenaeans, the Peoples of the Sea. This book provides more information than most readers will want to know about the mysteries of Troy, but it also presents answers (and raises a few questions) for those interested in details. Contains maps, photographs, diagrams, index.

WOOD, TIM, AND ROWENA LOVERANCE. 1992. *Ancient Greece.* New York: Viking. This richly-illustrated book features a series of acetate overlays which enables students to see a structure from the outside, then peel away a layer to look inside. Several entries provide useful information on the origins of the Greeks, the physical geography of Greece, and the importance of the sea to Greek life. Each begins with a short summary paragraph of the major ideas.

ZEMAN, LUDMILA. 1992. *Gilgamesh the King.* Montreal: Tundra Books. At last, a children's book which conveys the emotional power of this 5000-year-old Sumerian tale. This book tells the story of the friendship between Gilgamesh and Enkidu, while a second volume, *The Revenge of Ishtar* (1993), describes the hero's battle with Humbaba and the struggle between Gilgamesh and the goddess Ishtar. Zeman's extraordinary illustrations extend the story and provide stylized pictures of life in ancient Uruk. Zeman and her husband are creating a full-length animated film of the Gilgamesh epic.

OTHER RESOURCES ON STORYTELLING AND THE CLASSICS

RECORDED VERSIONS OF *THE ODYSSEY*

The Odyssey, told by Odds Bodkin, Rivertree Productions, P.O. Box 410, Bradford, NH 03221. Three-cassette boxed set, recorded live at the author's elementary school; as this book was being written, the talesman was considering releasing a newer and longer version. The storyteller accompanies himself on guitar and Celtic harp, includes masterful sound effects, and tells the tale dramatically through the distinct voices of dozens of characters. Odds Bodkin begins his version with Odysseus inside the Trojan Horse, and follows the hero chronologically through his adventures, omitting only the journey to the land of the dead. Rivertree also handles bookings for Odds Bodkin's storytelling performances.

In the Cyclops' Cave, told by Anne Bodman, HC 55, Box 180, Sturgis, SD 57785. This tape also includes "The Call to Troy" and "Homecoming." It is a straightforward telling of the tale, drawing in part on Robert Fitzgerald's poetic translations of Homeric similes. The storyteller skims over many episodes in the interests of time, but dwells at length on the dramatic encounter with Polyphemus. Especially moving is her rendition of the reunion of Odysseus and Penelope.

The Odyssey, radio play by Jabberwocky. Order from The Mind's Eye, P.O. Box 6727, San Francisco, CA 94101. Four cassettes. This adaptation features a full cast and musical interludes. Compared to the Bodkin or Bodman tapes, this version is closer to the structure of Homer's epic, starting with the gods on Olympus and only later switching to Odysseus as the focus of the action. Children accustomed to versions in which the story unfolds chronologically might need to be warned of the flashback structure of the original. Missing in this elaborate production, however, is the powerful voice of a single storyteller. Also available from Mind's Eye are taped versions of "Agamemnon," "Oedipus the King," "Antigone," and "The Execution of Socrates."

The Odyssey, told by Mary Sinclair, Serendipity Productions, 37 Estey Street, Brattleboro, VT 05301. A first version of the tape was recorded in

1993; a final version may be available by the time of this book's publication. Mary Sinclair follows the flashback structure of Homer's narrative.

ORGANIZATIONS

American Classical League
Miami University, Oxford, Ohio 45056
Phone: (513) 529-7741   FAX: (513) 529-7742

Now celebrating its seventy-fifth year, the ACL is an association of some 4,000 teachers and scholars around the country. Membership includes a subscription to *The Classical Outlook,* a quarterly journal, as well as a thrice-a-year newsletter and *Prima,* the journal of the affiliated Elementary Teachers of Classics. Members also receive a 20 percent discount from the Teaching Materials and Resource Center, which publishes an extensive catalog of its own; to avoid duplication, most of those materials are not listed in this bibliography. The League's annual Institute and Workshops, held late in June, combine classical scholarship with classroom pedagogy.

Each region also has a classics organization, from CANE (Classical Association of New England) to CACW (Classical Association of the Canadian West). Contact ACL for the organization nearest you. Regional associations sponsor their own conferences and workshops, ranging from an afternoon to ten-day institutes. Professors of classics in various universities have been helpful whenever requested, providing translations, texts in Greek, telephone consultations, storytelling, and general encouragement.

National Center for History in the Schools
University of California, Los Angeles
10880 Wilshire Blvd., Suite 761
Los Angeles, CA 90024-4108
Phone: (310) 825-4702   FAX: (310) 825-4723

The History Center offers dozens of teaching units for U.S. and world history, as well as a 70-page annotated bibliography of recommended teaching materials. The Center published *Lessons From History: Essential Understandings and Historical Perspectives Students Should Acquire* and is continuing to develop specific history standards for adoption and implementation in schools.

National Council for History Education, Inc.
26915 Westwood Rd., Suite B-2, Westlake, OH 44145-4656
Phone: (216) 835-1776   FAX: (216) 835-1295
e-mail: ae515@cleveland.freenet.edu

An outgrowth of the Bradley Commission on History in Schools, NCHE was established "to promote the importance of history in school and society." Actively lobbies and monitors efforts across the country to implement new standards in social studies. An attractive newsletter, *History Matters!,* presents updates on these efforts as well as excerpts from relevant publications and tips for more effective history teaching. NCHE also maintains a speakers' bureau to discuss curriculum reform or to work with teachers on inservice days.

National Storytelling Association
P.O. Box 309, Jonesborough, TN 37659
Phone: (800) 525-4514

In addition to publishing its own magazine devoted to storytelling, for twenty years this group has sponsored the National Storytelling Festival each year in October. Their focus is more folkloric than classic. They are a useful source of information for locating storytellers throughout the country, and their catalog includes books, audiocassettes, and videos of stories from varied traditions, as well as a selection of materials for teaching storytelling techniques.

Chapter opener scratchboard artists
Chapter 1, p. 3: Geoff Schellens
Chapter 2, p. 19: Ariel Rothstein
Chapter 3, p. 36: Margot Harris
Chapter 4, p. 50: Tiffany Willey
Chapter 5, p. 75: Lisbeth Liles
Chapter 6, p. 96: Holly Foltz
Chapter 7, p. 113: Caroline Edwards
Chapter 8, p. 129: Kate Nattie
Chapter 9, p. 143: Alexis Nelson
Chapter 10, p. 159: Eli Schned